4/ 80

Lord Minto and the
Indian Nationalist Movement
1905 to 1910

# Lord Minto and the
# Indian Nationalist Movement
## 1905 to 1910

BY

SYED RAZI WASTI

CLARENDON PRESS · OXFORD
1964

*Oxford University Press, Amen House, London E.C.4*

GLASGOW NEW YORK TORONTO MELBOURNE WELLINGTON
BOMBAY CALCUTTA MADRAS KARACHI LAHORE DACCA
CAPE TOWN SALISBURY NAIROBI IBADAN ACCRA
KUALA LUMPUR HONG KONG

PRINTED AND BOUND IN ENGLAND BY
HAZELL WATSON AND VINEY LTD
AYLESBURY, BUCKS

# FOREWORD

By THE RT. HON. EARL ATTLEE, K.G., P.C., O.M., C.H.

In this volume, which was written as a thesis for the degree of Doctor of Philosophy, Mr. Wasti has made a valuable contribution to Indian History. He shows the Indian scene from 1906 to the first world war with notable impartiality. His careful examination confirms, what many of us had already realized, that the senior partner in the Morley-Minto reforms was Minto not Morley, the Conservative Viceroy not the Liberal Minister. Events have moved so swiftly in the last half century that it is difficult to realize how insensitive to the signs of the times were the bureaucrats of those days. It is hard to realize how tardy was the realization by the Moslem Community of the need for political action.

Mr. Wasti has dealt with his subject with admirable objectivity and his book should be read by all students who want to understand the period at the beginning of the century when seeds were sown which were to ripen under the impact of two world wars.

# PREFACE

THERE was a need for an analytical study of Lord Minto's attitude towards Indian nationalism. He was the first Governor-General who emphatically stated that the Indian National Congress should be considered as 'an important factor' in Indian political life. He was thus responsible for changing Government policy, which, at least under Curzon, was to ignore the Congress. While he sympathized with the genuine aspirations of the educated Indians for political reforms, he took stringent measures to meet the terrorist movement. He also recognized the Muslim demand for separate representation. This was not a new policy, as the Government had always believed that the only suitable system of representation in India was the representation of various interests. He simply confirmed it and brought it to its logical conclusion by incorporating it in the Reform scheme. These decisions, taken during his regime, have affected the destinies of Indians. Historians have passed conflicting judgements on them.

With the opening of the private papers of Lord Morley at the India Office Library and the acquisition of Lord Minto's papers by the National Library of Scotland, it became possible to find some of the missing links and to go more deeply into certain problems. In preparing this book, besides the private papers of Minto and Morley, the official records of the Government of India and the India Office, the parliamentary papers and debates, newspapers and the contemporary and secondary sources have been consulted.

I was awarded a scholarship by the British Council for research on the hitherto unused papers of Minto and Morley. A grant from the Edwina Mountbatten Trust took me through the final stages of my research. Miss S. Clive Smith and Mr. David Hardman greatly helped me during my stay in England. The

Department of Education, Government of West Pakistan, granted me study leave. Librarians and staff of the India Office Library, the British Museum, the National Library of Scotland, the Senate House Library of the University of London, and the Indian Institute, Oxford, ungrudgingly gave me all the assistance I required. I take this opportunity to thank them all.

I am extremely grateful to Dr. K. A. Ballhatchet, under whose supervision I wrote my thesis for the degree of Doctor of Philosophy and presented it to the University of London in 1962. This book is a revised version of that thesis. Dr. Ballhatchet not only taught me the art of research and documentation, but also gave me complete freedom to develop my own ideas. I am, however, solely responsible for the views expressed and the mistakes, if any, in this book. I am indebted to my teachers, Professor A. L. Basham and Dr. P. Hardy of the School of Oriental and African Studies, University of London, Professor Namdar Khan, University of the Punjab, and Dr. Riaz-ul-Islam, University of Karachi, for their guidance and encouragement.

I gratefully acknowledge the honour done to me by Lord Attlee who, despite his serious illness in 1962, was generous enough to write the Foreword. My thanks are due to the Delegates of the Clarendon Press, who accepted the manuscript for publication.

My wife has been my constant companion during the preparation of this book. She not only typed the script and prepared the Index, but also gave me valuable suggestions and encouragement. I dedicate this book to her.

*Lahore,* S.R.W.
*November,* 1963

# CONTENTS

# ABBREVIATIONS

| | |
|---|---|
| *B.N.N.R.* | Bengal Native Newspaper Reports. |
| B.M. | British Museum. |
| Dept. Depts. | Department(s). |
| E.B. & A. | East Bengal and Assam. |
| H. of C. | House of Commons. |
| H. of L. | House of Lords. |
| Home Misc. | Home Miscellaneous. |
| I.N.C. | Indian National Congress. |
| I.O.L. | India Office Library. |
| *M.C.* | Minto Collection, National Library of Scotland, Edinburgh. |
| *M.P.* | Morley Papers, India Office Library, London. |
| N.L.S. | National Library of Scotland, Edinburgh. |
| Offg. | Officiating. |
| Parly Papers ⎱ P.P. ⎰ | Parliamentary Papers. |
| Pol. | Political. |
| Prog. | Proceeding(s). |
| P.N.N.R. | Panjab Native Newspaper Reports. |
| Sect. | Secretary. |

# INTRODUCTION

ON Curzon's resignation Minto was appointed Viceroy of India in 1905. Although Lady Minto was 'immensely proud that the choice should have fallen upon' him, she thought his appointment 'most unexpected' and 'a bolt from the blue'. She was pleased because it meant that Minto would follow in the footsteps of his great grandfather. But the reasons why she thought this appointment 'a bolt from the blue' were that Minto had 'no parliamentary experience' and 'disliked politics and the methods of politicians' and that he was succeeding 'one of the most brilliant men of the day'.[1] Minto was also conscious of the fact that the Conservative Government which had appointed him was tottering and that soon 'he would be the servant of a very different government'.[2] He knew that the task before him was not an easy one.

In India there was no Parliament but there was the problem of British parliamentary interference in Indian administration; there were no party politics as such but there was a political party with aspirations, and there was the aftermath of Curzon's administration. Curzon had ruled India, 'but without the necessary sympathy which would have endeared him to the people'.[3]

Curzon's lack of 'sympathy' had enraged a number of Indians. There was little that Curzon did which did not cause these Indians, Congressmen mostly, to pile up resentment—not against individuals only but against the entire régime and system of government. Gokhale, in his presidential address to the twenty-

[1] Mary, Countess of Minto, *India, Minto and Morley, 1905–1910* (London, 1934), p. 6. Minto himself was surprised on his appointment though it was 'the greatest appointment I have ever hoped for'—John Buchan, *Lord Minto* (London, 1924), p. 210.

[2] John Buchan, op. cit., p. 210.

[3] Lady Minto, *My Indian Journal* (Indian Institute, Oxford, 1905–6), vol. i, pp. 5–6. This *Journal* was a record of views and events which she started compiling even before the Mintos left for India.

first Congress, 1905, summed up Curzon's achievements and administration, finding a parallel in Aurangzeb. It was 'an attempt at a rule excessively centralised and intensely personal'. According to Gokhale it had 'the same strenuous purpose, the same overpowering consciousness of duty, the same marvellous capacity for work, the same sense of loneliness, the same persistence in a policy of distrust and repression, resulting in bitter exasperation all round'. His conclusion was that 'the most devoted admirer of Lord Curzon cannot claim that he has strengthened the foundations of British rule in India'. Gokhale was conscious of the new Viceroy's difficulties as well. He knew that these difficulties of the situation were not of Minto's creating and that he had a right to expect the co-operation of both the officials and the public in his endeavours to terminate a state of tension.[4]

Minto realized that it was his responsibility to restore the confidence of Indians in the British Government. He therefore decided to base his administration on the maxim 'that many a race has been won by giving the horse a rest in his gallops'.[5] While Curzon's watchword was 'efficiency', Minto, without proposing to sacrifice efficiency, adopted 'sympathy' as his watchword.[6]

In India, after a succession of religious and social reform movements, a political party had been founded in 1885. A. O. Hume, a retired Civil Servant, was one of its founders and Lord Dufferin, the then Viceroy of India, showed great interest in its origin, because he was anxious to ascertain the wishes of the people, which in the absence of a political party was not possible.[7] The Congress started as an association of moderate Indians who met annually at different places, debated certain problems, passed a number of resolutions and dispersed. Its membership

[4] *Report of the I.N.C.* 1905. Gokhale's Address, p. 7.
[5] *Speeches by the Earl of Minto* (Calcutta, 1911), p. 8.
[6] The earliest mention of this word 'sympathy' is found in Lady Minto's *Journal*, vol. i, 1905-6, pp. 5-6.
[7] Sir William Wedderburn, *Allan Octavian Hume, C.B.* (London, 1913), pp. 59-60.

was small and its members enjoyed good social positions. Most of them were liked by the officials in their individual capacities. Its resolutions, meetings and particularly its activities in England did unnerve a number of bureaucrats, yet on the whole this organization worked well and grew steadily. Besides securing political concessions from the Government, its aim was to develop into a national organization embracing all Indians, irrespective of sect, caste and religion. It was an uphill task, yet some of its leaders worked to achieve this end. What it required was a first-class political slogan to bring itself closer to the masses. There was another snag. The Muslims had not taken very kindly to the Congress and refrained from joining it in any number.[8] Thus before Curzon's régime, though the Congress had grown in size, it had not become a popular or national organization. Its reaction to Curzon's administration and particularly to the Partition of Bengal made it popular amongst the Hindus, but further disillusioned the Muslims. Whatever justifications and reasons might be put forward for it, the Partition and the way it was carried out gave a stimulus to the Congress activities. The Russian defeat at the hands of the Japanese in 1905 further encouraged Indian self-confidence, as a success of Asians over Europeans. Hence on his arrival Minto found the Congress a very formidable factor in Indian political life.

From its very early days the Congress had been asking for certain political reforms. The methods its leaders adopted to achieve these demands were constitutional and moderate. They approached the Government through resolutions, deputations and petitions. As the personnel of the Government kept on changing, so, correspondingly, did the fortunes of the Congress leaders. Some looked into their demands sympathetically, some brushed them aside. In the first category was Dufferin and in the second Curzon. Curzon loved India and her agricultural masses but intensely disliked the educated 'Babus'. He considered the Congress demands extravagant and impracticable. This antipathy of the Government towards the moderate Congress

[8] See Appendix I, p. 221.

aspirations encouraged the rise of a new group whose ideas seemed more attractive to the younger generation. They were tired of the 'mendicant' methods of the moderate leaders and started thinking of other methods to force the Government to accept their demands. While the moderates were asking for 'self rule' on the model of 'self ruling colonies', they demanded complete *Swaraj* (independence). The moderates believed in the use of slow constitutional methods to achieve their ends; they wanted immediate results and did not hesitate to adopt extreme methods. Thus grew an extremist school within the Congress, threatening its very existence as a moderate political party.

One of the factors behind the rise of this extremist group was a revulsion against western culture. Many feared that before it their own culture and religious heritage might disappear. The effects of the Brahmo Samaj and its off-shoots further horrified them.[9] It was thought that India might be Europeanized as a result of British rule.

Consequently religious movements developed which glorified Hinduism and belittled western culture.[1] The Arya Samaj aimed at the revival of the past glory of Hinduism and of faith in the infallible Vedas.[2] In the Punjab, Lala Lajpat Rai was not only its staunch supporter but a congressman with extreme views. In Bengal, B. C. Pal and the brothers Aurobindo and Barindra Ghose were leaders of the extreme group in the Congress. In Maharashtra its leader was B. G. Tilak.

Tilak's speeches and writings denounced the activities of the

[9] The Brahmo Samaj was a reform movement started by Raja Ram Mohan Roy (1772–1833) in 1828, in the hope of rationalizing and liberalizing Hinduism in the light of modern science, western deist philosophy, Christianity and Islam. The movement was later on divided in other groups, like that of Keshab Chandra Sen, which seemed more offensive to the orthodox Hindus. B. C. Pal was an exception as he was a member of the Brahmo Samaj and a leader of the extremist group.

[1] It was mainly as a result of the insistence of the extremists that in 1906 the Congress passed a resolution urging the people to set up educational institutions 'on national lines and under national control'–*Report of the I.N.C.*, p. 98.

[2] It was started by Swami Dyanand Saraswati in 1875 at Calcutta.

moderate leaders as ineffective and aroused a militant Hindu nationalism, which, because it affected them as well, antagonized the Muslims. From the Government's point of view the activities of the extremists had become a very serious problem. Some hot-headed young men from Bengal and the Maharashtra had also organized themselves as a militant group. Imitating in their ways the techniques of European terrorists and anarchists, they took their cue in the main from the Irish Sinn Fein and other European revolutionaries.

The Muslims had held themselves aloof from political activities, mainly because of their backwardness in western education. Sir Syed Ahmed Khan, who had become a prominent Muslim leader, faced immense opposition from the Conservative Muslims, when he advised his co-religionists to learn English. His main aim was to enable the Muslims to overcome their sense of humiliation and grief at the loss of their power and to avail themselves of new opportunities by acquiring western education and professing their loyalty to the British. Despite opposition in certain quarters his movement was gaining strength and English education was becoming popular. But the Hindus had become politically and socially awakened. Earlier in the century Raja Ram Mohan Roy had made them conscious of the advantages of learning English and rationalizing and liberalizing Hinduism. The Brahmo Samaj contributed to some extent towards the political consciousness of the Hindus. Dwarkanath Tagore's Landlords' Association was founded in 1833 and in 1851 was founded the British Indian Association, mainly consisting of the rising middle-class Bengali Hindus, though its organ the *Hindu Patriot* helped to spread its activities beyond Bengal. The educated Hindus were also deriving their inspiration from such English thinkers as Burke, Sheridan, Fox and Mill. These political currents running through India also affected those Muslims who were receiving an English education. Sir Syed's Translation Society, founded in 1864 at Ghazipur but later transferred to Aligarh, enabled Muslims to read translations of Rollins's *Ancient History*, Mill's *Political Economy*, Elphinstone's *History of India*, and Malcolm's *History of Persia*. In April 1865 the Muhammedan Literary Society was formed by Nawab Abdul Latif of Bengal. Its activities acquainted the Muslims of Bengal, if not of other provinces, with some aspects of western culture and English literature, though it did not play any significant part in creating political consciousness among them. Sir Syed succeeded in establishing the Muhammedan Anglo-Oriental College at Aligarh in 1875. It was the fulfilment of Sir Syed's aim. The College became the centre of Muslim activities and produced the future Muslim leaders of India.

Though in a speech on 10 May 1866, before the British Indian Association, Sir Syed did talk about the need for a body which could make known to the British Parliament their requirements and wishes, he remained aloof from any political activity, even to the extent of declining Syed Ameer Ali's invitation to lend his support in the formation of the Central National Muhammedan Association in 1877.[3] It was, in Ameer Ali's opinion, the birth of the Indian National Congress which opened Syed's eyes.

When the Congress was founded in 1865 Sir Syed felt bound to advise the Muslims about the line they should adopt. His aim was not to separate the Hindus and the Muslims; he had the best interests of his community at heart. He clearly saw the superiority of the Hindus and the Muslim backwardness in the field of education. He was convinced that western political institutions were quite unsuitable to the Indian people. For centuries, in fact, India had been without politics or at least without any party politics, and a thorough grounding in western education was indispensable for any political understanding.[4]

---

[3] Syed Ameer Ali, Memoirs in *Islamic Culture,* vol. v, No. 4, p. 540. 'In 1877 when I founded the Central National Muhammadan Association, we respectfully invited him (Sir Syed) to give his valuable support but he declined.'

[4] R. B. M. R. Hassaan, *The Educational Movement of Sir Syed Ahmed Khan (1858–1898),* Ph.D. thesis 1960, University of London, suggests that Sir Syed's educational programme was not devoid of political consideration. It was meant to prepare the Muslims for political understanding and solidarity amongst themselves.

The Congress itself was a loyal organization and its aims were not revolutionary, but he felt that Muslim alignment with any political organization would jeopardize the mission of his life. They were not ready for political activities. To keep their attention away from this predominantly Hindu organization he founded the Muhammedan Educational Congress in December 1886 (the word 'Congress' was changed to Conference in 1890). The Conference met regularly and the Muslims remained aloof from the Congress with few exceptions and despite the attempts of some of the Congress leaders.[5] This Conference proved to be a forerunner of the All-India Muslim League as most of the leaders who attended this Conference in 1906 formed themselves into a political party.

On 28 December 1887 Sir Syed openly attacked the Congress in a speech which he delivered before a large gathering of prominent Muslims in Lucknow.[6] He made three main points—that the Hindus and Muslims were 'two different nations' in spite of many things in common; that representative institutions were unsuited to Indian conditions as this system would lead to the permanent subjugation of the Muslims by the Hindus because of their numerical strength; and that Indian Muslims must depend on the British to safeguard their interests and secure their effective representation in administration. In short, the Congress aims were not suitable to Indian conditions and the Muslim alignment with such an organization would lead them nowhere.

[5] The number of Muslim delegates attending the Congress sessions between 1885 and 1905 amply suggests that they were not very interested in it. Fluctuation in their numbers was due mostly to the convenience of the place where the session was held. Between 1885 and 1910 there were only two Muslim Presidents of the Congress out of twenty-six: Badruddin Tayabji, Madras, 1887; and M. R. Sayani, Calcutta, 1896. See Appendix I. S. N. Banerjea in A Nation in Making (London, 1925) on p. 108, says that the Muslim delegates were even given return fares. In the 4th Congress a resolution was passed which forbade the introduction of resolutions for discussion if one community was strongly opposed. Even then the Muslims did not join the Congress in any number.

[6] The Pioneer, 11–12 January 1888. The Times, 16 January 1888, also referred to the speech as 'one of the most remarkable political discourses ever delivered by a native of India'.

Fiery speeches and writings of the extremist Hindu leaders had powerfully stirred the imagination of young Hindus, some of whom had even committed serious crimes.[7] This political stir amongst the Hindus affected the younger generation of the Muslims also. They too began to feel restive.

The Indian Councils Acts of 1892 further brought home to the Muslims that if Government policy was moving towards a representative or responsible form of government it was high time for them to do something to safeguard their interests. As a minority community they had not been able to secure their due share under the new elective system. The Government's attempt to nominate some Muslims to the Legislative Councils had failed to satisfy the Aligarh School. Sir Syed himself, after the passage of the 1892 Act, had realized that the time had come when the Muslims should unite politically for the safeguarding of their interests. The meeting of the leading Muslims on 30 December 1893 and the formation of the Muhammedan Anglo-Oriental Defence Association of Upper India were signs of a change in his attitude towards Muslim political associations.

Though differences between Hindus and Muslims were of long standing, the Devanagri-Persian script controversy in 1900, the agitation at the time of the Partition of Bengal,[8] and the Congress claim to be the sole representative national party, while it had only a few Muslim members, perturbed the Muslim leadership after Sir Syed's death in 1898 and posed it an anxious problem. They started thinking of various methods for safeguarding the Muslim interests and preventing the younger generation from joining the Congress. Thus at the time of Minto's arrival in India the Muslims were very anxious to embark on a political career.

All of Minto's difficulties were not in India. In England the Conservative Ministry resigned in December 1905, and a

---

[7] Communal riots in Poona and Bombay, 1893, Rand murder in 1897, &c. Rowlatt Committee's Report puts the blame on Ganpati festival. See p. 1.

[8] S. N. Banerjea, op. cit., p. 124.

Liberal Government came into power.[9] The well-known Liberal John Morley assumed charge of the India Office. His views and his past record were well known, so his appointment as Secretary of State for India put new heart into Indian sympathizers in general and the Indian leaders in particular. Gokhale welcomed his appointment and the Congress considered this liberal advent as the 'return of hope and joy' for India. Morley was conscious of this effect of the change of events; as he put it in his *Recollections,* 'this coincidence between the uneasy stir there and the ascendency here of parliamentary groups all agreeing strongly in a general temper of reform constituted a serious element in the situation at Simla and Whitehall alike.'[1] Minto, though Conservative by temperament and political proclivities, was not averse to change and like Morley sensed from the beginning that something had to be done to pacify the irritated educated Indians. They both agreed on principles but differences occurred in details. Morley was extremely sensitive on certain points and tended to interfere in the details of Minto's administration. As a philosopher he was sceptical and as a politician he was cautious. Minto, being a practical man, learnt quite early that he had to be extremely tactful in his relations with Morley.

For a very long time the Indian nationalists had been trying hard to secure supporters in Parliament through whom Indian views on various problems concerning India could be brought to the notice of the British public. Though an attempt was made in 1889 it was not until 1893 that an Indian parliamentary Committee was finally established. Sir William Wedderburn, W. S. Caine and J. E. Ellis were its founders. By 1906 this committee of about 154 members had grown to 200.[2] In the new House of

---

[9] In the 1906 General Election 377 Liberals, eighty-three Irish Nationalists and fifty-three Labour members were returned to the House of Commons, as against 157 Conservatives. *The Annual Register, 1906* (London, 1907), p. 12.

[1] John Viscount Morley, *Recollections,* vol. ii, p. 150.

[2] For a detailed account of the activities of early Indian nationalists in England see Dr. Mary Cumpston, 'Some Early Indian Nationalists and Their Allies in the British Parliament, 1851–1906', *English Historical Review,* vol. lxxvi, No. 299, April 1961, pp. 279–97.

Commons the Indian sympathizers consisted not only of retired Anglo-Indians like Sir Henry Cotton and C. J. O'Donnell, but Labour members like Keir Hardie and Radicals like F. C. Mackarness and Dr. V. H. Rutherford. They demanded quick action to redress Indian grievances and harassed Morley by not only asking searching questions regarding Indian administration, but by taking a spirited and active part in Indian debates. The members of the Indian parliamentary Committee kept themselves well informed and in close touch with the Indian leaders—both moderates and extremists. Their speeches in the House of Commons were fully reported in the Indian papers. They exerted immense pressure on Morley and Morley on his part pressed Minto. Minto never liked this parliamentary interference in Indian administration. Morley and Minto differed on this point. In general the Labour, the Radical and most of the Liberal members supported and presented the Congress views in the House, while Conservatives like Ronaldshay and Earl Percy supported the Muslim demands.

There were certain other influences which hindered Minto's administration at times. For instance in India Anglo-Indian opinion was hostile to change and in England the House of Lords and the Conservatives were unwilling to allow the Government to adopt a liberal line such as would be indicated by the appointment of an Indian on the Viceroy's Executive Council. The Radicals, on the other hand, demanded much more radical changes in Indian administration and bitterly criticized strong Government action against extremists. Since the improvement of means of communication the interference in the day-to-day Indian administration by the India Office had increased. Morley was, perhaps, more inclined than any previous Secretary of State to interfere in the details of Indian administration. Then there were visiting M.P.s like Keir Hardie and journalists like H. W. Nevinson who were no supporters of the Indian bureaucratic machinery. They visited India, attended public meetings and openly criticized the Government. They encouraged the nationalists, but did not make things easier for the Government.

The Indian Press had also become quite powerful and bitterly criticized some of the Government's actions.

An attempt has been made in this study to discuss and analyse Minto's policy towards Indian aspirations—the Congress demand for more representation on the Councils of the Government and the Muslim demand for separate representation.

Quite soon after his arrival in India Minto formed his opinion about Indian nationalism; unlike Curzon he decided not to ignore the Indian demands but to listen to them and meet them as far as possible. He recognized the Congress as an important factor in the situation and tried to befriend the moderate leaders, who accepted this opportunity and helped the Government in carrying out its policies. Gokhale, Moti Lal Ghose, Rash Behari Ghose and others were frequent visitors to Government officials, especially to Dunlop Smith. The exit of the extremists after the Surat session in 1907 eased the work of the moderates and the Government, too, decided to back them up openly.

One of Curzon's legacies was the Partition of Bengal. Minto accepted this as a 'settled fact', but he realized that there was some justification for the agitation against it, because of the way the Partition had been carried out. Unlike the agitators he did not think that both Hindus and Muslims were against it. In his opinion it was mainly Calcutta Hindu leaders who had started the agitation and Fuller by his tactless policies had aggravated the situation. With a view to eliminating any appearance of partiality or discrimination against any community, he did not hesitate to accept Fuller's resignation, although he knew that at least amongst the Muslims Fuller was popular.

To combat the militant strain in nationalism he adopted a firm policy. Various repressive measures were passed, but he always impressed upon the Local Governments that they should use repressive measures cautiously. He did not hesitate to redress wrong-doing and admit his mistakes, as in the case of Lajpat Rai; but where he believed that his action was justified he resisted the strongest pressures to revise his policy, as in the case of nine Bengali deportees.

Minto thought the Congress demand for 'self-rule' an impossibility. He firmly believed that the character of the Indian Government must remain autocratic, but it could be tempered by giving Indians a larger representation on the Legislative Councils and more share in the administration of their country. He even fought for the admission of an Indian to the Executive Council, from which the Indians were barred by tradition.

The Muslims, who had gradually become conscious that they had fallen behind the Hindus in the political race, approached Minto for safeguards for their interests. The deputation that met Minto on 1 October 1906 was organized by Mohsin-ul-Mulk, who had the support and co-operation of other Muslim leaders. Morley's budget speech of 1906, which indicated an extension of the representative element on the Legislative Councils, was the cause of this sudden stir amongst the Muslims. They demanded separate representation for themselves, and Minto accepted their cogently worded plea. In agreeing with this demand he was not so much accepting a new principle of separate Hindu and Muslim representation, as maintaining the old idea that the Indian society consisted of 'interests'—social groups or hereditary trades—rather than territorial areas.

It is not correct to suggest that the Muslim deputation and their demands were inspired or engineered by the Government. As has been explained in this study, and as Minto's correspondence with Hare suggests, the Government was not even aware of what the Muslims intended to ask for in their address. Minto and Hare were thinking to find ways and means to pacify the Muslims, who were agitated at Fuller's resignation. They did not discuss the question of separate representation. The organization of the Muslim deputation and the framing of their demands were solely the work of the Muslim leaders under Mohsin-ul-Mulk's guidance.

When the All-India Muslim League was founded in December 1906 it did not receive the degree of Government patronage that the Congress had received from the hands of Lord Dufferin; amongst its organizers there were not present any ex-I.C.S.

officers and M.P.s of the calibre of A. O. Hume and Sir William Wedderburn. Its main aim was to fight for separate electorates. Morley, who had whole-heartedly approved of Minto's commitment, subsequently changed his mind, but the League presented its case so ably that the Government after all decided to accede to this demand. It was a big achievement for such a new political party, with practically no experience of political tactics. Though Gokhale accepted the introduction of separate representation as the only solution of existing differences other Congress leaders interpreted it as an attempt to divide India into two hostile camps—Hindus and Muslims.

Minto has been blamed for this 'Machiavellian' policy. The question naturally arises whether the decision to concede the Muslim demand was because of a policy of 'divide and rule', resulting in differences between the Hindus and Muslims; or whether it merely recognized the cultural and religious differences that already existed between the two. Almost every historian agrees that those differences had always existed between the two communities. The Muslims, though no less patriotic or nationalist than the Hindus, were worried at the prospect of their being swamped by the Hindu majority. The Hindu majority had not been able to satisfy them that the joint electorates would help Hindus and Muslims to develop a national outlook in political matters. Past experience had shown the Muslims that the only possible way to safeguard their interests was to ask for separate representation. Hence they strove to achieve this aim and were able to convince the Government that they must be given separate representation.

Moreover, Minto wanted to secure the representation of various classes and interests on the Legislative Councils. There is no evidence whatsoever to suggest that his policy was based on 'divide and rule'. He sincerely thought that separate representation would eliminate the causes of irritation between various classes and that the Government would benefit by the presence of all important interests on her Councils. He had two objects in mind. Firstly, it would satisfy important classes like the Muslims and without separate representation there was no chance of their getting sufficient representation. Under the 1892 Act not only the Muslims but other interests like that of the landholders had not been able to secure proper representation on the Legislative Councils. Minto was not concerned with the representation of Muslim interests only. He desired all those who had a stake in the country to be represented in one form or another. His proposal for a Council of Princes was based on this very idea. Secondly, with larger representation of these interests and classes, he hoped, the causes of unrest would disappear and the foundations of the British *Raj* would be strengthened. This was perhaps more dominant in his policies because, with a view to suppressing sedition and combating unrest, he did not hesitate to veto the Punjab Colonies Bill in opposition to his Council and accepted the resignation of Fuller, knowing full well that it would irritate not only the Civil Service but also the Muslims.

He carried out his policies with tact, sympathy and firmness. He did not weather the storm completely, but at least mitigated some of its consequences. His policy towards the Muslims was successful. They did not join the ranks of dissatisfied Indians. Even the Montagu-Chelmsford Report admitted this: 'Throughout the troubled days of 1907–1910 the Muhammadans, with a few unimportant exceptions, held severely aloof from the revolutionary movement, and retained their traditional attitude of sturdy loyalty, secure in the feeling . . . that their interests were safe in the hands of the Government.'[3]

The moderate Congress leaders were also satisfied. The Congress session of 1908 expressed a deep sense of gratification. The 1909 session saw a change in the Congress attitude towards the Government because of the announcement of separate representation, but in 1910 the Congress accepted it as a necessary evil. The reforms had encouraged the moderate leaders and discredited the extremists.

As to whether Minto or Morley was more responsible for the reforms there is sharp difference of opinion. Morley remained

[3] *Report on the Indian Constitutional Reforms*, 1918, Cd. 9109, p. 22.

contented with *The Times*'s verdict that 'Viceroy and Secretary of State both seem to have come simultaneously to very much the same conclusions, and both worked in a spirit of cordial co-operation to carry their joint ideas.'[4] Lady Minto did not agree. She urged upon Morley, before and during the publication of his *Recollections*, that her husband should be given priority in thinking out the reform scheme. 'I cannot share your content to leave the claim for priority and originality where it was put by *The Times* in 1914. I remembered so well Minto's letter to you suggesting the Reforms which, after living in the country for some time and mixing with all creeds and classes, he felt must inevitably come. Your answer is also fresh in my memory. The proposal to have an Indian member on the Viceroy's Executive Council was surely entirely his.'[5]

John Morley's *Recollections* was published in 1917, three years after Minto's death. This book is based entirely on his letters to Minto, lacks certain important details and fails to give an adequate idea of Minto's reactions to some of Morley's suggestions. It suggests that in many matters Morley's will prevailed. It gives us an impression that many important decisions were taken by Morley, while Minto meekly submitted. It credits Morley, in the most modest way, with originating and initiating a number of reforms. Though it gives an idea of Morley's strong likes and dislikes (particularly in the matter of deportees) it fails to convey Minto's feelings towards this problem. Thus in

[4] John Viscount Morley, op. cit., p. 340.
[5] See Lady Minto's correspondence in the Minto Collection in the National Library of Scotland, Edinburgh. It gives an idea of the methods that were adopted by Lady Minto and Dunlop Smith to minimize Morley's part in it and how they arranged to influence reviewers in various papers. Morley showed the manuscript of his *Recollections* to Dunlop Smith at Lady Minto's instance and was willing to make certain changes, but refused to hand it over to another person when she insisted that a third person should judge his account. He told her that it was his memoirs, and as to Minto's part in this affair, some day his biography would be written and that would present affairs from his angle. Minto had died in 1914. He assured Lady Minto, 'I am convinced that no mischief will be done either to truth, or to that loyal good feeling which Minto and I were so happy in maintaining.' Morley to Lady Minto, 20 November 1916.

many ways it is insufficient and gives a one-sided picture. Morley himself took shelter behind the thought that it was his auto-biography, and so must necessarily concern him. Its publication hastened Lady Minto's endeavours to get her husband's bio-graphy published. Harcourt Butler, the Educational member of the Viceroy's Council, and after him Harold Stuart, another Civil Servant, and a Secretary of the Government of India in Minto's time, were approached. But both declined to comply, owing to their preoccupations and their official positions.[6] Ultimately John Buchan wrote and published *Lord Minto* in 1924, a year after Morley's death. This is a well-written biography of Minto, but in it his Indian administration forms a very small part. Buchan based his chapters on India on Minto's private papers and tried to present the whole case from Minto's point of view. But he had very little space at his disposal, and so could not go into greater detail.

Realizing that the part that Minto had played in moulding the destinies of the Indian people was too important to be described in this biography, Lady Minto published *India, Minto and Morley* in 1934. She took great pains in presenting the events of 1905-10 in greater detail, and endeavoured to support the story with quotations from the letters of Morley and Minto and from her own *Indian Journal*. Her *Indian Journal* is preserved in the Indian Institute, Oxford, and is very interesting and illuminating. It contains many beautiful photographs and descriptions of Indian scenes. Lady Minto tried to describe some Indian per-sonalities and her book gives us an idea of the warmth and sympathy that the Mintos felt towards India and Indians. Both her book and her *Journal* are understandably partial to Minto —she presents him in the brightest possible colour. In *My Indian Journal* she criticizes the Indian Press for attributing the reforms to Morley. In some of his letters to his friends Minto also seems to have suffered from the obsession that the credit for these

[6] Correspondence between Lady Minto, Harcourt Butler and Harold Stuart is preserved in a loose packet of letters in the Minto Collection in the National Library of Scotland.

reforms was gradually shifting towards Morley. E. Montagu, the Under-Secretary of State for India, had said in the House of Commons, 'Lord Morley and his Council, working through the agency of Lord Minto, have accomplished much.'[7] Lady Minto thought Montagu's reference to Minto in his speech 'positively insulting'. She states, 'In this I see the hand of Morley, who has never quite forgiven Rolly for having stated publicly that he was the author of the reforms, for which Morley had hitherto been given the entire credit.'[8]

Such an obsession in the minds of both Minto and Lady Minto becomes understandable when we look through the pages of the *Native Newspaper Reports*. A great majority of vernacular news-papers considered that Morley was solely responsible for reforms. They considered that Minto had spent his time in big-game hunting and extravagant tours. Morley's parliamentary speeches and other utterances were fully reported. Unlike Curzon Minto made few public speeches. His correspondence with Morley was extremely secret and private. Thus it was not possible for the Press to follow Minto's part in these reforms.

But before we lay the responsibility for these reforms upon any individual's shoulders there are a number of different questions to consider—who thought of them first and then who did more to bring them about or to overcome opposition. The climate of opinion was also important. In India and in England the Congress and the Muslim League were exerting their influences. The role played by the leaders of these parties was also significant. Dun-lop Smith, in one of his notes in Lady Minto's *Journal*,[9] explained that the Viceroy initiated the reforms because, before leaving for Simla in the spring of 1906, he discussed these matters with the Lieutenant-Governor of Bengal and some members of his Council. Moreover, on 24 May 1906 Minto wrote to Morley that he was in favour of giving the native population of India 'as large

[7] *Hansard,* House of Commons, vol. xix. (11 July–3 August 1910), 26 July 1910, Col. 1,984.

[8] Lady Minto, op. cit., vol. ii, pp. 271–2, 9 August 1910.

[9] Ibid., 1908, pp. 238–42, dated 6 September 1908.

a share in the Government as we can give'. Dunlop Smith's statement has the greater significance because the Congress had been urging such reforms, and the *Bengalee*, on 20 February 1906, had suggested that certain reforms should be brought forward now—namely the enlargement of Legislative Councils; permission to move amendments in connexion with the Budget; Indian representation in the Viceroy's Executive Council and in the Indian Council in London; separation of judiciary from executive, &c.

The *Indian Mirror* on 30 May 1906 also advocated such reforms. Minto as the man on the spot must have felt the need to inform himself of the opinion of his colleagues on these matters. Of course, he must have been conscious of the fact that if he had not prepared himself for such exigencies he would have been unprepared when the new Liberal Ministry decided to embark on reform. Moreover, his own inclinations, as could be deduced from his public and private utterances and letters, show that he was genuinely interested in administering India with 'sympathy' and in giving a proper hearing to the demands of the loyal, moderate, educated Indians. But it was decidedly Morley who on 15 June 1906 asked Minto to set the ball rolling in the direction of reform. Minto did yeoman's work in mastering the details and carrying out a remarkable transformation in the conservative outlook of his colleagues. He was faced with more difficulties than Morley. His colleagues, many a time, disagreed with him; the Local Governments sometimes kept him in the dark,[1] and sometimes fought him tooth and nail on petty details.[2] Over and above all these was hostile Anglo-Indian opinion. Then there were the activities of the terrorists and the extremists and

---

[1] See Chapter I.

[2] Sir George Clarke, Lord Sydenham, *My Working Life* (London, 1927), pp. 236–7. He was the Governor of Bombay and very proudly writes that his Government fought hard with the Central Government on many details. Even Morley had to warn him: 'Forgive me for saying so, but were I in your place, I would not fight too hard over every disputable point with G. of I. . . .' But Clarke says, 'It was impossible to explain that I was not fighting the G. of I, but only two or three officials . . .'

the moaning of the moderates, who every time brought it to his notice that if nothing was done there would be grave consequences. There were sectarian and religious differences. The Secretary of State himself presented a problem. He was sensitive, sceptical, autocratic and was prone to interfere in petty details. Minto had a tremendously difficult job.

Morley had difficulties but they were not so grave. True, the House of Lords was conservative, but the House of Commons was more radical than the Secretary of State himself. The Indian Council was almost a nonentity so far as its powers were concerned. *The Times* was occasionally angry, but never hostile. Despite that, Morley was sometimes slow to react. The influence of the retired Anglo-Indians was one of the reasons.

Amongst the Indian leaders Gokhale played a prominent part. Morley and Minto had confidence in him and he was able to keep the Congress in order after the Surat split. Even the angry outbursts of the 1909 session were mollified in the 1910 session, when the Congress resolution regarding the regulations was extremely docile. But there was not a single Muslim leader who enjoyed the confidence of either Minto or Morley. Whatever the Muslims were able to achieve for themselves was because of pressure through the League rather than any policy of favouritism or patronage on the part of the Government. There was, on the other hand, an intense feeling prevalent that the Liberals, like the Labour Party, were unsympathetic to Muslim interests, and at one time Morley had to explain to the Aga Khan that he was not anti-Muslim, whatever other Liberals thought about Islam.[3] As Morley liked Gokhale and listened to him and there was a strong parliamentary group that expressed the predominantly Hindu Congress views, the Muslim leaders felt that Morley was more under the Hindu or anti-Muslim influence than any Muslim influence.

With all these points before us it seems quite fair to agree with *The Times*'s view that 'Viceroy and Secretary of State both seem to have come simultaneously to very much the same conclusions...'

[3] Morley to Minto, 18 February 1909. *M.P.*

The political climate in India and England paved the way for them and, despite some hairsplitting controversies over details, the reform scheme was the result of their joint ideas and remarkable understanding of the Indian political situation.

CHAPTER ONE

# MINTO AND THE INDIAN
# NATIONAL CONGRESS, 1905–1907

By 1905 the Congress had become a formidable organization. Though it remained mainly a Hindu organization, its membership had grown considerably. Curzon's undisguised contempt for the Congress[1] and his emphasis on an efficient rather than a representative system of government gave a greater impetus to this movement to grow from an association of moderate, constitutionally inclined members to a bitterly critical one. The return to power of the Liberals after the Conservative defeat at the General Elections of 1905 and the appointment of John Morley as the Secretary of State for India was claimed by the moderate Congress leaders to be 'the return of hope and joy' for India and they hoped that now the Government would consider their claims patiently, wisely, and sympathetically.[2] Surendranath Banerjea and others went to the extent of flattering Morley by calling him their 'political Guru'.[3]

[1] Curzon thought the 'Congress was tottering to its fall' and he would 'assist it to a peaceful demise'. Curzon to Hamilton, 18 November 1900, *Hamilton Papers*, vol. xviii, I.O.L.

[2] *Report of the I.N.C.*, 1905, Introduction, pp. 3–4. Such a change was expected and the Congress leaders were preparing to place their demands before the new Government. In its twentieth Session, 1904, Wedderburn introduced a resolution in favour of sending a Congress deputation to England. See also S. K. Ratcliffe, *Sir William Wedderburn and the Indian Reform Movement* (London, 1923), p. 137.

[3] *Report of the I.N.C.*, p. 65. Gokhale in his presidential address said, 'Large numbers of educated men in this country feel towards Mr. Morley as towards a master, and the heart hopes and yet trembles as it had never hoped or trembled before. He, the reverent student of Burke, the disciple of Mill, the friend and biographer of Gladstone,—will he courageously apply their principles and his own to the government of this country, or will he too succumb to the influences of the India Office around him and thus cast a cruel blight on hopes which his own writings have done so much to foster?' Ibid. p. 17.

Through presidential addresses and resolutions the Congress had been pressing for the extension of representation in the Executive and Legislative Councils of the Government of India since 1892, the year when the Indian Councils Act was passed.[4] It was in 1905, that the demand for 'further extension and reform of the supreme and provincial Councils' became intensive.[5]

The Congress demanded 'a real voice in the Government of the Country' and recommended an increase in the number of elected members and the right to divide the councils on financial matters. Gokhale in his presidential address went even further. While admitting that 'our destinies are now linked with those of England', he demanded the same 'form of Government which exists in the self-governing Colonies of the British Empire.'[6]

Yet Morley was cautious and despite his liberal ideas he was reluctant to move quickly. Immediately on his arrival Minto gathered all the information he needed to form his opinion of the Congress and wrote to Morley that 'I think myself it is a mistake to attempt to ignore the existence of the Congress. The section of the population it represents will never, I am convinced, possess the grit to play a leading part in the Government as a whole, but it does represent Indian advanced thought on many subjects which must affect the future administration of the country, and it will be the greatest mistake to attempt to set the Congress aside and to refuse to have anything to do with it as a factor in the present history of India.' He also expressed his inclination to receive a Congress deputation (Curzon refused to receive any such deputation from the Congress), 'provided of course that the deputation is a well selected one representing influential members'.[7] Minto thought that Gokhale 'represents the best elements in the Congress' and that 'one can do a good deal by keeping in

---

[4] (a) Presidential address, 1895, p. 14. Ibid. 1898. (b) Resolution xiv, 1898, p. 108. Ibid. 1898. (c) Resolution xii, 1899, p. 33. Ibid. 1899. (d) Presidential address, 1899, pp. 21–2. Ibid. 1899.

[5] Resolution ii, p. 23. Ibid. 1905.

[6] Ibid. 1905. Presidential address, p. 13.

[7] Minto to Morley, 3 April 1906. *M.P.*

touch with such leaders as S. N. Banerji and Moti Lal Ghose'.[8] Minto's view, thus, was that the Congress was an important factor in the Indian political life and it would do immense good to make friends with the moderate leaders of the Congress.[9]

Morley was, on the other hand, sceptical. He had 'no particular liking for that school [the Congress], yet he wanted to look deeper into 'their notions'. His suggestion to Minto was 'to consider rather slowly whether it would be well to accede to their request for an interview. It is not to be settled off hand, I think, either way'.[1] After his interviews with the Prince of Wales who had returned from India, and Gokhale,[2] who had gone to see him, Morley came to this conclusion that 'there it [the Congress] is, whether we like it or not (and personally I don't like it)'. The Prince of Wales told him that the Congress was 'becoming a great power for evil', but Morley thought 'that it will mainly depend upon ourselves whether the Congress is a power for good or evil', and he comforted Minto by saying that 'all depends on you and me keeping step'.[3]

Commenting on Gokhale's speech at the Benares Congress meeting (1905) Minto had earlier expressed his views about popular representation. 'His [Gokhale's] ideas and his ambitions certainly appear to me high spirited and patriotic, but one can-

[8] Minto to Morley, 9 May 1906. See also Minto to Morley, 28 May 1906 and 27 June 1906. *M.P.*

[9] Minto to Morley, 2 May 1906: 'it would be best not to ignore it [the Congress].' Ibid.

[1] Morley to Minto, 19 April 1906. Ibid.

[2] During his stay in England, Gokhale, besides his many meetings with Morley, met H. Campbell-Bannerman, the Prime Minister. This interview was without Morley's knowledge which upset him very much. He wrote to the Prime Minister pointing out that it would have been better had the Secretary of State been informed about this interview beforehand, as there was every likelihood of Gokhale's making capital out of it. The Prime Minister, however, assured him that it was 'innocent' and 'unimportant'. See Morley to Campbell-Bannerman, 2, 4 August 1906. *Campbell-Bannerman Papers*, vol. xviii (ff. 288). (41223. B.M.) See also F. A. Hirtzel's Diary, 9, 23 May; 12, 26 June and 1 August 1906. *Home Misc.* 864, I.O.L.

[3] Morley to Minto, 11 May 1906. *M.P.* See Morley, op. cit, p. 171. Morley omitted those words which he thought would betray his dislike of the Congress.

not disguise from oneself the risk that would surround popular representation on any large scale in the government of this country.' He explained that the Indian Empire was composed of many races, some of them far behind the Bengali standard of intellectual development, but more war-like and it was very doubtful whether these races would 'put up with Bengali ascendancy in the administration of India'.[4] Minto was thus of the opinion that it would be dangerous 'to import into India English political institutions'. He admired the British constitution, but 'our constitution . . . is the result of a long course of historical experience unknown to India.' He would never encourage its blind imitation by the Bengali.[5]

Morley agreed, '*Fundamental* difference between us, I really believe there is none. Not one whit more than you, do I think it desirable, or possible, or even conceivable, to adopt English political institutions to the Nations who inhabit India. Assuredly not in your day or mine. But the *Spirit* of English institutions is a different thing, and it is a thing that we cannot escape even if we wished, which I hope we don't.'[6]

Both of them had become aware of the growth of a new spirit in India—Morley from what he had been told,[7] and Minto from what he saw. That is why Minto was more emphatic in his desire to consider the Congress as one of the chief factors in the situation. He surprised Morley when he expressed his willingness to receive a Congress deputation, if it came to him.[8] His admiration for 'perfectly loyal and moderate' Indians belonging to the educated class was great and he thought that this loyalty entitled the members of this class 'to a greater share in the Government of India'. Moreover, there was another fear 'if we do not [conciliate this class], we shall drive it into the arms of the Congress leaders'; and by the Congress leaders he meant the leaders of the

[4] Minto to Morley, 3 January 1906. *M.P.*
[5] Minto to Morley, 16 May 1906. Ibid.
[6] Morley to Minto, 6 June 1906. Ibid.
[7] Morley to Minto, 6 June 1906. Ibid.
[8] Minto to Morley, 3 April 1906. Ibid; Morley to Minto, 25 April 1906. Ibid.

extremist group.[9] In another letter Minto informed Morley that Gokhale was also very anxious that if nothing was done, 'the whole younger generation of India is going over to the extremists' side' and they were attracted by the extremist doctrines of 'getting rid of British rule'.[1]

As early as March 1906[2] Minto discussed with some members of his Executive Council possible changes, such as the appointment of an Indian to his Executive Council, but the members of his Council were not favourably inclined to the idea, so he dropped it. In a letter on 28 May 1906, Minto stated that he had been thinking of 'a possible counterpoise to Congress aims' and suggested that 'we may find a solution in the Council of Princes'.[3] Morley was sceptical. 'What would the Council discuss? What power of directing or influencing the executive? How far could they be allowed to look into the secrets of Government?' he asked. But he admitted, 'it is with the liveliest satisfaction that I perceive in your letter of the 28 May how much cool, equitable and penetrating reflection you are giving to all our puzzles'.[4]

Morley knew that he had no practical knowledge of Indian affairs,[5] that India was not England; and that one cannot transplant British institutions wholesale into that country, whatever the Congress or others might think. He was of the opinion that India had reached in her political evolution a stage between the old strictly bureaucratic régime, and government by representative and constitutional institutions. And it was after becoming sure that Minto was thinking in the same direction of administrative reform that Morley suggested, 'Either do you write me a despatch, or I'll write you one—by way of opening the ball' before 'the demands will widen and extend into "National" reasons, where I at least look with a very doubting and suspicious eye.'[6]

[9] Minto to Morley, 27 February 1907. *M.P.*
[1] Minto to Morley, 5 March 1907. Ibid.
[2] John Buchan, op. cit., p. 231.      [3] Minto to Morley, 28 May 1906. Ibid.
[4] Morley to Minto, 22 June 1906. Ibid.
[5] Morley to Minto, 21 June 1907. Ibid. 'I do not know the Indian ground ...'
[6] Morley to Minto, 15 June 1906. Ibid.

Minto readily fell in line with Morley but expressed the desire that the initiative should come from the Government of India, being the Government on the spot and to avoid any misgiving in the minds of the people that the Government of India had been forced.[7] It was a statesmanlike suggestion and Morley acquiesced. Minto accordingly appointed a Committee of his Executive Council with Sir A. Arundel as its chairman on 16 August 1906.[8] The Committee was to give its opinion on four points: a Council of Princes or their representation on the Viceroy's Legislative Council; a Native Member for the Viceroy's Executive Council; increased representation on the Viceroy's Legislative Council and that of Local Governments; and prolongation of the debate on Budget and powers to move amendments.[9]

Besides the consideration of changes in administration Minto diverted his attention to finding out the immediate causes of political stir in India and in Bengal particularly the Partition of Bengal was one of the most ticklish questions. The Partition of Bengal announced on 3 December 1903 and carried out on 16 October 1905[1] had given a great shock to the Congress leaders and stirred up a violent nationalism in Bengal. The Congress considered it a calculated move against the national unity and solidarity. It was thought 'a most arbitrary and unsympathetic evidence of irresponsible and autocratic statesmanship'.[2]

In his very first letter Minto informed Morley of the situation in Bengal. He was not content with the official interpretation of the happenings in Bengal. Official opinion was unanimous in its approval of Partition. He was told that the agitation was really not due to any genuine national feeling in India, but due to the

[7] Minto to Morley, 5 July 1906. *M.P.*
[8] Minto to Morley, 15 August 1906. Ibid.
[9] Secret Minute circulated for Honourable Members of Committee's information, 15 August 1906. Ibid.
[1] For a detailed account of events leading to Partition see P. C. Ghosh, *Development of the Indian National Congress, 1892–1909* (Calcutta, 1960), pp. 95–128. For Bengali Muslim attitude towards Partition see Sufia Ahmed, *Some Aspects of the History of the Muslim Community in Bengal (1884–1912)*. London University Ph.D. Thesis, 1960, pp. 320–429.
[2] *Report of the I.N.C.* 1904, Presidential address, p. 46.

'loss of a certain amount of business, especially legal business, which now migrates from Calcutta to the large cities of Eastern Bengal, and that this feeling had been fanned into blaze by wire-pullers at Calcutta under the influence of other wire-pullers at home connected with the National Congress'. The Indian Press had been violent, asserting that Partition had been carried out regardless of Bengal national sentiment and local feeling, and that it had been aimed to a great extent at the *Swadeshi* movement in support of the local industries which the Government was accused of hoping to destroy. Minto's opinion was that 'there is no doubt a great deal of truth in the assertion that the agitation has been unscrupulously fostered, and that influence has been brought to bear upon the student class and the universities to join the movement. But at the same time I cannot but think there is much more genuine feeling in the movement than the official mind is prepared to admit. . . . I cannot help suspecting that local feeling has been treated with some want of sympathy in aiming at what in the official mind is considered necessary for administrative machinery.' Minto thought that if the East Riding of Yorkshire were for the best possible administrative reasons handed over to Lincolnshire, one would hear a good deal about it and 'I believe it is incorrect to deny the existence of a somewhat similar feeling here,'[3] though the Muslims who largely preponderated in Eastern Bengal appeared to be generally satisfied with what had occurred.[4] He, however, firmly believed that Partition was 'very necessary' and that 'the agitation was settling down'.[5]

As the Prince and Princess of Wales were touring India at that time Minto thought it advisable to call Gokhale for an interview and asked him to stop the agitation pending reappraisal of the whole situation by his Government. This interview had a marked effect on both. Gokhale told Dunlop Smith that 'His Excellency shows sympathy and understanding' and Minto gained

---

[3] Minto to Morley, 13 December 1905. *M.P.*
[4] Minto to Morley, 20 December 1905. Ibid.
[5] Minto to Morley, Memorandum, 5 February 1906. Ibid.

'through him a real insight into the aspirations of the Hindus.'[6]

The Bengali Hindu leaders headed by Surendranath Banerjea had started this agitation for the revocation of the Partition. They held protest meetings which were attended by other Congress leaders as well. Their processions and chanting of *Bande Mataram*,[7] a song disliked by the Muslims of Eastern Bengal particularly, were considered a danger to the peace of the new province. This agitation unwittingly united the leaders of extreme views with the moderate thinking ones against the Government. It further gave birth to the Boycott movement—the Indians were to boycott British goods with a view to compel the British Government to listen to their demands. This method had worked in Ireland and it was hoped that it would work in India as well. The boycott was supplemented by increased emphasis on the *Swadeshi* movement which sought to correct the industrial helplessness of the country.[8] With these political and economic weapons, the Bengali Hindus sought the redress

[6] Mary, Countess of Minto, op. cit., p. 20. T .V. Parvate, *Gopal Krishna Gokhale* (Ahmedabad, 1959), pp. 310–11, does not agree with Lady Minto's account of this interview. According to him, 'Gokhale could not be the theatrical courtier that he is made out to be by the Countess of Minto, as turning round to the Viceroy's Private Secretary and indulging in fulsome flattery'. Parvate seems to have missed the point Lady Minto was trying to make. What she wanted to convey was that Gokhale was impressed by the Viceroy's sympathetic attitude.

[7] H. W. Nevinson, *The New Spirit in India* (London, 1908), p. 15. This song 'Hail Motherland' was disliked by the Muslims. Because 'Motherland' was identified with the Hindu goddess Kali and the song was full of Hindu imagery. It was taken from Bankim Chandra's novel *Ananda Math* (The Abbey of Bliss). The *Pioneer*, 27 September 1906, suggested that it would be better if the agitators invent some cry with 'less disagreeable associations' than the pure Hindu cry 'Bande Mataram', which is so unpalatable to the Muslims.

[8] S. N. Banerjea, op. cit., p. 191. '...the *Swadeshi* movement had already come into existence. At any rate the *Swadeshi* spirit was abroad. It was in the air. There was a growing party among the educated community who espoused it. Our industrial helplessness was attracting attention in an increasing measure; and it was readily perceived that the boycott would be a double-edged weapon, industrial and political, in its scope and character.'

of their grievances. But it placed the Congress in a difficult position, for it brought Muslim and Hindu interests into sharp conflict.

The Muslims, except a few, did not join these protests and demonstrations and remained aloof. They opposed the Congress demand for the revocation of Partition and did not join the *Swadeshi* movement, as besides being an economic movement, to which probably they would not have objected,[9] it had a strong religious colouring which attracted the Hindu masses. *Swadeshi* meetings opened and closed with Hindu songs, *Bande Mataram* being one of them. Besides, in order to symbolize the continued unity of the Bengali race the *rakhis* (thread wristlets) were distributed. The Muslims did not like all these manifestations of a movement which was supposed to be economic. They abstained from its meetings. Even some Hindus were coerced to attend these meetings and use *Swadeshi* goods. The *Hitavarta*, Calcutta, gives a story of a representative of the Bhattacharya family in the village of Mahespur, District of Jessore, who visited various families urging them to use *Swadeshi* goods. The defaulters were told that they would be ex-communicated.[1]

Besides these *Swadeshi* meetings a new festival was celebrated in Calcutta. It was the Shivaji festival and Tilak himself spoke at one

---

[9] The Muslims were not opposed to *Swadeshi* as such. The weavers in Bengal were mostly Muslims and it was in their interest. This is further borne out in a letter from Adamji Peerbhoy, President of the Muslim League Session 1907, to Dunlop Smith dated 25 March 1908, which he sent with 'a small true *Swadeshi* article' as a wedding present to Lady Ruby Elliot. Lady Minto, *My Indian Journal*, 1908, p. 77.

[1] The *Hitavarta*, Calcutta, 24 December 1905. *B.N.N.R.*, 1905. Fortnightly report from the Government of Eastern Bengal and Assam, 8 October 1906. Chief Sect. of E.B. & A. Government to Government of India, 6, 8, 23, 26 October 1906, 5 November 1906. *Home Progs.*, August–December 1906, 7313. S. N. Banerjea, op. cit., pp. 202–3, shows how Pundit Kali Prosanna Kabyavisard, editor of the *Hitabadi*, introduced a new element in *Swadeshi* meetings by beginning them with patriotic songs. For a comprehensive account of the *Swadeshi* leaders' tactics to make the movement popular see also J. R. McLane, *The Development of Nationalist Ideas and Tactics and the Policies of the Government of India, 1897–1905*. London University Ph.D. Thesis, 1961, Ch. VI.

of the meetings.[2] This festival was first celebrated in 1896 at the Fort of Raigarh in honour of the birthday of Shivaji, a Maratha Chieftain, who had fought against the Mughal army. He had assassinated Afzal Khan, a general of the Bijapur Army treacherously. Tilak had exonerated Shivaji from the charge of murdering Afzal Khan by suggesting that for national reasons he was justified in doing so. The revival of the Maratha glory in the shape of the Shivaji festival had undoubtedly stirred the Maratha imagination, but it was intensely disliked by the Muslims. Its celebration in Bengal naturally affected the Muslim public opinion towards any movement with which those Hindus were associated who were celebrating the Shivaji festival. While the *Sandhya*, the *Bharat Mitra*, and the *Yugantar* praised Tilak and Shivaji,[3] the *Soltan*, in most conciliatory terms suggested to the Hindus that if they must celebrate such festivals, why not find some hero who would not be as obnoxious and unpalatable to the Muslims as Shivaji was. It asked the Hindus, 'How can our Hindu brethren wipe away from the page of history the record of Shivaji's inhuman conduct towards Afzal Khan and his army? Cannot the annals of the Hindu race point to a single hero whom even the tongue of slander will not dare call a chief of dacoits or a treacherous man?'[4] Such were the questions which remained unanswered and the cleavage between the two communities widened.

The Boycott movement placed the Muslims in an awkward position and the refusal of some Muslim traders and vendors to agree to boycott British goods led to rioting. One such instance occurred in Mymensingh in Eastern Bengal in 1906. Thus the tactics adopted by the Hindu leaders to mobilize public opinion against the Partition led to strong differences between Hindus and Muslims. That is why this anti-Partition agitation of the

---

[2] D. V. Thamankar, *Lokmanya Tilak* (London, 1956), pp. 65–66, says that the festival was being celebrated in Calcutta before Tilak was invited in 1906. See also Ram Gopal, *Lokmanya Tilak* (Bombay, 1956), pp. 234–6.

[3] The *Sandhya*, Calcutta, 7 June 1906; the *Bharat Mitra*, Calcutta, 9 June 1906; the *Yugantar*, Calcutta, 10 June 1906. *B.N.N.R.*, 1906.

[4] The *Soltan*, Calcutta, 8 June 1906. Ibid.

Congress Hindus, originally directed against the British Government, had the appearance of being aimed at the Muslims who had supported Partition.

Minto's first important public utterance in India was his reply to an address from the Indian Association on 12 January 1906. The address dealt mostly with the situation in Bengal. Minto's reply was careful but firm. He made it clear that he would be misleading the bearers of the address if he in any way appeared to encourage in them a hope of the reversal of the policy already agreed upon.[5] He was an administrator and his duty was to carry out the policy already approved by the Secretary of State. He told them unhesitatingly that the reasons they had given for the revocation of the Partition were not shared universally, so far as he knew. He explained that he was no opponent of *Swadeshi*, 'it is only the abuse of the word to which I object'.[6] His reply naturally pleased neither the deputationists[7] nor the Bengali Press.[8] The *Indian Mirror* thought that Minto's reply 'has disillusioned the people' and would not restore public confidence and that he was ill-advised in accepting the official version of the facts as gospel truth. It suggested to Minto that he should not allow himself to be too much under the influence of bureaucracy.[9] The *Amrita Bazar Patrika* was of the opinion that instead of giving the reply in a purely 'official way', Minto might have said that he could not commit himself to an expression of opinion on the difficult points raised. Such a reply would not have offended the people, whereas the reply he actually had given had wounded their feelings and created the impression

[5] In his letters to Morley, Minto explained that first he thought of telling the deputation that like all other British subjects they had a right to approach the House of Commons for the redress of their grievances if any. But that meant more trouble, so he changed his mind and gave them no such hope. Minto to Morley, 3, 17 January 1906. *M.P.*

[6] *Speeches of the Earl of Minto* (Calcutta, 1911), p. 28.

[7] Lady Minto, *My Indian Journal*, vol. i, 1905–6, p. 45.

[8] *B.N.N.R.*, 1906. To keep himself informed of the day-to-day position, Minto asked for fortnightly reports from the Lt.-Governors of the two provinces besides these newspaper reports.

[9] The *Indian Mirror*, 14, 18 January 1906. *B.N.N.R.*, 1906.

that 'he favoured the official party at the cost of the nation'. It, however, advised the people not to lose heart as their cause was just and if the Viceroy could not redress the Bengali grievances, the Secretary of State and Parliament would do it.[1] According to the *Charu Mihir*, Minto's reply had made the people despair of getting any redress of their grievances.[2] The *Sri Sri Vishnu Priya-o-Ananda Bazar Patrika* thought that it 'has disappointed the Bengali people'.[3]

But there were still hopes that the question of the Partition would be raised in Parliament and that the new Ministry would undo the unjust act. In the House of Commons some Liberal members, H. Roberts, Sir Henry Cotton, C. J. O'Donnell, T. Hart-Davies, and D. M. Smeaton, pressed Morley for a reconsideration of the Partition.[4] Sir Henry Cotton explained that the Bengali race, with all their faults, were the principal section of the Indian Community who had inspired the new national patriotism in which was centred the hope and destiny of their country. This Partition was designed to weaken the Bengali ascendancy. The object of the Partition was to strike a blow at the intelligence and enterprise which had taken a form that the officials did not approve of. The wish of the people of Bengal was that the old state of things should be restored and that they might still be placed under one government. He admitted the practical difficulties of undoing the Partition but suggested that 'it was possible to meet the feeling in India by some modification of the existing arrangement'. With regard to the Hindu-Muslim differences he admitted that it was partially true that the Muslims had not joined the protest meetings, but they were absolutely at one with the Hindus in this demand for revocation of Partition. On what evidence he based his statement he did not

---

[1] The *Amrita Bazar Patrika*, 15, 16 January 1906. Ibid.

[2] The *Charu Mihir*, Mymensingh, 16 January 1906. Ibid.

[3] The *Sri Sri Vishnu Priya-o-Ananda Bazar Patrika*, Calcutta, 18 January 1906. Ibid.

[4] *Hansard*, House of Commons, 4S, vol. 152 (February–March 1906). 26 February 1906, Cols. 811–15; 822–30; 833–6; 837; 838–42.

clarify.[5] T. Hart-Davies was not sure whether it was a 'Machia-vellian policy' framed by the late Government, but he was of opinion that it was part of 'the wild policy' followed by the late Government in China, South Africa and the Somaliland. He, therefore, suggested that considering the new spirit prevalent in India, the new Government should respond to the aspirations of the people.[6] C. J. O'Donnell informed Morley that it was possible 'to do away with what had been done'.[7] Earl Percy, on the other hand, stated that there was no doubt that the Partition had given rise to a great deal of discontent. But, in his opinion, it not only subserved the interests of administration, but it actually secured far better grouping than had hitherto existed both of language and nationality by recognizing the preponderance of the Muslim element in the North and amalgamating the Uriyah-speaking populations of the West.[8] Morley's reply was a definite 'no' to any suggestion of reconsideration of the Partition. In his opinion the Partition was a 'settled fact'.[9]

The Bengali Press, which had pinned their hopes to the new Government for revocation of the Partition, was shocked at Morley's statement. The *Hitavadi* thought that 'elevation to power has a levelling effect in the field of politics. The charm of office makes men belonging to widely different political creeds express the same views about political incidents'. John Morley was the classic example of this, because he supported the Par-tition on the same grounds on which his predecessor in the India Office supported it. It, therefore, urged the people to do something that should make Morley repent one day for having supported the Partition. Let him not say that the agitation was subsiding. The authorities must be brought to their senses by a thorough boycott of English goods. *Bande Mataram* should henceforth be 'our only instrument instead of prayers and petitions'.[1] The *Sandhya* sarcastically stated that it was happy that

---

[5] *Hansard,* House of Commons, 4S, vol. 152 (February–March 1906), 26 February 1906, Cols. 822–30.

[6] Ibid. Col. 837.     [7] Ibid. Col. 836.     [8] Ibid. Col. 847.     [9] Ibid. Col. 844.

[1] The *Daily Hitavadi,* Calcutta, 28 February 1906. *B.N.N.R.* 1906. On 2 March 1906, it stated that Morley's statement 'has created the greatest

Morley had rejected their plea of revoking Partition, because it had served 'to open our eyes to the true nature of *feringis*[2] and indicate to us the true means of getting divided Bengal re-united.' In its opinion 'the harsher Sir B. Fuller's strokes will become, the more Lord Minto and Mr. Morley will spurn at us, and the fiercer the course of official oppression on students will grow, and the more the *feringi* will exhibit his true nature, the closer will the divided parts of Bengal be drawn together in bonds of unity. Life comes through death. Life will not come to us so long as death does not overcome our false political agitation, unnatural love for *feringis*, our despicable want of self-reliance and the ideas and superstition which an alien education has generated in us'.[3] The *Bengalee* urged Morley to think again as 'Liberalism becomes a very meaningless creed if it is to tolerate or perpetuate evils simply because they are settled things'. It advocated a vigorous agitation to show that they were not slackening in their demand.[4] The *Amrita Bazar Patrika* and the *Indian Mirror* also urged for a stirring to inform the entire British public opinion of the actual state of things.[5] The *Amrita Bazar Patrika* thought that Morley's statement resembled the decision of King Habu Chander (a legendary King), who once ordered a person to be hanged on charges of murdering another. But the King could not take back his order when the alleged murdered person appeared in his court.[6] It wondered what had happened to Morley. He was silent and acquiescing in the perpetuation of wrong. It decided to place no hope either in Liberals or Tories but appeal to the Labour Party—the working classes of

suspicion in the public mind as regards British justice. The national crisis has become all the more acute. But it will not do to remain inactive ... A stirring agitation must be got up again and the entire British public informed of the actual state of things'.

[2] A Persian word, meaning foreigner, originally used for Europeans, but later on acquired a contemptuous meaning.

[3] The *Sandhya,* Calcutta, 28 February 1906. *B.N.N.R.,* 1906.

[4] The *Bengalee,* 28 February, 2 March 1906. Ibid.

[5] The *Amrita Bazar Patrika,* 28 February 1906; the *Indian Mirror,* 28 February 1906. Ibid.

[6] The *Amrita Bazar Patrika,* 2 March 1906. Ibid.

England.[7] With regard to Morley's statement that the agitation was subsiding, the *Indian Mirror* stated that he had been misinformed. It was true that the first paroxysm of grief had passed, 'but the grief is still there—silent, settled and unabated'.[8] The *Dacca Gazette* simply said, 'so, after all, the fate of Bengal is sealed!'[9]

While this controversy was going on in the Press with regard to Minto and Morley's policy towards the Partition of Bengal, Fuller's administration of Eastern Bengal and Assam had also taken a very controversial turn which ultimately resulted in his resignation. The most important decision Minto had to take early in his administration was the acceptance of Sir J. Bampfylde Fuller's resignation. Fuller had become the object of Congress attacks because of some of his tactless expressions and attempts to fight the agitation. His attitude had annoyed the Congress leaders and the *Bengalee,* the Congress's most vociferous organ, wrote strongly against him.[1] The Bengali Press opposed Fuller for three reasons. He was appointed to a province the creation of which the Bengali Hindu Press did not like. Secondly, he tried to suppress the Bengali Hindu agitation sternly by banning its meetings and the cry of *Bande Mataram* because a large section of the Muslim population in Eastern Bengal did not approve of these and there was danger of disorder in the province. Thirdly in an attempt to redress the Muslim grievance of meagre representation in the provincial administration he exposed himself to the charge of partiality. The Bengali Press was owned by Hindus. The Muslims had no papers of their own except one or two weeklies which had a very poor circulation.

[7] The *Amrita Bazar Patrika,* 25, 27 May 1906. *B.N.N.R.,* 1906.

[8] The *Indian Mirror,* 3 March 1906. Ibid.

[9] The *Dacca Gazette,* Dacca, 5 March 1906. Ibid.

[1] The *Bengalee,* 24 June 1906. The extracts from the Press in the *B.N.N.R.,* 1906, show the intense dislike the Bengali Hindu Press had for Fuller. He was called 'Muhammad Tughlak of East Bengal' (the *Sanjivani,* 26 April 1906); 'Shaista Khan II' (the *Bengalee,* 1 May 1906; the *Amrita Bazar Patrika,* 3 May 1906), &c. The period of his Lt.-Governorship was called a period of great 'Zulum' (tyranny).

The *Swadeshi* and Boycott movements had attracted students from schools and colleges and they were taking an active part. The Government disliked their participation, so on 10 October 1905, even before the new Province came into existence, the Government of Bengal issued a circular with regard to the participation of school and college students in political agitation. The magistrates and collectors in each district were instructed to take notice of students taking part in political activities. They were directed to inform the heads of schools and colleges that in the event of the students of any particular institution taking part in such a movement, its grants-in-aid and other privileges would be withdrawn. Its students would not be permitted to compete for scholarships and scholarship holders would not be admitted there. The institution would, however, not be punished, if it was found to be making sincere efforts to prevent such disorders, but then it was obliged to give the names of the offenders to the authorities. The magistrates and collectors were given powers to take either disciplinary action themselves or ask the educational authorities to punish the students concerned.[2]

Fuller issued a similar circular on 16 October 1905. According to this circular the district authorities were to furnish the names of prominent residents of their districts who had been taking a leading part in the agitation. It also stated that the Government would take a lenient view except in one particular case, 'the scandalous vernacular broad sheets which have been in circulation', and the authorities were asked to spare 'no pains' to discover any persons who have been disseminating them.[3] These 'broad sheets' were various circulars that the Bengali leaders issued encouraging people to maintain boycott of foreign goods and agitate. Most of these were issued anonymously, but wher-

---

[2] Circular from Government of Bengal to Magistrates and Collectors, 10 October 1905. *Parly. Papers,* Cd. 3242. J. R. McLane, op. cit., gives a number of instances where students took an active part in *Swadeshi* and boycott movements.

[3] Semi-official circular from Government of Eastern Bengal and Assam to the Commissioners of Rajshahi, Dacca, Chittagong, and heads of all other districts, 16 October 1905. *P.P.* Cd. 3242.

ever the authors were brought to the Government's notice, they were warned, made to withdraw or punished. In the Government's view these circulars tended to excite people and were thus a danger to the maintenance of law and order in the province. For instance, in Barisal, Aswini Kumar Dutt and some other leaders had issued one such circular. Fuller called them for an interview and asked them to withdraw their circular, which they did. They agreed to withdraw it because, in their own words, it 'contains certain expressions that may tend to lead people to commit breaches of the peace'.[4] The Bengali Press alleged that in this meeting Fuller's behaviour was rude and he did not even ask the leaders to sit down. The *Sanjivani*, therefore, asked 'should Lord Minto not think of removing such a man who was so much deprived of the sense of gentlemanliness?'[5]

Nevertheless the Boycott leaders took no notice of Fuller's circulars and the students were encouraged to take an active part in political affairs.[6] A volunteer corps of the teachers and students of the Banwari Lal High School and the Victoria High School at Sirajganj in the Pabna district was formed with a view to guarding against the sale of foreign goods in the town.[7] The activities of this corps led to difficulties. Their first conflict was with the Marwaris, who traded in foreign cloth. On 15 November 1906, they tried to stop them from loading their carts with this cloth, and in the afternoon they even went to the extent of assaulting a certain Carberry, an officer of the Bengal Bank.[8]

[4] The *Daily Hitavadi*, 24 November 1905, *B.N.N.R.*, 1905.

[5] The *Sanjivani*, 28 December 1905. Ibid.

[6] S. N. Banerjea, op. cit., p. 196. See also, *Home Progs. Public/Political*, January–March 1906 (7311); April–July 1906 (7312); August–December 1906 (7313); January–April 1907 (7587); May–August 1907 (7588); September–December 1907 (7589); July–December 1907 (7590). Fortnightly reports on Partition, agitation and the Boycott movement in Bengal from the Governments of Bengal and Eastern Bengal and Assam.

[7] Inspector of Schools to D.P.I., Eastern Bengal and Assam, 2 January 1906, Para. 3. *P.P.* Cd. 3242.

[8] Government of East Bengal and Assam to the Registrar, Calcutta University, 10 February 1906, Para 2. *P.P.* Cd. 3242. *The Times*, 14 November 1906.

The Government took serious notice of the whole affair. The inquiries of M. P. Chatterji, Inspector of Schools, Rajshahi Division, showed that the boys of the two schools had violated the rules laid down by the Government, and he recommended that they be punished.[9] The Education Department, after considering the report, recommended to the Lieutenant-Governor that the Banwari Lal High School and the Victoria High School, Sirajganj, be brought to task. Fuller, accordingly, asked the Syndicate of the Calcutta University to withdraw 'the recognition extended to these two institutions'.[1]

The Government of India wanted to take a lenient view, and thought the action of the Lieutenant-Governor rather tactless. He was, therefore, requested to withdraw his recommendations.[2] The school authorities attempted to come to an amicable settlement as well. Fuller was willing to withdraw his recommendations, if the boys concerned paid a small fine. But the negotiations broke down. The Congress leaders from Calcutta, who had become interested in this affair, did not want to let this opportunity go. So they influenced the local people and the school authorities not to come to any terms with Fuller. Fuller, in the meanwhile, arranged for a new Government School to replace the other two and was even willing to re-affiliate the two schools if they acknowledged their past errors. But all attempts at negotiation failed. Fuller thought that his stooping down would weaken his authority and he would not be able to maintain public order in the province. In an attempt to carry the Government of India with him, and knowing little that things could take a different shape, he wrote to Minto that 'these orders [for the withdrawal of Fuller's recommendations to the Syndicate] may be re-considered, or that, if I am to give effect to them, my resig-

[9] Inspector of Schools to the D.P.I., Government of East Bengal and Assam, 2 January 1906, Para. 8. *P.P.* Cd. 3242.
[1] Government of East Bengal and Assam to the Registrar, Calcutta University, 10 February 1906. *P.P.* Cd. 3242.
[2] Government of India to Fuller, 5 July 1906. *P.P.* Cd. 3242. Minto to Morley, 5 July 1906. *M.P.*

nation may be accepted'.[3] Minto promptly accepted his resignation.[4]

This was the immediate cause of his resignation.[5] When the papers regarding Fuller's resignation were presented to Parliament every effort was made to explain that the agitation had nothing whatsoever to do with his resignation, but the Viceroy's reference to the 'present situation'[6] when suggesting withdrawal of Fuller's recommendations regarding schools betrays the fact that the political agitation did play a part in it. Minto has since been blamed for bowing before the agitation, much to the agitators' pleasure.[7] It has been suggested that this showed weakness and that he betrayed the Civil Service by not upholding one of its members, and the Muslims who had come to look upon Fuller as the champion of their cause. It has also been alleged that Minto agreed to revert to even harsher measures later on, than those for which Fuller was compelled to resign in August 1906.[8]

Despite the fact that Fuller wrote to Minto 'we have to be careful not to commit ourselves to Musalman interest,'[9] some of his actions, during the nine-month period of his Lieutenant-Governorship, positively antagonized the Hindu leaders. His circular, curtailing the right of public meetings, preventing the cry of *Bande Mataram*, and the prosecutions in this connexion; his attempts to redress the genuine under-representation of the

[3] Fuller to Minto, 15 July 1906. *M.C.*

[4] Telegram, Viceroy to Lt.-Governor of East Bengal and Assam, 3 August 1906. *P.P.* Cd. 3242.

[5] The same immediate cause is given in the *Summary of the Administration of the Earl Minto, in the Home Department, November 1905 to November 1910* (Simla, 1910), p. 6. *M.C.*

[6] Government of India to Fuller, 5 July 1906. *P.P.* Cd. 3242.

[7] The *Bengalee*, 7 August 1906. 'This [Fuller's resignation] would point to the potency of the Bengali Press.' Also see the *Amrita Bazar Patrika*, 6, 7, 8 August 1906, *New India*, 4 August 1906. The *Indian Mirror*, 7 August 1906, thought it 'a welcome relief'; the *Hindoo Patriot*, 7 August 1906, 'it should prove a lesson and a warning to officials of his class'. Only the *Soltan*, 10 August 1906, and the *Mihir-o-Sudhakar*, Calcutta, 10 August 1906, both Muslim papers, praised Fuller and thought it a loss to Muslims.

[8] V. Chirol, *Indian Unrest* (London, 1910), p. 88.

[9] Fuller to Minto, 26 November 1905. *M.C.*

Muslims in the public services,[1] and his casual remark that out of two of his wives, the Hindu and *mehtar*, the latter was his favourite,[2] were enough to make the Hindus angry. The Government of India did not approve of his handling of the case concerning an indecent assault on a *mehtar* (sweeper) woman. On 21 March 1906, Gokhale brought this to the notice of the Government of India by asking questions in the Legislative Council. He enquired the reason as to why the *Weekly Chronicle* of Sylhet had been boycotted by the Government of Eastern Bengal and Assam. If it had committed some crime why were criminal proceedings not instituted against it? Arundel, on the information supplied by the local Government, told him that the paper had published a false report of an indecent assault on a sweeper woman named Mangli by a Gurkha policeman at Barisal and produced statements of Mangli and her husband Gunpati. As to criminal proceedings he explained that the local Government considered that no useful purpose would be fulfilled by instituting criminal proceedings and therefore decided to withdraw from the newspaper certain facilities. On making further enquiries, the Government of India came to know that J. E. Dickinson, Assistant Superintendent of Police, in his enquiry, 14 December 1905, had stated that 'I have no hesitation in believing that an assault was actually committed on the woman, probably with the intent to outrage her modesty, but there are many suspicious circumstances and discrepancies which prevent

---

[1] Fuller to Minto, 26 November 1905. *M.C.* The *Amrita Bazar Patrika*, 12, 15 and 16 June 1906; The *Bengalee*, 14 June 1906; The *Hindoo Patriot* 14 June 1906; *Power and Guardian*, 17 June 1906; the *Indian Mirror*, 24 June 1906; the *Indian Nation* fiercely criticized the policy of the Government of Eastern Bengal and Assam to provide larger employment to the Muslims and considered the Government's circular which was issued to invite suggestions in this matter 'a humiliating document'. The *Bengalee* blamed the Muslims for apathy towards English education which caused meagreness of their numbers in Government jobs. It considered the Government's policy a sinister move to curry favour with the Muslims and create a rift between Hindus and Muslims.

[2] Morley to Minto, 5 October 1906. *M.P.* See H. W. Nevinson, op. cit., p. 192.

my crediting the story, or rather imputation that her assailant was a Gurkha sepoy . . .' The assault was committed on the night of 10 December 1905. On 11 December, Babu Rajani Kanta Das, Chairman of the Barisal Municipality, came to T. Emerson, the District Magistrate, with papers explaining that a Municipal overseer was deputed to make enquiries when a complaint of the assault was made to him. Since the woman did not wish to proceed further, he suggested that the matter be dropped. But the Magistrate deputed Dickinson to make the enquiry. On 13 December 1905, the *Weekly Chronicle* of Sylhet published the report of the crime under 'Gurkha oppression at Barisal'. On 19 December the report came to the notice of Fuller while on tour at Barisal. He sent for the papers of the enquiry and consulted the Legal Remembrancer as to the propriety of prosecuting the newspaper for libel, but was advised that such a prosecution would probably fail on technical grounds. Fuller demanded an apology from the paper. Since it was not done, Government advertisements and other special facilities were withdrawn from this paper. The Government of India took a serious view of the whole case, and blamed the local Government for not supplying them with full details,[3] thus compelling them to make unsatisfactory answers to Gokhale's questions. The Government of India was satisfied and agreed with Dickinson's enquiry that an assault had been made and that the action of the local Government with regard to the newspaper was wrong. As the Editor was not guilty of specific misconduct in the sense in which he was accused, the local Government was asked to withdraw the disabilities imposed by them on the *Weekly Chronicle*.[4]

Fuller's action in connexion with the Bengal Provincial Conference held at Barisal on 14 April 1906 was not approved by the Government of India. The Conference was to be held at Barisal and the delegates came from various parts of Bengal. The cry of *Bande Mataram* was forbidden throughout Eastern Bengal and

---

[3] Government of India to Government of Eastern Bengal and Assam, 31 May 1906. *Home Progs.* (Public), April–July 1906. 7312.
[4] Ibid.

Assam.[5] Rajani Kanta Das, Secretary of the Reception Committee, was almost in daily contact with T. Emerson, the District Magistrate. Aswini Kumar Dutt was the President of the Reception Committee. A few days before the arrival of the delegates, both of them called on Emerson, who told them that he would not allow any processions or shouts of *Bande Mataram* in the streets of Barisal during the Conference. They agreed to abide by his orders.[6] On 13 April the delegates arrived in two steamers which reached Barisal *ghats*[7] at about 7 p.m. Surendranath Banerjea was in the steamer that came from Narainganj. Abdul Rasul, the President of the Conference and other delegates from Calcutta came in the steamer from Khulna. When the steamers reached the *ghats*, the delegates on them began to shout *Bande Mataram*. But about 3,500 people, who had assembled on the shore to receive them, did not respond. The Calcutta delegates felt very sad at the apathy of Barisal people and some even refused to eat until the cry of *Bande Mataram* was heard publicly in the streets. F. E. Kemp, District Superintendent of Police, was also present there. He went on board the Narainganj steamer and explained to Banerjea the Government orders and asked him to stop those who were shouting. Banerjea questioned the legality of the order, but Kemp told him that he had not come to discuss Government orders with him. Wiser counsels, however, prevailed and the delegates stopped shouting and silently went to Raja Bahadur's *haveli*.[8]

---

[5] Fuller's circular to Commissioners of Dacca, Chittagong, and Rashahi Divisions, 8 November 1905. *Home Progs*. April–July 1906. 7312.

[6] Emerson's report, no date. The orders were verbal. Ibid.

[7] Pier.

[8] Residence, literally a palace. S. N. Banerjea's account of the arrival of the delegates differs with this only in one respect. He does not mention the presence of Kemp and says that the delegates decided to stop shouting, because they did not want to compromise the position of their hosts who had made an agreement with the authorities. He also states that they had decided not to shout *Bande Mataram*, only for that time, but otherwise they had agreed that the cry would be uttered throughout the Conference proceedings and that the local leaders concurred with this decision. S. N. Banerjea, op. cit., pp. 220–1.

Next day the police came to know that the delegates were in-
tending to take out a procession and shout *Bande Mataram* in
the streets with a view to test the legality of the Government
orders. Kemp thought it a great risk to the maintenance of law
and order in the town, so he secured an order from Emerson, 'to
prevent the holding of this procession and, if any attempt was
made to carry it out to disperse it and arrest the ringleaders'.[9]
The delegates began to collect at Raja Bahadur's *haveli* and the
procession left for the *Pandal*, an assembly place outside Brajo
Mohan College, at 2 p.m. Abdul Rasul and his wife left in a
carriage and other leaders including Banerjea, Moti Lal Ghose,
editor of the *Amrita Bazar Patrika* and Bhupendra Nath Basu,
were in the first row. According to Banerjea they had already
decided to take out a procession and shout *Bande Mataram* with
'full concurrence' of the Barisal leaders, and also apprehended
that the police would interfere and might even use force. The
delegates had, therefore, been warned by their leaders not to
carry any sticks or *lathis*[1] and the instructions were 'loyally
carried out'.[2]

The Police, armed with regulation *lathis* under Kemp, were
present outside the *haveli*. As the first rows of the procession
were not orderly lines, they let them pass by. But when about
forty members of the Anti-Circular Party[3] led by K. K. Mittra,
editor of the *Sanjivani*, came out of the *haveli*, they were in rows
of two and four and had badges of *Bande Mataram* pinned on
their chests. The police tried to disperse them, but they refused
and forced their way in an attempt to carry out their march.
At this the police started beating them. Kemp's report suggests
that the delegates were shouting *Bande Mataram* and when they
were asked to stop, they resisted and this resulted in a scuffle with

[9] Emerson's note, no date. *Home Progs.* April–July 1906. 7312.
[1] Long bamboo sticks.
[2] S. N. Banerjea, op. cit., p. 221.
[3] Anti-Circular Party was founded in Calcutta to protest against the various
circulars about schools, *Bande Mataram* and boycott issued by Fuller. Mittra
was later on deported for 'seditious activities'. He was a prominent member
of the Brahmo Samaj.

the police.[4] Banerjea states that the delegates started shouting after they had been beaten.[5] Newspaper reports are also very confusing. It is not easy to determine responsibility for the start of the actual happening, but it is clear that the police did show grave high-handedness. The sight of so many processionists seemed to have unnerved the police officer and he ordered the police to use force. The procession was illegal because the authorities had not been approached for permission beforehand. The police action too, seems unjustified, because the reports of H. Le Meseurier, Officiating Commissioner of Dacca, Emerson and Kemp, had not been able to provide any evidence that this show of force was necessary.

A great pandemonium ensued and the people began to shout *Bande Mataram*. Banerjea and other leaders turned back and Banerjea accepted the responsibility for breaking the law and was accordingly arrested. Banerjea was brought before Emerson and was fined for breaking the law as well as contempt of court.[6] Here, too, the nervousness of the officers-in-charge was apparent. Banerjea was summarily tried and Emerson seemed to have shown his ill-temper while conducting the trial. Emerson maintained that the fact that the procession through the town had been forbidden was known to Banerjea. He could have secured permission from the District Superintendent of Police, but he did not. This does not seem very convincing, because the Government of Eastern Bengal admitted that section 30(i) of the Police Act (Act V of 1861) gave power to the police to control such processions but did not extend to the total prohibition of such processions. If the Magistrate or the police wanted to prohibit the procession, they could have issued orders under the

[4] Kemp's report, 16 April 1906. *Home Progs.* 7312.
[5] S. N. Banerjea, op. cit., p. 222.
[6] Banerjea presents the whole incident of his arrest in a most dramatic style and suggests that his arrest was pre-arranged. The fact was that Kemp had already the orders to arrest the ringleaders and Banerjea was extremely anxious to court arrest and assume responsibility in order to gain popularity.

Criminal Procedure Code.[7] No such orders had been issued as far as the first day's proceedings were concerned. Kemp's action, even if it was intended to stop the processionists shouting *Bande Mataram*, seemed high-handed, because the Government had not been able to produce any evidence that there was any immediate danger of a Hindu-Muslim clash. Local officers took a faulty decision and acted outrageously. Even the Officiating Chief Commissioner of Dacca did not know about it till quite late. Fuller pleaded that it was a difficult situation and the officer concerned was under great pressure.[8]

Another interesting feature of all these proceedings is the absence of local leaders. Throughout these incidents, it seems, the local leaders had been pushed aside and the Calcutta leaders took the responsibility of testing the legality of the Government order against the cry of *Bande Mataram*. Newspaper reports clearly show that the Calcutta delegates, particularly the members of the Anti-Circular Society under K. K. Mittra, were determined to have their own way. There is more evidence to suggest this. On 15 April, Kemp received reports from Inspector Kali Kishore Chaudhri and Girija Kanta Bal that the delegates intended to take out a procession. He asked Emerson to pass an order under Section 144, Criminal Procedure Code, for stopping the Conference, because it would not otherwise be possible to stop the procession. Emerson issued the orders. Before carrying out the orders, Kemp approached Rajani Kanta Das, who at first denied any knowledge of the procession, but after consultation with other leaders he confirmed it. He, however, gave no assurance that *Bande Mataram* would not be shouted.[9] The Conference was ultimately stopped under Emerson's orders.

[7] Emerson's report; P. C. Lyon, Chief Secretary to Government of E.B. & A. to Secretary, Government of India, Home Dept. no. 45, dated 25 April 1906. *Home Progs.* 7312.

[8] Report of H. Le Mesurier, Offg. Commissioner of Dacca Division, 18 April 1906. Government of E.B. & A. to Government of India, 25 April 1906. *Home Progs.* 7312. The newspaper reports, no doubt, suggest that the Muslims did become uneasy after the Barisal events.

[9] Rajani Kanta Das to Kemp, 15 April 1906. *Home Progs.* 7312.

Kemp's reason in securing prohibition of the Conference was that it was not possible to control such a huge procession.

The whole incident had a melodramatic touch. The main characters were three—Banerjea, leading the Calcutta delegates, Kemp, the Superintendent of Police and Emerson, the Magistrate. Between them a situation was created which undoubtedly agitated the political atmosphere and brought Banerjea into the limelight, but discredited Fuller's Government. Determination of the Calcutta leaders to test Fuller's circular against *Bande Mataram* cannot be denied. In this they received loyal but unenthusiastic support from Barisal leaders. Kemp's nervousness gave the whole affair a colour which ordinarily it would not have acquired. Emerson's conduct at Banerjea's trial was also not blameless.

The Government of India was immediately approached and an enquiry was demanded.[1] Dr. V. H. Rutherford, J. Ward, and Sir Henry Cotton asked questions in the House of Commons.[2] But the Bengali Press was most indignant. The *Bengalee* wrote violently about the whole incident and called the events at Barisal the 'climax of brutality' and thought that Surendranath Banerjea's arrest was the 'brilliant *coup d'état* of the *Jungly Lat*'.[3] The *Daily Hitavadi* questioned: 'Is this British rule or the régime of Nadir Shah?' It was not sure whether 'such anarchy prevailed even in the time of Shaista Khan'. It further informed the English officials that they were bound by law, and that a repetition of the *Zulum* of the *Badshahi* and *Nawabi* regime was an impossibility in these days of civilization. In its opinion Emerson was 'a dog unfit even to touch the shoes of Babu Surendranath'.[4] The *Indian Mirror* and the *Sri Sri Vishnu Priya-o-*

[1] A. Chaudhri to Dunlop Smith, telegram, 15 April 1906. Abdul Rasul, President of the Conference to Dunlop Smith, telegram, 16 April 1906. Ibid.

[2] *Hansard*, House of Commons, 4S, vol. 156 (26 April–10 May 1906), 1 May 1906, Col. 42.

[3] The *Bengalee*, 15, 17 April and ff., 1906. '*Jungly Lat*'—Wild Master, uncivilized ruler meaning Fuller.

[4] *Daily Hitavadi*, Calcutta, 15, 17, 20 April 1906. *B.N.N.R.*, 1906. Reference to Nadirshah and Shaista Khan—*Badshahi* (Muslim Kingship) and *Nawabi*

*Ananda Bazar Patrika* requested Minto to set things right in Eastern Bengal by recalling Fuller.[5] The *Amrita Bazar Patrika,* the *Sanjivani,* and the *Sandhya* were all violently hostile.[6] The *Indian Empire* could not 'help crying out that the glory of the British Government in India has departed . . .'[7] In the opinion of the *Hindoo Patriot,* the Government of Eastern Bengal and Assam had acted 'outrageously, senselessly and illegally', but it suggested that passion and prejudice had done enough harm and both the Government and the people should learn to be more tolerant and more solicitous for the welfare of the country.[8] But the *Englishman* put all the blame on the Calcutta leaders as they deliberately chose Barisal with 'the mischievous idea of making trouble'.[9]

Fuller withdrew the circular banning the cry of *Bande Mataram* after this great stalemate and as a face-saving device, the Government of India suggested that he might base its withdrawal on the good behaviour of the Barisal people in standing aloof during recent agitation.[1] Morley announced this withdrawal in the House of Commons.[2]

Minto had not liked Fuller's handling of the situation. He wrote to Morley, 'In Fuller's case one cannot put one's finger upon any particular act of his for which he could be justly

must be noted. While under-rating the British regime, the aim of the Congress papers was to solicit Muslim support. It is doubtful whether such comparisons would have brought Muslims nearer to the Hindus.

[5] The *Indian Mirror,* 17, 18 April 1906. The *Sri Sri Vishnu Priya-o-Ananda Bazar Patrika,* 19 April 1906. *B.N.N.R.,* 1906.

[6] 17, 18, 26 April 1906. Ibid.

[7] The *Indian Empire,* 24 April 1906. Ibid.

[8] The *Hindoo Patriot,* 18, 19, 20 April 1906. Ibid.

[9] The *Englishman,* 16 April 1906.

[1] The Government of India to Government of E.B. & A., telegram, 4 May 1906. *Home Progs.* 7312. B. C. Pal addressing a meeting of about 4,000 people at Barisal on 1 March 1907 said that *lathis* were shown to the people to stop their agitation but when they had made the Government understand that they also had *lathis,* and bamboo groves behind their homes, the *Bande Mataram* circular was withdrawn, not as a favour but through fear. C.I.D. Report of B. C. Pal's speech. *Public Letters from India,* 1907, vol. xxxv.

[2] *Hansard,* House of Commons, 4S, vol. 157 (11 May-25 May 1906), 14 May 1906, Col. 177.

recalled. His proclamations, his dealings with the schools, the story of the Mehtar woman, and lastly this unfortunate murder appeal case,[3] have been rather illustrations of want of tact and of good judgment than anything more serious'.[4] But Minto explained more fully in a letter to Sir V. Chirol, written quite some time after the incident. 'The question I had to deal with was, not whether his action towards the school was right or wrong, but how in the world to get a dangerous man away from a position, his retention of which would quite certainly have produced a conflagration in Eastern Bengal. He was hysterical and absolutely unsuited for a position full of risk and requiring infinite tact'.[5]

Both Minto and Morley agreed that Fuller was not the right man to tackle the delicate situation in Eastern Bengal and Assam.

[3] Udoy Patani was sentenced to death for murder and was accordingly hanged. His execution became a cause of great resentment, because he was hanged before his appeal could reach the Viceroy. A number of questions were asked in the House of Commons and Morley admitted that a mistake had been committed in the sense that Udoy Patani was hanged before the decision of the Government of India with regard to his sentence. Since the Government of India was convinced of the crime committed by Udoy Patani it was doubtful that his appeal would have been accepted, yet the fact that he was hanged before the Government of India's decision does reflect a grave mistake on the part of the Local Government. The Local Government was negligent in the sense that it did not give much time for Udoy Patani's appeal to reach the Government of India and the execution of the sentence. The date of his execution was fixed by the Sessions Judge for 21 May 1906. The prisoner's appeal was turned down by the Lt.-Governor on 12 May. On Sunday 13 May the prisoner orally appealed through the Superintendent to the Government of India. On 15 May the Local Government sent the papers under registered cover marked 'immediate' to the Government of India, but these did not come into the hands of the Government of India until 10 o'clock on the morning of Monday 21 May. He was executed at 7 o'clock the same morning. Morley's statement in the House of Commons, 12 July 1906. *Hansard*, House of Commons, 4S, vol. 160 (4 July–16 July 1906), Col. 1047.

[4] Minto to Morley, 5 July 1906. *M.P.*

[5] Minto to Chirol, 18 May 1910. *M.C.* In reply Chirol wrote that all that had been told him about Fuller 'takes me, I confess, by surprise. I am inclined to think that to the present day he ascribed his dismissal merely to the difference of opinion between the Government of Eastern Bengal and Assam and the Home Department with regard to matters of school discipline'. Chirol to Minto, 23 May 1910. Ibid.

'Fuller, the Lieutenant-Governor, though a pleasant man to talk to, does not at all impress me as likely to take a level-headed course of action, and there has been very stupid mismanagement there lately', wrote Minto to Morley.[6] A few days after the Barisal incident, Minto wrote that he was 'somewhat doubtful of the good judgment of the local Government, and I cannot but suspect that things might have been better managed the other day at Barisal.'[7] In spite of all his dislike of Fuller's tactlessness, Minto did not want him to be made a 'scape-goat' on public grounds.[8] He further thought that Fuller's removal from the Lieutenant-Governorship would be looked upon as a victory gained by the Bengali leaders and would have a mischievous effect throughout India.[9] Morley, on the other hand, did not have that cool and unperturbed mind. His continuous harassment in the House of Commons regarding Fuller's actions made him extremely impatient. He wrote to Minto, 'Granted that Curzon's choice of Fuller for a difficult post was not happy; granted that it may be wise to "save his face"; I still cherish a lively hope that bye-and-bye some means may be found of removing him to a post more sympathetic to him. If the agitation subsides, so be it. If not, I must say frankly that it will be impossible for me to carry both Partition and Fuller on my back'.[1]

Fuller himself provided an opportunity. Minto and Morley thought it a 'stroke of luck',[2] and both heaved a sigh of relief.[3] Fuller was, on the other hand, stunned with this decision to

[6] Minto to Morley, 29 March 1906. *M.P.*

[7] Minto to Morley, 25 April 1906. Ibid.

[8] Minto to Morley, 16 May 1906. Ibid.

[9] Minto to Morley, 27 June 1906. Ibid.

[1] Morley to Minto, 3 May 1906. Ibid. See T. V. Parvate, op. cit., pp. 209–10. Gokhale's letters to Krishna Swami, 8 June 1906 and N. A. Dravid, 6 July 1906. Since his arrival in England Gokhale had been pressing Morley for Fuller's transfer and Morley had virtually promised him to make an announcement in this regard. See also F. A. Hirtzel's Diary, 14 May, 2, 10, 11, 23 July 1906. *Home Misc.* 864. I.O.L.

[2] Minto to Morley, 25 July 1906; Morley to Minto, 20 September 1906. *M.P.*

[3] Minto to Chirol, 18 May 1910. *M.C.* 'I never was so relieved in my life as when he resigned.'

accept his resignation, as he had not expected it. His only objection, when he placed his case before Morley, was that he was not given an opportunity to explain and he received no clear indication of the line of policy to follow.[4] Minto defended his action, which he himself was so reluctant to take, with the thought that if he had asked Fuller to come to Simla and discuss matters with him, it would not have been possible to get rid of him. The officials in Simla would have exerted all their influence in favour of Fuller.[5] Moreover, 'there was no policy, entailing a change in the nature of his administration, advocated by the Government of India. We assumed that he would administer his province and enforce law and order in a reasonable manner with the machinery at his command, but he did not act reasonably or judiciously . . .'[6]

Fuller was himself responsible for his undoing.[7] He was rash, tactless and impulsive, though 'shrewd, eager,—quite well-fitted for Government work of ordinary scope'.[8]

The agitators were jubilant at Fuller's fall, but the Muslims started an agitation condemning the Government of India's

[4] Morley to Minto, 5 October 1906. *M.P.*

[5] Lady Minto, op. cit., vol. ii, 1905–6, p. 179 and pp. 241–3. 'The members of [the] Council, whom Rolly [Minto] consulted, feared that, if his resignation was accepted, the impression throughout India would be that the agitation had brought about the desired result, and that they would howl all the louder, in order to obtain further concessions. Rolly decided that this danger was preferable to the risk of keeping on Sir Bampfylde, with the probability of having to recall him at some future date, so accepted his resignation.' Lady Minto thought that Fuller was a rash, 'hot-headed and impetuous Irishman'. See also Dunlop Smith's note on Fuller's resignation in the same *Journal*, 1908, pp. 227–37.

[6] Minto to Morley, 28 October 1906. *M.P.*

[7] Morley to Minto, 5 October 1906. Fuller missed another chance, when it was suggested that he should be appointed to the Secretary of State's Council and Morley had almost made up his mind to do so. He published a letter in *The Times*, 6 June 1908, criticizing the Government policy. This made Morley change his mind immediately. Morley to Minto, 8 June 1908. Ibid.

[8] 'People ask me,' he [Sir Andrew Fraser] said, 'was it Lord Minto's doing or Mr. Morley's doing; I say it was Fuller's doing.' Morley to Minto, 14 September 1906. Ibid.

action. Minto, Morley and Sir Arthur Godley all thought it a good sign. 'As long as it does not get out of control it will be useful to us,' Minto thought.[9] 'I cannot help being rather pleased at the demonstrations which are being made in his favour. They will be a most useful reminder to people in this country—some of them in high positions—that the Bengali is not everybody in India,' wrote Godley to Minto.[1]

But Fuller's fall did not solve the problem of Partition. There was still hope of discussion in Parliament and a possible reversal of the action taken. The agitation against the Partition was kept alive. Minto did not think it desirable that in India 'a change of Government at home should be looked to as likely to bring the reversal of decisions arrived at here'. The Government of India had a strong point—not to surrender to agitation by unsettling the settled fact. This would also mean betraying the Muslims in Eastern Bengal who 'appear to be generally satisfied with what has occurred'.[2] In a later letter Minto informed Morley that even Gokhale said that he 'was not opposed to Partition, that he recognized Mohammedan claims and so on; that he knew the anti-partition feeling in Bengal was really nothing but sentimental'.[3] Dr. A. Mukerji, Vice-Chancellor of Calcutta University, had earlier informed Minto that the anti-Partition agitation was the work of disappointed agitators.[4] All these opinions of leading Indians had helped Minto to form his opinion about this complex problem. And the 'settled fact' remained settled during Minto's Viceroyalty, despite Morley's dictatorial assertion that 'I had only to lift my finger, and the H. of C. would instantly have passed a resolution that would have overthrown the "settled fact" in a trice'.[5]

[9] Minto to Morley, 22 August 1906. *M.P.*
[1] Godley to Minto, 20 September 1906. *M.C.*
[2] Minto to Morley, 20 December 1905. *M.P.*
[3] Minto to Morley, 5 November 1907. Ibid.
[4] Minto to Morley, 16 May 1906. Ibid.
[5] Morley to Minto, 24 January 1907. Ibid. See also S. N. Banerjea, op. cit., p. 283: '. . . it was clear that Lord Minto would do nothing to modify the Partition.'

While Minto and Morley were shaping their policy towards Indian aspirations, the Congress leaders were busy in making their voice more effective. A section of them becoming tired of the 'mendicant policy' of the moderate Congress leaders, tried to divert the line of action. Earliest symptoms of this extremism appeared at the Benares Congress of 1905, but the first open rupture manifested itself in the Calcutta Congress of 1906.

By a clever move, the extremists were hoodwinked and Dadabhia Naoroji was invited to preside over the deliberations of the 1906 session of the Congress at Calcutta.[6] The extremists were not willing to take it lying down. Tilak, in a speech on 7 June, had already said that the days of protests and prayers had gone and nothing would be achieved unless the demand was backed by 'solid force'. His conclusion was that nothing much should be expected 'from a change in government'.[7]

The Congress session of 1906 thus heard the speeches of Tilak, B. C. Pal and Aurabindo Ghose, along with the moderately worded speech of the President and other moderate leaders.[8] Dadabhai Naoroji declared that the goal of the Congress was to attain 'Swaraj' or 'self-government',[9] and a resolution was also passed which said that 'the system of government obtaining in the self-governing British colonies should be extended to India'.[1] Minto thought Naoroji's address 'very long and impractical' and

[6] The extremists wanted Tilak to be the Congress President, but the moderates did not, so Surendranath Banerjea wrote to Naoroji, who agreed to come. R. P. Masani, *Dadabhai Naoroji* (London, 1939), p. 497. Minto also thought it a good thing, but doubted whether Naoroji would be able 'to control some of the firebrands he has to deal with', Minto to Morley, 18 November 1906. *M.P.*

[7] *Speeches and Writings of Tilak* (Madras, 1918), pp. 24–25.

[8] Minto realized that the time had come when the moderates should be given a 'a pat on the back'. He not only opened the Industrial Exhibition, but tried to repair the damage done by Curzon's policy towards the Congress by even permitting such high officials, as the Lieutenant-Governor, Lord Kitchener, and Dunlop Smith, to attend the garden party given by the Maharaja of Darbhanga to receive the Congress delegates. Minto to Morley, 26 December 1906. *M.P.*

[9] *Report of the I.N.C.* 1906, Presidential Address, p. 21.

[1] Ibid. Resolution.

the type of administration he had foreshadowed as 'impossible'.[2]
Morley, however, thought that 'this gives me plenty to think
about, and sows the seeds of plenty of difficulties, great or small,
for me in the next session of the House of Commons'.[3] Minto
was keenly interested in Dadabhai's views, but was surprised
when he went away without seeking an interview, 'which', he
wrote, 'I would gladly have given him'. Minto suspected 'his
[Naoroji's] not doing so was out of regard to "extremist" susceptibilities'.[4]

It is interesting to note that this session of the Congress did not
take any notice of either the Muslim Deputation that had met the
Viceroy, or the contents of their Address to him and the Viceroy's
reply. Nor did any speaker try to discuss or mention the various
demands of the Muslims and the fear that they had expressed of
being subjected to a Hindu majority if a representative form of
government was introduced. The Viceroy's reply must have
startled the Congress leaders. The number of Muslims attending
this session was not very encouraging, for out of 1,663 delegates
forty-five were Muslims, of whom twenty-four were from Bengal. Moreover, the Nawab of Dacca's scheme of an All-India
Muslim Confederacy was already in circulation and the Congress
papers had not only discussed and criticized this scheme, but
had also laughed at the idea of any independent Muslim organization. The All-India Muslim League was meeting for the first
time in those very days in Dacca.

Perhaps the Congress leaders were too much occupied with
their own difficulties to think very seriously about the nascent
Muslim movement, except for a slight reference in Surendranath
Banerjea's speech. Dadabhai Naoroji, however, in his presidential address, did try to enlist the support of the Muslims by
quoting Sir Syed Ahmed and saying that he was 'a nationalist to

[2] Minto to Morley, 2 January 1907. *M.P.* Minto also informed Morley that
'there has been a stiff fight in Congress between the Extremists and
Moderates, resulting, as far as one can see at present, in the complete success
of the latter.'
[3] Morley to Minto, 27 December 1906. Ibid.
[4] Minto to Morley, 16 January 1907. Ibid.

the backbone'. He hoped that 'the wise and patriotic counsel of that great man' his Muslim friends 'will take to heart'. He emphasized 'that our emancipation depends upon the thorough union of all the people of India without any obstruction'.[5] Surendranath Banerjea, speaking 'as a member of the Hindu Community', desired 'to tell my Mahommedan fellow-countrymen that we notice with satisfaction the political ferment which we witness in the great Islamic community in India. We rejoice at the growing aspirations of the Mahommedan Community. From us Hindus, you will receive nothing but sympathy and co-operation, for we recognize that you are brothers linked to us by an inseparable destiny. Hindus and Mahommedans let us stand on a common platform...'[6] The remarks of the Chairman of the Reception Committee, Dr. Rash Behari Ghose, on the other hand, might have antagonized those Muslims who were urged to join the Congress. In an attempt to emphasize that the Muslims were well represented he said, 'with the exception of some Nawabs and Khan Bahadurs in the Eastern province who are now weeping like the poor Queen of Carthage for Sir Joseph Fuller, you will find on the Reception Committee almost all the most prominent men of Bengal, Behar and Orissa...' And it was those very Nawabs and Khan Bahadurs who were laying the foundations of the All-India Muslim League.

The Congress, despite its growing strength, showed grave weaknesses. Its leadership was hopelessly divided and it worked under conflicting principles. Gokhale was liked by Morley and Minto and he was the foremost leader, but he was weak and lacked unifying magnetism. Morley thought 'he [Gokhale] had a politician's head',[7] but 'as a party manager', he 'is a baby'.[8] Gokhale had a difficult task. Morley had clearly told him that to implant English political institutions in India was a dream but 'for reasonable reforms in your direction, there is now an

[5] *Report of the I.N.C.* 1906. Presidential Address, p. 32.
[6] Ibid. *1906.* Speech, S. N. Banerjea, p. 77.
[7] Morley to Minto, 2 August 1906. *M.P.*
[8] Morley to Minto, 31 October 1906. Ibid.

unexampled chance'. Morley frankly told Gokhale that the chance of such reforms might be spoilt by the perversity and unreasonableness of some members of the Congress. Though Gokhale assured Morley that he would see that nothing unpleasant happened and that he had taken steps in that direction,[9] he knew that the Congress was in danger.

The moderates succeeded in averting a showdown at the 1906 session at Calcutta, but they could not save a split in the Congress when it met on 26 December 1907 at Surat. The 1906 Congress session had disclosed the existence within the Congress of a body of extreme opinion opposed to the severely constitutional methods of the older generation. There the two parties wrangled fiercely, amongst other things, over the propriety of the boycott as a political weapon of universal application. The older men looked upon the boycott movement and its connected activities as a temporary expedient, the adoption of which had been forced upon them; not as a normal method of political agitation. There was also the question whether the boycott should be economic or extend to other aspects of the West; i.e. law courts &c. However, embarrassed as they were by the Secretary of State's declaration that the Partition must be accepted as a settled fact, the moderates retained control of the situation, though they allowed the resolutions on self-government, national education, and the *Swadeshi* and boycott movements and tolerated the heated tone of the speeches.

The next session of the Congress was to have been held at Nagpur, but due to some local differences, the meeting place was changed to Surat. Rumours started spreading from early November 1907, that the twenty-third session of the Congress would

---

[9] Morley to Minto, 2 August 1906. *M.P.* See also T. V. Parvate, op. cit., pp. 212–13. Gokhale's letter to Dravid, 3 August 1906, '. . . I want you to do what you can to prevent any *ungenerous* criticism of Mr. Morley in the press. See Mr. Kelkar and with him see Mr. Tilak if necessary and beg them in my name to exert their influence for the sake of our common country to discourage any declaration on the part of the Indian Press just at present of want of faith in Mr. Morley . . .' Natesh Appaji Dravid was one of the first members of Gokhale's Servants of India Society and one of his closest friends.

have nothing to do with the four resolutions of the preceding session, i.e. resolutions on self-government, national education, *Swadeshi* and boycott of foreign goods. At Calcutta the Congress passed these resolutions, but for the Surat Session 'slight verbal alterations had been made in one or two of them to remove ambiguity'. For instance, the resolution on Self-Government was changed from 'the system of government obtaining in the self-governing colonies' to 'the self-government enjoyed by other members of the British Empire'; later on Gokhale even inserted 'self-governing' before 'members of the British Empire'. The *Swadeshi* resolution was changed from 'to stimulate the production of indigenous articles by giving them preference over imported commodities even at some sacrifice' to 'to stimulate the consumption of indigenous articles by giving them preference where possible over imported commodities'. Nevinson suggests that the 'omission of the words "even at some sacrifice" was due to the inaccuracy of the newspaper copy, from which the resolution was taken'. Similarly a clause in the resolution about national education was modified from 'to organize a system of education —literary, scientific, and technical—suited to the requirements of the country on national lines and under national control' to 'to organize an independent system of education—literary, scientific, and technical—suited to the requirements of the country'. Gokhale again defended the alteration on the ground that it was more restrained in form and 'more in accord with what was being actually attempted in different parts of India'. The change in the resolution on boycott was criticized most. Previously it was that the Congress was 'of opinion that the Boycott movement inaugurated by Bengal by way of protest against the Partition of that province was and is legitimate'. The wording of the new resolution was, 'This Congress is of opinion that the Boycott of foreign goods resorted to in Bengal by way of protest against the Partition of that province was and is legitimate.' Earlier this could have been interpreted as suggesting the boycott of foreign goods, education, foreign authority, foreign appointments, foreign justice, &c., but now it was specifically restricted to 'foreign goods'.[1] On the eve of the session, the extremists under the leadership of Tilak encamped themselves at three miles distant from the Congress camps. Despite numerous refutations and denials, rumours continued to spread. Then arose the difficulty over the election of the President. The Moderates wanted Dr. Rash Behari Ghose and the extremists Lala Lajpat Rai, on whose refusal they put up another man. The real clash came on 26 December 1907, when Dr. Ghose's name was proposed and Surendranath Banerjea rose to address the assembly. The audience did not want to listen to him and cried for Lajpat Rai and Tilak. The session ended in pandemonium and it was adjourned *sine die*.[2]

People were expecting it. Gokhale, Minto and Morley expected it.[3] Gokhale thought that this split would encourage bureaucracy to put down both sections without much difficulty. They would brush Gokhale and his friends aside on the ground that they had no large following in the country and would put down the new party for sedition.[4] Minto thought this whole line of argument 'trash'. He knew that the reforms would not be welcomed by the extremists, but he expected that 'he [Gokhale] could have played a great game if whilst asserting his own political honesty he had recognized our good intentions and done his best to assist the Government of India'.[5] Minto construed 'Gokhale's letters to Wedderburn simply as indicating that for the present he has lost the game and feels that our recognition of

[1] H. W. Nevinson, op. cit., pp. 250–3. See also *Reports of the I.N.C. 1906*, 1908. *The Surat Congress*. I.O.L. Tract No. 1042.

[2] *Report of the I.N.C. 1908. Home Progs.* (Public), vol. 7872, January–March 1908. For a more detailed account of the Surat Split, see also P. C. Ghose, op. cit., pp. 163–83.

[3] Minto to Morley, 9 October 1907. *M.P.* Morley to Minto, 26 December 1907. Morley feared that this split might not result in the defeat of moderates, who were to be backed.

[4] On 11 October 1907 Gokhale wrote to Wedderburn, 'The outlook at this moment is as dark as could be . . . If a split does come, it means a disaster . . . ' Morley to Minto, 31 October 1907. *M.C.*; Minto to Morley, 5 November 1907, 'He [Gokhale] was very disappointing as to the future.'

[5] Minto to Morley, 23 November 1907. *M.C.*

political interests other than those of the party he represents has for the present scotched his wheel'. This disappointed Minto.[6]

Events at Surat did not prove to be so disastrous. Minto thought it 'a great triumph for us', because the extremists had disappeared from the Congress and he hoped for 'a reasonable recognition by the moderates of our intentions'. Gokhale and other moderates also heaved a sigh of relief.[7]

[6] Minto to Morley, 30 November 1907. *M.P.*
[7] Minto to Morley, 2 and 15 January 1908. Ibid.

# CHAPTER TWO

# THE ORIGIN AND GROWTH OF THE ALL-INDIA MUSLIM LEAGUE

## 1906–1910

IT was not until 1900 that the seeds of an independent Muslim political party on an All-India basis were sown. Talking about the origin of the Muslim League, Syed Ali Imam said in 1908, 'It is nearly a decade since Nawab Viqar-ul-Mulk Bahadur called an informal meeting of leading Mahommedans of India at the house of my esteemed friend Mr. Hamid Ali Khan of Lucknow. I was present in that meeting. After the necessary deliberations, the gathering broke up and all of us who had taken part in it felt the absolute necessity of political organisation of our own.'[1] In other words, some prominent Muslims, who were destined to play an important part in Muslim politics later on, had decided to organize a political party long before the supposed 'British imperial policy' which helped the birth of the Muslim League.[2]

Nawab Viqar-ul-Mulk, who had settled at Amroha, U.P., after his retirement from Hyderabad and who had not taken an active part in public affairs, became active during the Hindi-Urdu controversy in 1900. Articles were published in the *Aligarh Institute Gazette*. The revival of the Muhammedan Anglo-Oriental Defence Association was advocated. He toured the country and a meeting was also held at Lucknow in October, 1901, where it was decided to form a political association to safeguard Muslim interests. The support was not very encouraging as the Muslims were still very reluctant to deviate from the path which had been laid down by Sir Syed, though in July 1903,

[1] Syed Ali Imam, *Presidential Address*. Amritsar Session, All-India Muslim League, 1908.
[2] See W. C. Smith, *Modern Islam in India* (London, 1946), p. 246.

the Muhammedan Political Association was formed at a public meeting of the Muslims held at Saharanpur, U.P.[3]

The agitation over the Partition of Bengal which took the shape of an anti-Muslim agitation, especially when the *Bengalee*, an influential Congress organ, began to criticize the Muslim leaders particularly Nawab Salimullah of Dacca for their support of Partition, further antagonized the Muslims.[4] They started to think in terms of finding the best ways of counteracting the Congress agitation. But as the leadership was still in the hands of landholders or members of the upper middle class, they were very slow to react because of their vested interests. Moreover, they had great hopes of the Government. Sir Syed had done much to emphasize to the Government the loyalty of the Indian Muslims and it was hoped that the Government would not betray them in the face of an anti-Government agitation. Curzon's announcement that the new province would give them extra opportunities of emerging from their backward state had given them further confidence. But there were no signs of any decrease in the fervour of the agitation, despite the fact that Morley had declared Partition a 'settled fact'.[5] The Barisal events and the acceptance of the resignation of Fuller, who was considered to be a champion of the Muslim cause, made them extremely uneasy.[6] A wave of resentment ran across the whole sub-continent. Hundreds of telegrams poured into the Governor-General's office and heavily attended meetings were held at

[3] The *Pioneer*, 31 July 1903.

[4] In Bengal, at least, the agitation over the Partition and the Muslim reaction to that widened the gulf between the two communities. See N. C. Chaudhri, *Autobiography of an Unknown Indian* (London, 1951), pp. 233–7. He describes how 'a cold dislike for the Muslims settled down in our hearts, putting an end to all real intimacy of relationship'. The Hindus nicknamed Nawab Salimullah 'the one-eyed', p. 234.

[5] *Hansard*, House of Commons, 4S, vol. 152 (February–March 1906), Col. 844. Morley's Speech, 26 February 1906.

[6] See Chapter I. Fuller was given an extremely touching send-off by the Muslims. Newspaper reports of the period contain many statements of the Muslim leaders and organizations throughout the country condemning the Government action and praising Fuller. The *Englishman*, 7, 8, 9, 11, 13, 15, 18, 25 August; 3, 5, 7, 11, 13, &c., September 1906. See also *B.N.N.R.*, 1906.

almost every important town of India and even at some lesser known places, which had no connexion with the movement whatsoever.[7] The resignation of Fuller stirred up the Muslims[8] just as the Partition and *Swadeshi* movement had popularized the Congress. These largely-attended meetings of the Muslims at places that had not been affected by the Partition or the resignation of Fuller indicated their keenness to join in some organization to press for the safeguard of their interests. It further showed that the Muslims had realized that the time had come when something should be done to bring to the notice of the Government the existence of a community which was intensely loyal and which had not resorted to the methods of the agitators to safeguard their interests. And the documents show that the Government, too, was beginning to realize the Muslim uneasiness.[9]

But before resorting to the methods adopted by the Congress, they wanted to approach the Government in the most constitutional and peaceful way and the opportunity was provided when Morley in his Budget speech expressed his desire to consider the proposals for reforming the Legislative Councils[1] and Minto appointed a Committee to look into the matter and suggest some reforms. The Muslim leaders decided to act promptly.

Nawab Mehdi Ali Khan, better known as Mohsin-ul-Mulk, who had succeeded Sir Syed to the secretaryship of the Aligarh College, wrote a letter from Bombay on 4 August 1906 to the Principal of his College, W. A. J. Archbold, who was staying in Simla during the summer vacation: 'You must have read

[7] For instance Multan in the Punjab. The *Englishman*, 5 September 1906. See also *B.N.N.R.*, 1906.

[8] Lady Minto also admits this in *My Indian Journal*, vol. ii, 1905–6, p. 201, though she omitted the relevant sentence from her book, *India, Minto and Morley*, p. 45. The complete sentence is 'The Younger generation were wavering, inclined to throw in their lot with the advanced agitators of the Congress, then came Fuller's resignation. A howl went up that the loyal Mahommedans were not to be supported, and that the agitators were to obtain their demands through agitation'.

[9] Hare to Minto, 1 September 1906. *M.C.*

[1] *Hansard*, House of Commons, 43, vol. 161, 20 July 1906, Col. 588.

and thought over Mr. John Morley's speech on the Indian
Budget. It is very much talked of among the Mohammedans of
India, and is commonly believed to be a great success achieved
by the "National Congress".

'You are aware that the Mohammedans already feel a little
disappointed, and young educated Mohammedans seem to have
a sympathy for the "Congress"; and this speech will produce a
greater tendency in them to join the "Congress". Although there
is little reason to believe that any Mohammedans, except the
young educated ones, will join that body, there is still a general
complaint on their part that we (Aligarh people) take no part in
politics, and do not safeguard the political rights of Mohammedans, they say that we do not suggest any plans for preserving
their rights, and particularly do nothing and care nothing for the
Mohammedans beyond asking for funds to help the college. I
have got several letters drawing attention particularly to the new
proposal of "elected representatives" in the Legislative Councils.
They say that the existing rules confer no rights on Mohammedans; and no Mohammedans get into the Councils by election;
every now and then the Government nominates a stray Mohammedan or two by kindness, not however on the ground of his
ability, but of his position, who is neither fit to discharge his
duties in Council nor is he considered a true representative of his
community. If the new rules now to be drawn up introduce
"election" on a more extended scale, the Mohammedans will
hardly get a seat, while Hindus will carry off the palm by dint
of their majority, and no Mohammedan will get into the Councils
by election.

'It has also been proposed that a memorial be submitted to His
Excellency the Viceroy to draw the attention of Government to a
consideration of the rights of Mohammedans.

'I feel it is a very important matter, and, if we remain silent,
I am afraid, people will leave us to go their own way and act up
to their own personal opinions.

'Will you therefore inform me if it would be advisable to
submit a memorial from the Mohammedans to the Viceroy, and

to request His Excellency's permission for a deputation to wait on His Excellency to submit the view of Mohammedans on the matter?'[2]

It was in reply to this letter that Archbold wrote his famous letter of 10 August 1906, which many have since quoted pointedly without referring to what Mohsin-ul-Mulk had written. Syed Tufail Ahmed Mangalori first published the 'gist' (*Khulāsa*) of Archbold's letter without mentioning the source.[3] This gist was translated verbatim by Achyut Patvardhan and Asoka Mehta in *The Communal Triangle*.[4] From there it was copied by G. N. Singh in his *Landmarks in Indian Constitutional and National Development*,[5] by B. M. Chaudhri, in *Muslim Politics*,[6] and Ram Gopal, in *Indian Muslims*.[7] Mohammed Noman accepted the letter without contesting its authority or verifying the date or contents or trying to trace the letter to which it was a reply.[8] Lal Bahadur, however, does not mention it: though his conclusions do not differ from those other writers, that Archbold was the prime mover and originator of the idea of a Muslim deputation to the Viceroy,[9] thus supporting the thesis that the British aroused the Muslims as a counterpoise to Congress aims.

Archbold's letter to Mohsin-ul-Mulk could not be traced (except as reproduced in various books) but the correspondence between Archbold, Dunlop Smith and Mohsin-ul-Mulk suggests that Archbold was acting on behalf of and under instructions from

[2] Mohsin-ul-Mulk to Archbold, 4 August 1906, enclosed with Minto to Morley, 8 August 1906. *M.P.*

[3] Tufail Ahmed Mangalori, *Musslmanon Ka Roshan Mustaqbil* (Urdu), 1938, pp. 348–9.

[4] Published at Allahabad in 1942, p. 62. Dr. W. Cantwell-Smith, perhaps, based his views on this letter quoted in Patvardhan's book when he says, 'this group of Muslims and the government together decided on an imperial policy of special British favour for communalist and loyal Muslims', p. 286. W. C. Smith, op. cit.

[5] Published at Delhi in 1950. There is no mention of Archbold's letter in the first edition of this book published at Benares City in 1933.

[6] Published at Calcutta in 1946, p. 15.

[7] Published at London in 1959, p. 97.

[8] M. Noman, *Muslim India*, 1942, p. 72.

[9] Lal Bahadur, *The Muslim League*, 1954.

Mohsin-ul-Mulk and not vice versa. Mohsin-ul-Mulk soon established contact with Dunlop Smith and corresponded with him
directly. Moreover some of Archbold's suggestions appear to
have been turned down. He was in favour of the deputation
supporting the system of nomination while the deputation suggested election of their representatives.[1]

Mohsin-ul-Mulk's letter was put before Minto through Col.
Dunlop Smith, his private secretary. This letter reached Minto
at a time when he was seriously thinking about political reforms.
Being aware of the trends of the new Liberal Government, he
was preparing himself to outline a policy which should meet
with the Indian aspirations. Until then the Congress's voice was
the only voice that had reached him. Mohsin-ul-Mulk's letter
explained to him the feelings of a loyal but politically important
Indian community. Realizing the importance of this letter he
immediately forwarded it to Morley.[2] After telling him that the
telegraphic accounts of his speech 'have excited a good deal of
interest', Minto wrote, 'I think it is worthwhile to enclose you a
copy of a letter to Mr. Archbold, Principal of the Aligarh
College, from Mohsin-ul-Mulk, the manager of the College. It
was only put before me to-day and is important in illustrating
the trend of Mohammedan thought, and this apprehension that
Mohammedan interests may be neglected in dealing with any

---

[1] Archbold to Dunlop Smith, 9, 20, 22 August 1906; Dunlop Smith to
Archbold, 10, 21 August 1906; Mohsin-ul-Mulk to Archbold, 18 August
1906. This letter suggests that Archbold did send a draft of the formal application and Mohsin-ul-Mulk circulated it amongst his friends. But it was not
liked. Mohsin-ul-Mulk wrote, 'I am sure nobody will like the opening phrases
which give an assurance of deliberate aloofness from political agitation in
future. Probably also they will not like me to represent their cause to the
Government without the means of a political association.' M.C.

[2] Morley was well-informed and Minto had Morley's complete support and
confidence. G. N. Singh is wrong in suggesting that 'It is certainly most surprising but nonetheless it is an important fact that Lord Morley was not only
not consulted but appears to have been deliberately kept in the dark about the
mischievous move until Lord Minto had committed the Government to the
policy of granting to the Muslim community both weightage and separate
political representation.' Landmarks in Indian Constitutional and National
Development, 1950, p. 194.

increase of representation on the Legislative Councils. I have not had time to think over the advisability of receiving the proposed deputation, but am inclined to do so. There have been other signs besides the letter to Mr. Archbold pointing in the same direction, and there is no doubt a natural fear in many quarters lest perpetual Bengalee demands should lead to the neglect of other claims to representation throughout India; so that we must be very careful in taking up these questions to give full value to the importance of other interests besides those so largely represented by the Congress'. Minto was not unaware of the presence of various interests besides the Congress and knew that their claims could not be overlooked, but he was very cautious and not very enthusiastic about Mohsin-ul-Mulk's suggestion. He feared that the Congress would not look favourably at any attempt to recognize other claims than those put forward by it.[3]

Nevertheless he was willing to receive any deputation.[4] Writing from Agra on 3 April 1906, Minto says, 'In a Reuter which had just reached me I see it is stated that you have been asked to advise me to receive deputations from the "Congress" and that you replied that you saw no reason for taking the initiative. Curzon refused to receive any deputations of the sort, but my own inclination is certainly to do so, provided of course that the deputation is a well selected one representing the influential members. I think myself it is a mistake to attempt to ignore the existence of the Congress. The section of the population it represents will never, I am convinced, possess the grit to play a leading part in the Government of India as a whole, but it does represent Indian advanced thought on many subjects which must affect the future administration of the country, and it will be the greatest mistake to attempt to set the Congress aside and to refuse to have anything to do with it as a factor in the present

[3] Minto to Morley, 8 August 1906. *M.P.*
[4] Besides the Muslim deputation, Minto received many important deputations. (a) Rajput Deputation at Agra, 10 January 1907; Report in the *Bengalee*, 11 January 1907. (b) the Orthodox Hindu Deputation, &c.

history of India.' On 2 May 1906, some six months before he actually received the Muslim deputation, he wrote to Morley, 'I see that the other day you were asked a question in the House as to my willingness to grant an interview to representatives of the Congress,[5] and you allude to such a possibility in your last letter to me. My inclination would certainly be to grant such an interview, although one would have to be careful about it. I think we are bound to look upon the Indian National Congress as a factor in Indian politics, and that it would be best not to ignore it.'[6]

Morley was rather cautious, 'with no particular liking for that school, I wish that I could see a little deeper into what may be good and useful in their notions. *The Times* is going, I believe, to write in the sense of giving them a reasonable hearing. You will no doubt consider rather slowly whether it would be well to accede to their request for an interview. It is not to be settled off-hand, I think, either way.'[7] A few days later he writes, 'As I showed in my letter that crossed yours, I am a very cautious person (caution being sometimes disguised) . . . Your language about receiving a deputation from the Congress is quite a surprise to me,—but a highly agreeable surprise.'[8]

Thus, Minto was willing to receive even the Congress deputation, though the suggestion never materialized, presumably due to lack of enthusiasm on the part of the Congress leaders themselves.

Minto's aim was to acquaint himself with the views of all those groups of the Indian population who were to be affected

---

[5] C. E. Price asked Morley this question. Morley replied, 'I am confident that the Governor-General of India will be inclined to give a sympathetic hearing to any person or collection of persons having a fair and reasonable claim to be heard.' He stated that the Viceroy would use his discretion as to the recognition of such persons and that he saw no reason for taking any initiative in the matter. *Hansard*, House of Commons, 4S, vol. 155 (30 March–25 April 1906), 2 April 1906, Col. 148.

[6] Minto to Morley, 2 May 1906. *M.P.*

[7] Morley to Minto, 19 April 1906. Ibid.

[8] Morley to Minto, 25 April 1906. Ibid.

by the contemplated changes in the structure of the Indian Government, and the Muslim deputation was not the only deputation he received during his Viceroyalty; he received many more, some equally prominent.

Morley, on the other hand, thought it 'an excellent occasion for vindicating our entire and resolute impartiality between races and creeds, and deprecating any other construction of either language used by Government or action taken. We view all these questions in genuine good faith.'[9] Encouraged by Morley's enthusiasm Minto replied, 'I have not yet got a copy of the Aligarh Address. It will be capital opportunity for making clear our position, and the line I shall try to take will be exactly as you say in the direction of indicating our entire and resolute impartiality between races and creeds. I shall say this clearly and strongly, but the position is a ticklish one, and one will have to think over very carefully all that must and must not be said. Arundel's Committee is dealing with the very points you mention—the representation of races, creeds and interests.'[1]

Normally the Viceroy was given beforehand a copy of any address to be presented to him, so that he could prepare his reply in time; but a copy of the Muslim address had not reached Minto even by 19 September 1906,[2] though he was in the meanwhile considering the pros and cons of the coming event. Minto had already decided to receive the deputation but he was not quite sure about their demands. The Muslims in Eastern Bengal were very agitated over Fuller's resignation. Minto naturally suspected that the situation in Bengal would loom large in the deputation's address. Moreover the Congress Press was trying to establish that the contemplated Muslim deputation was not a

[9] Morley to Minto, Telegram, 27 August 1906, *M.P.*

[1] Minto to Morley, Telegram, 31 August 1906, letter, 29 August 1906. Ibid.

[2] It was at a meeting of the Muslim representatives at Lucknow on 15 and 16 September that the text of the address was finalized. The *Englishman*, 17 September 1906. Minto to Morley, 19 September 1906. *M.P.* Dunlop Smith to Mohsin-ul-Mulk, 13 September 1906, in reply to Mohsin-ul-Mulk's letter of 7 September 1906: 'I am to request you that a copy of the proposed address may be furnished to me for His Excellency's information as early as possible.' *M.C.*

representative one and it was the work of the frustrated Bengali Muslim leaders who had been disappointed at Fuller's resignation.[3] So with a view to acquainting himself with the situation in Eastern Bengal and the Muslim feelings there, he wrote to Sir Lancelot Hare, the new Lieutenant-Governor of Eastern Bengal and Assam, who was quite popular amongst the Hindus as well then.[4]

Hare's letters did not add much to Minto's knowledge. He already knew through Mohsin-ul-Mulk's letters and newspaper reports about dissatisfaction amongst the Bengali Muslim leaders. Hare's information was significant only in one respect that it was an official opinion. After telling Minto that the Muslims were capable of staging a more effective agitation under the leadership of *Moulvis* (Religious leaders) than the Hindus, Hare suggested that the Government of India should give them an assurance that the Government was in sympathy with their hopes and aspirations and would help them, as far as possible, 'without undue favour or detriment to other classes'. He, however, added that great uneasiness would prevail among them in case the members of the deputation were not considered representatives or were not heeded.[5]

Minto was still completely unaware of the contents of the Address. In his letter to Morley on 10 September 1906, he states, 'I am to receive the Mohammedan deputation on the 1st of October, and if I can succeed in saying the right thing it may have a great effect on the present position. My answer must of course depend considerably on the points put forward, but, from what I hear, the Address is likely to be moderate in tone. I should like, if possible, to avoid direct allusion to Fuller and to go

---

[3] *B.N.N.R.*, 1906. The *Hitavadi*, Calcutta, 21 September 1906; the *Amrita Bazar Patrika*, 7, 14 September 1906; the *Bengalee*, 9 September 1906, to mention only a few.

[4] Ibid. The Congress Press in Bengal approved and applauded Hare's appointment as Lieutenant-Governor of Eastern Bengal and Assam. He had officiated in this capacity in Bengal as well during Sir Fraser's absence.

[5] Hare to Minto, 1 September 1906; Hare to Dunlop Smith, 1, 18 September 1906. *M.C.*

generally on the lines that our rule is based on an administration which aims at recognizing and safeguarding the welfare of all interests and creeds. I would gladly not touch on "Partition", though no doubt Mohammedan feeling and Mohammedan interests would be very adversely affected by any idea that reconsideration was possible, and it would have a great effect on the future to assure the deputation that our decision is definitely taken and that they need have no fear as to the stability of the new province.'[6] Morley was equally anxious about the outcome of the deputation.[7]

While this correspondence was going on between the Viceroy and the Secretary of State and they were thinking of possible answers to an address about the contents of which they had no knowledge as yet, Mohsin-ul-Mulk busied himself in arranging the signatures and ascertaining the views of various prominent Muslims. Muslim Associations and Anjumans were consulted. The draft memorial which was prepared by Nawab Imad-ul-Mulk S. H. Bilgrami in collaboration with Mohsin-ul-Mulk was discussed and finalized at a meeting at Lucknow on 16 September 1906.[8]

Minto received the Muslim Deputation on 1 October 1906. Thirty-five prominent Muslim leaders from all over India gathered in the Ball Room of the Viceregal Lodge at Simla. Their leader was a young man of twenty-nine years, H. H. Aga Sir Sultan Mohamed Shah Aga Khan from Bombay, who besides being the head of the rich Ismaili sect of Muslims had

[6] Minto to Morley, 10 September 1906. *M.P.*

[7] 'Your talk to the Mahometans next Monday will become the centre of Indian interest. I am looking forward to it pretty keenly, as you may guess—with perfect assurance that you will hold sound and straightforward language.' Morley to Minto, 26 September 1906. *M.P.*

[8] (i) A. H. Albiruni, *The Makers of Pakistan* (Lahore, 1950), p. 92.
  (ii) M. Noman, op. cit., p. 71. On page 74, Noman wrongly considers Nawab Imad-ul-Mulk and S. H. Bilgrami as two persons. Nawab Imad-ul-Mulk was S. H. Bilgrami's title.
  (iii) S. H. Bilgrami, *Addresses, Poems and other Writings* (Hyderabad, Deccan, 1925), pp. 139–44.
  (iv) See Note by Dunlop Smith on Mohsin-ul-Mulk dated 11 November 1907. Lady Minto, op. cit., vol. ii, 1907, pp. 286–7.

close and friendly relations with prominent British people.[9] Mohsin-ul-Mulk and other sponsors of the deputation had had a hand in his selection, and he had been hastily summoned from his tour abroad.[1] Other members of the deputation were not elected representatives of the Muslims, but they did command respect, popularity and considerable influence in their respective areas and represented many professions and various shades of opinion. This galaxy of men presented such an impressive and delightful scene in the afternoon's garden party at Viceregal Lodge[2] as to make even Morley wish that he could 'have moved about' among them.[3]

The Address that they presented was extremely moderate in tone. It conveyed the impression that the deputationists were politicians by compulsion rather than by choice, and were forced by contemporary developments to speak out concerning the fears of their community regarding its future position and status under the contemplated changes in the administrative set-up.

After praising British rule which brought 'peace, security, personal freedom, and liberty of worship' to the peoples of India, the address criticized the existing system of representation in Municipalities, District Boards and Legislative Councils, and dwelt on the political importance of the Muslims as a community of over sixty-two millions. Morley's Budget speech had hinted at

[9] Incorrect date and place are given in:—
    (a) H. J. Greenwall, *His Highness the Aga Khan* (London, 1952): 'Early in 1896 . . . went to Delhi to call on the Viceroy', p. 16, on p. 126, the date was corrected.
    (b) Stanley Jackson, *The Aga Khan* (London, 1952): 'Meanwhile, in Delhi, the Aga Khan headed a Moslem deputation . . .', p. 49.
    (c) Sir George Dunbar, *India and the Passing of Empire* (London, 1951): '. . . a deputation of the All-India Moslem League, and backed by the Government of India which in this matter had Gokhale's support.' p. 171. The All-India Muslim League was not in existence at that time.
[1] This selection did not please Nawab Syed Muhammad, a member of the Viceroy's Legislative Council, who himself aspired to lead this deputation. Minto to Morley, 4 November 1906. *M.P.*
[2] Mary, Countess of Minto, op. cit., p. 47.
[3] Morley to Minto, 26 October 1906. *M.P.*

the possible increase in the Legislative Councils. Hence it was submitted that they might be given 'adequate recognition as an important factor in the state' and it was urged that 'the position accorded to the Mohammedan community in any kind of representation, direct or indirect, and in all other ways, affecting their status and influence, should be commensurate not merely with their numerical strength, but also with their political importance, and the value of the contribution which they make to the defence of the Empire'. It was hoped that 'due consideration' would be given 'to the position which they occupied in India a little more than a hundred years ago'. It was emphasized that the system of election or nomination to the Legislative Councils prevailing hitherto had failed to give them proper representation, and it was hoped that this discrepancy would be removed by granting them the right to send their own representatives through separate electorates. The insufficient Muslim representation on the Bench, Municipalities, District Boards and on the Senate and Syndicates of the Indian Universities was also brought to the notice of the Viceroy.

In the address a specific system of representation was suggested:

1. 'That, in the cadre of the Council, the proportion of Mohammedan representation should not be determined on the basis of the numerical strength of the community, and that, in any case, the Mohammedan representatives should never be an ineffective minority.

2. 'That, as far as possible, appointment by election should be given preference over nomination.

3. 'That, for purposes of choosing Mohammedan members, Mohammedan landowners, lawyers, merchants, and representatives of other important interests of a status to be subsequently determined by Your Excellency's Government, Mohammedan members of the Provincial Councils and Mohammedan Fellows of Universities should be invested with electoral powers to be exercised in accordance with such procedure as may be prescribed by Your Excellency's Government in that behalf.'[4]

[4] The Muslim Address, Para. 14. *M.P.*

They also sought protection of their interests in the event of the appointment of an Indian to the Viceroy's Executive Council and solicited help in the foundation of a Muslim University. The address ended on a note of loyalty to the British Raj.[5]

The points raised in this address were discussed at length by the Viceroy, the Secretary of State for India and others in their private and official correspondence. Minto's reply, though non-committal, was extremely sympathetic. He said that he realized that the Muslim claim was not merely that they should be represented 'as a community' but that their position should be estimated not merely on their numerical strength but in respect to their political importance and their service to the Empire. He agreed with the deputationists that 'any electoral representation in India would be doomed to mischievous failure which aimed at granting a personal enfranchisement regardless of the beliefs and traditions of the communities composing the population of this continent,' and assured them 'that their political rights and interests will be safeguarded in any administration with which I am concerned.'[6] It is worthwhile noting that none of the critics of Government policy or the supporters of the Congress views asked any questions at that time in Parliament with regard to Minto's reply.

Morley telegraphed his approval and appreciated 'its high qualities,'[7] and he read the account of the proceedings in *The Times*, not 'with anxiety', but 'with lively interest', as he thought the address 'was admirable alike in spirit, in the choice of topics, and in the handling',[8] and he maintained the same tone of appreciation in his other letters[9] till the controversy arose over his electoral college scheme. 'Among other good effects' of this 'Mahometan deliverance', he wrote, 'was that it had completely deranged the plans and tactics of our Cottonians[1]: that is to say

[5] The Muslim Address, Paras. 15, 16, 17. *M.P.*
[6] Minto's reply. Ibid.
[7] Morley to Minto, telegram, 4 October 1906. Ibid.
[8] Morley to Minto, 5 October 1906. Ibid.
[9] Morley to Minto, 11 and 19 October 1906. Ibid.
[1] A group of M.P.s in the House of Commons, extremely sympathetic towards the Congress, whose chief spokesman was Sir Henry Cotton.

it has prevented them from any longer presenting the Indian Government as the ordinary case of the bureaucracy *versus* the people. I hope that even my stoutest radical friends will see that problem is not quite as simple as this'.[2] Minto's brother, Hugh Elliot, also congratulated him on his address. 'I don't think the answer & tone of it would have been improved, & there seems to be only one opinion in the papers here as to its wisdom & fittingness. I am glad to see that the Indian papers appear to be as well pleased as the English ones'.[3] John Buchan considers Minto's reply 'most sagacious and tactful'.[4]

But the Congress Press commented differently. While most of them praised its prudence, the Congress papers sensed the beginning of a never-ending imperial policy which would result in the perpetuation of British rule, by exploiting rivalries between the various communities of India.[5] The Congress leaders were naturally very worried and suspected that the Muslims were being put up as opponents of political reforms. The *Amrita Bazar Patrika* tried to minimize the importance of the deputation by suggesting that it was not an 'all-India' deputation and that it was a 'got up affair fully engineered by interested officials'.[6] The *Bengalee* published various editorials. On 13 September 1906, it appealed to the Muslims to co-operate with the Hindus in presenting a united front to the Government and promised to meet the Muslim 'brethren half-way'. But the appeal did not evoke any response. It first denounced the whole idea of a Muslim deputation,[7] and when it realized that it could not be stopped, admitted that the deputation was 'as thoroughly representative and influential as could be desired.'[8] It expressed its happiness

---

[2] Morley to Minto, 19 October 1906. Ibid.

[3] Hugh Elliot to Minto, 8 October 1906. *M.C.*

[4] John Buchan, op. cit., p. 243.

[5] The *Hindu Patriot*, 5 October 1906; The *Sanjivani*, 11 October 1906; the *Hitavadi*, 12, 14 October 1906; The *Weekly Chronicle*, 24, 31 October 1906; *B.N.N.R.*, 1906.

[6] The *Amrita Bazar Patrika*, 2, 3 October 1906.

[7] The *Bengalee*, 9 September 1906.

[8] The *Bengalee*, 29 September 1906.

that 'among the deputation there are several Mahomedan leaders who are as level-headed as they are loyal and patriotic.'[9] But it soon changed its tone after publishing a full account of the proceedings.[1] In the course of five editorials it asserted that the deputation 'was composed most exclusively of Mahomedan leaders of the old school, that some of the important Mahomedan Provinces' and 'the educated section' were accorded a lamentably inadequate representation; that 'the reply of the Viceroy must have been rather disappointing to the deputation'; that the deputation was 'the first fruit of educational movement' among the Muslims; that the address was 'moderate and sober'; that they also detested 'nomination' like the Hindus and wanted 'election'. It strongly opposed the Muslim demand for separate representation as it considered it 'not only indefensible in theory', but it would create 'serious political difficulties'.[2]

The Anglo-Indian Press, like the *Pioneer,* and the *Englishman,* heartily expressed its approval of the proceedings and shared the opinion of *The Times* that the memorial was the 'only piece of original political thought which has emanated from modern times.'[3]

Minto himself was very anxious to 'avoid appearing to take sides', but he could not help 'heartily acknowledging the soundness of the Mohammedan arguments', and was pleased that 'the members of the Deputation were more than satisfied'[4] with his answer. He was, however, pained when Hare told him of the 'attempts of the *Amrita Bazar Patrika* and the *Bengalee* to belittle the Mohammedan deputation, and the lying assertions that this and the recent 16th October meetings to celebrate the Partition have been got up by the Government officials',[5] and when one 'Madras English Paper' stated that he had 'missed a magnificent opportunity of pitching into Surendra Nath Banerjee

[9] The *Bengalee,* 30 September 1906.
[1] The *Bengalee,* 2 October 1906.
[2] The *Bengalee,* 3, 4, 5, 6, 9 October 1906.
[3] *The Times,* 2 October 1906.
[4] Minto to Morley, 4 October 1906. *M.P.*
[5] Hare to Minto, 20 October 1906. Ibid.

and his friends! apparently with the idea that I should have made an onslaught on Congress ideas'. 'Whatever one may think of them', he explained, 'it is really extraordinary that there should be anyone so narrow and short-sighted as to imagine that the Mahommedan Deputation gave me an opportunity of attacking Bengali sentiment.'[6]

Mohsin-ul-Mulk told Dunlop Smith that the Muslims were genuinely pleased and satisfied, as this 'clear and sympathetic recognition of the rights of the Mohammedans' and 'historic declaration of the policy of the Indian Government' had 'put a new heart' into them.[7]

Thus the Muslim Deputation which waited on the Viceroy on the morning of 1 October 1906 at Simla, was not 'engineered' by the Government to offer 'a staunch resistance to all nationalist ambition and activity.'[8] There is no evidence that Mohsin-ul-Mulk was 'at the beck and call of the Government of India',[9] or that Archbold was its originator, or that the 'inspiration came from Simla',[1] or that it was a 'Command performance';[2] or that it was 'a counter-poise to the Congress aims.'[3]

[6] Minto to Morley, 9 October 1906. *M.P.*

[7] Mohsin-ul-Mulk to Dunlop Smith, 7 October 1906. Ibid.

[8] Lal Bahadur, *The Muslim League* (Agra, 1954), p. 33.

[9] Ram Gopal, *Indian Muslims, 1858–1947* (London, 1959), p. 97.

[1] C. Y. Chintamani, *Indian Politics Since the Mutiny* (London, 1940), p. 91. Though some years later C. Y. Chintamani himself favoured separate electorates, as they reduced the tension between the Hindus and the Muslims—Evidence before Reforms Enquiry Committee, on 18 August 1924—Shafaat Ahmad Khan, *What are the Rights of the Muslim Minority in India* (Allahabad, 1928), p. 92. C. H. Philips, *India* (London (n.d.)) '. . . the charge has often been made that the British deliberately applied such a "divide and rule" policy. Morley and Minto, indeed, were not unaware of the possible advantages of this course, but there is no evidence to suggest that they consciously sought it. Had they set themselves to introduce parliamentary government of the English kind into India, then their recognition of separate electorates would have been a mischievous act, but they clearly had no such intention in mind', p. 108. Evidence, moreover, is now available that at least in this particular case they were not the prime movers.

[2] Maulana Mohammed Ali's expression in 1923, quoted in various books (i.e. G. N. Singh, op. cit., 1950, p. 205). See also the *Cambridge History of India*, vol. vi (Delhi, 1958), p. 618, which contains certain inaccuracies.

[3] B. M. Chaudhuri, *Muslim Politics in India* (Calcutta, 1946), p. 15.

To subscribe to such opinions is to distort history and to underrate both Muslim political aspirations and the integrity and intellectual capability of Muslim leadership. Archbold's close contact with high Government officials might have facilitated the work of the Muslim leaders in approaching the Viceroy and presenting the memorial to him, but it did not in any way seem to have inspired them. The inspiration came from within rather than from without. In fact, when Muslims roused themselves from their lethargy and began to learn English, they naturally looked for responsible offices as Hindus had previously done, but found the doors to the public services practically closed upon them. Lord Ripon's Government had introduced Local Self Government in India, and mixed electorates had been made the entry to elective seats on the local bodies. The Muslims found it almost impossible to enter these bodies through mixed electorates. Mixed electorates had also been instituted in the universities under Lord Curzon's Indian Universities Act, but no Muslim could enter the Senates under this system. By the beginning of the twentieth century the struggle between the Haves and the Have-nots was becoming very acute. The announcement of the consideration of further constitutional reforms led Muslim leaders to take prompt action in order to safeguard their community's interests.

The Muslim leaders, who had gathered in Simla to present an address to Minto, put their heads together and informally discussed the question of forming an association with a view to safeguarding the interests of their community in India.[4] It was at that time that, the Aga Khan writes, 'Mohsin-ul-Mulk and I, in common with other Muslim leaders, had come to the conclusion that our only hope lay along the lines of independent organisation and action, and that we must secure independent political recognition from the British Government as a nation within a nation.'[5] Moreover Syed Ameer Ali, who founded the Central National Muhammadan Association in 1877, and had since been

[4] *The Times*, 6 October 1906. Report from its Correspondent.
[5] The Aga Khan, *Memoirs* (London, 1954), p. 76.

urging the Muslims to organize into a distinct political group, again emphasized the need of a political party in an article in the *Nineteenth Century*.[6]

But Nawab Salimullah Khan of Dacca, who could not join the deputation because of an eye operation,[7] took the first concrete step. He circulated a letter which contained a scheme for 'the Muslim All-India Confederacy'.[8] The aims and objects of this 'Confederacy' were to support the Government 'whenever possible' and to protect the interests of the Muslims. It also aimed at controverting the growing influence of the Congress and to win back those Muslims who had joined the Congress by providing them with a scope for public life. In other words the Nawab was suggesting a political party with the sole aim of protecting and propagating the Muslim cause. The scheme definitely had a little scope and was defective, but the scheme was the embryo from which the League emerged.

The *Bengalee* strongly criticized the scheme and hoped that the Muslims would not agree to this. It did not even like the name— 'the Moslem All-India Confederacy, reminds us of the Mahratha Confederacy of old and the Khalsa Confederacy of more recent times. Why should the Nawab assume a bellicose name when sycophancy is to be the watchword of the Association?'[9] The *Times of India* considered his circular 'ill-advised and indiscreet', though it appreciated the need of an association to unify the activities of the numerous Muslim associations in existence.[1] The *Beharee* characterized the scheme as 'hopelessly preposterous' and calculated to embitter the relations between Hindus and Muslims. It hoped that none of the Muslims would associate with 'the Salimullah tomfoolery'.[2] The *Pioneer* thought that

[6] Syed Ameer Ali, 'India and the New Parliament', *Nineteenth Century*, August 1906, pp. 257–8.

[7] The *Englishman*, 27 September 1906.

[8] Full text with editorial comments. The *Bengalee*, 14 December 1906.

[9] The *Bengalee*, 14 December 1906.

[1] The *Times of India*, 18 December 1906.

[2] The *Beharee*, 21 December 1906. *B.N.N.R.*, 1906. Comments of the Congress Press were not at all favourable.

'the Mohammedan community do need an authoritarian medium for the expression of their views. Failing it, the legitimate influence they should exercise is often lost'.[3] The *Englishman* expressed similar views. It published a letter by one 'J. B', who liked the Nawab's scheme and suggested that such a formation of Muslim political association was essential in the country's interest.[4] Thus while the Congress Press criticized and disliked the scheme, the Anglo-Indian Press appreciated and admitted the need of an all-India Muslim organization.

The Nawab's scheme became the basis of discussion at Dacca on 30 December 1906. Those delegates, who had assembled there from all parts of India to attend the All-India Muhammadan Educational Conference, met in a session after the Conference, under the presidentship of Viqar-ul-Mulk and decided to form the All-India Muslim League.

The meeting of these delegates began two hours later than the advertised time, but it was 'most enthusiastic'. Mohsin-ul-Mulk thanked the Nawab of Dacca for his hospitality and 'expressed satisfaction at the spirit and enthusiasm shown by the people of the new province'. Viqar-ul-Mulk took the chair and in his introductory speech in Urdu he said, 'Time and circumstances made it necessary for Mohammedans to unite in an association so as to make their voice heard above the din of other vociferous parties in India and across the wide seas to England. Unless united in support of one another and working in loyal unison with the Government of India the Moslem majority who, through misfortunes and errors, had fallen from their once high estate, were in danger of being submerged by the enormous Hindu flood'. He further said that there was a need for maturer guidance for the younger generation who were 'too hot, too frothy', and for showing complete loyalty to the Government. The Viceroy's reply to the Simla Deputation was cited as a great encouragement for the Muslims.[5]

[3] The *Pioneer*, 14 December 1906.
[4] The *Englishman*, 27 September 1906.
[5] The *Englishman*, 31 December 1906 and the *Pioneer*, 2 January 1907.

The Nawab of Dacca, introducing the Scheme, explained that under normal circumstances 'The movement might perhaps not have been heard of' but now the times were such that 'only those who cried loudest had a chance of being heard'. The Muslims had decided to abandon their traditional policy and come into the political field because now the Government was convinced of their loyalty and they themselves had acquired sufficient knowledge of the tricky hazard of politics. 'The resolution he was moving was framed to secure the protection and advancement of political rights and interests without prejudice to loyalty to the rulers or goodwill to their Hindu neighbours.[6]

The resolution was seconded by Hakim Ajmal Khan of Delhi and supported by a dozen speakers. Copies of this and other resolutions were sent to the Government of India and the Secretary of State for India.[7] The resolution was: 'Resolved that this meeting composed of Musalmans from all parts of India, assembled at Dacca, decided that a Political Association be formed styled All-India Moslem League, for the furtherance of the following objects:

(a) To promote, among the Musalmans of India, feelings of loyalty to the British Government, and to remove any misconception that may arise as to the intention of the Government with regard to any of its measures.

(b) To protect and advance the political rights and interests of the Musalmans of India, and to respectfully represent their needs and aspirations to the Government.

(c) To prevent the rise, among the Musalmans of India, of any feeling of hostility towards other communities, without prejudice to the other aforementioned objects of the League.'

A provisional Committee, with power to add to its members, was formed with Nawabs Viqar-ul-Mulk and Mohsin-ul-Mulk as Joint Secretaries, with a view to framing a constitution for the League within four months, and was authorized to convene a

[6] The *Englishman,* 31 December 1906. The *Pioneer,* 2 January 1907.
[7] Public Letter, Calcutta, 10 January 1907. *Proceedings of the Home Department (Public),* February 1907, vol. 7587. January–April 1907.

representative meeting of Indian Muslims at a suitable time and place to put the constitution before that body for final approval and adoption. A resolution condemning the anti-Partition agitation was also passed.

Thus on 30 December 1906, the All-India Muslim League was founded.[8]

The formation of the League was received by the Indian Press with mixed feelings. The *Englishman* thought that it 'will provide an effective answer to the Congress as well as affording an avenue for the publication of Mahommedan aspirations', and

---

[8] The following writers give wrong dates for the establishment of the All-India Muslim League:

(1) J. Ramsay Macdonald, *The Government of India* (London, 1919). 'In 1912 the Moslem League was founded', p. 13. See p. 18 as well.

(2) V. Chirol, *India, Old and New* (London, 1921), p. 136, states that the League was founded 'in 1905'.

(3) A. E. Dodd, *A Short History of the British Empire* (London, 1925), pp. 2–7 (Year 1910).

(4) G. T. Garratt, *An Indian Commentary* (London, 1928), p. 133, gives 1907 as the year and calls Ali Imam its founder.

(5) T. Murray Titus, *Indian Islam, A Religious History of Islam in India* (London, 1930), states that the Aga Khan was its President.

(6) W. H. Moreland and A. C. Chaterjee, *A Short History of India* (London, 1936), p. 451, mentions the year 1908.

(7) Mohammed Noman, *Muslim India* (Allahabad, 1942), p. 64, mentions that the name 'Muslim League' was first given to an association in the Punjab, which held its first meeting in 1906, and Azim Hussain, in his father's biography, *Fazl-i-Hussain* (London, 1946), p. 96, gives credit to his father for coining the name.

(8) Frederick Sykes, *From Many Angles*, an Autobiography (London, 1942), p. 482, mentions 1907.

(9) Eric A. Walker, *The British Empire, Its Structure and Spirit* (London, 1943), p. 112 (Year 1908).

(10) H. Plaskett and P. Jordan, *Government of Britain, The Commonwealth Countries and the Dependencies* (London, 1950), p. 287 (Year 1908).

(11) David Thompson, *World History from 1914 to 1950* (London, 1954), pp. 25, 28 (Year 1907).

(12) J. C. Powell-Price, *A History of India* (London, 1955), p. 599, states that 'the Muslim League had been founded in 1905 with a view to representing Muslims' special claims . . .'

(13) A. Gledhill, *Pakistan, the Development of its Laws and Constitution* (London, 1957), p. 27 (Year 1908).

(14) T. G. P. Spear, *India, Pakistan and the West* (London, 1958), p. 207 (Year 1907).

admitted that 'it was high time that the Mahommedans of India found a voice'.[9] Assuring *The Times*, which had expressed its doubts whether the League would make for peace,[1] the *Englishman* in a lengthy editorial said that its fears were uncalled for, as 'the new body is a thing not only to be welcomed with cordiality, but to be fostered, for it is in its essence sane, not hysterical, solid not frothy, sensible not absurd, representative not artificial'.[2] It published a number of letters explaining the policy of the League and replying to the criticisms of the Congress Press. The *Times of India* and the *Daily Telegraph* of Lucknow also welcomed its formation, as it was 'founded on the safe and sure rock of loyalty to the British raj'.[3] The *Pioneer*, Allahabad, and the *Civil and Military Gazette*, Lahore, remained almost neutral. The former stated earlier that 'the Mahomedan Community do need an authoritative medium for the expression of their views. Failing it, the legitimate influence they should exercise is often lost.'[4] But it did not bother to welcome or denounce the formation of such a body except for opening its columns for the League's news and Muslim correspondents. The latter merely printed Reuter's report of *The Times*'s editorial.[5]

While most of the Anglo-Indian Press was supporting the Muslim cause in the absence of any effective Muslim organ, it was the Congress Papers, and the *Bengalee* especially, that opened an attack on its organizers and on the League itself. The *Bengalee* often called it 'Salimullah League'[6] and 'Nawab Salimullah's latest fad'.[7] After commenting on *The Times*'s editorial, saying that '*The Times* does not evidently feel happy over the establishment of the Mahommedan League', it predicted that, 'it will, if it seeks to fulfil its mission, fraternize with the Congress, and eventually coalesce with it. If not, it will go the way

[9] The *Englishman*, 1 January 1907.
[1] *The Times*, 2 January 1907.
[2] The *Englishman*, 5 January 1907.
[3] Quoted in the *Englishman*, 10 January 1907.
[4] The *Pioneer*, 14 December 1906.
[5] The *Civil and Military Gazette*, Lahore, 4 January 1907.
[6] The *Bengalee*, 18 January 1907.
[7] Ibid. 10, 18 January 1907.

of the Patriotic Association of the late Sir Syed Ahmed.'[8] The *Bengalee* also alleged that 'the League and its branches are engineered mostly by Government pensioners or ex-officials, or gentlemen who are compelled to solicit Government assistance in their family or pecuniary difficulties.'[9] M. Haque, Barrister-at-Law[1] and a prominent member from Behar, tried to repudiate some of the charges levelled by the *Bengalee* in a letter to the *Englishman*.[2] He denied that the League was the work of Nawab Salimullah of Dacca or that it was engineered by old pensioners and needy persons, and strongly condemned the efforts of the 'Bengali Press' which was trying to misrepresent the aims and objects of the League and to sow dissension amongst the Muslims. Maulvi Rafiuddin Ahmed, Barrister-at-Law, a prominent member of the Simla Deputation and a leader from Bombay, also gave a long interview to the Press and explained the genesis, scope and aims of the League.[3] The *Bengalee*, however, showed its dislike of the League by not giving a detailed report of its formation, but instead publishing a lengthy account of a rival meeting of the 'Bengal Mahommedan Association', which was to have been presided over by Nawab Syed Muhammad of Madras. The *Bengalee* opened its columns for the correspondents of that Association.[4] The *Hindustan Review* was not very critical of the League. It welcomed the stir amongst the Muslims and refrained from commenting on separatist tendencies amongst them, because in its opinion 'the choice of methods is a question of detail, what is of more consequence is the principle.'[5]

The formation of the League was not favourably received in Britain and to a great extent went unnoticed. *The Times* thought it an inevitable outcome of the Congress movement and an

[8] The *Bengalee*, 6 January 1907.
[9] Ibid. 6, 8, 9 January 1907.
[1] Later President of the All-India Muslim League in 1915.
[2] Letter dated 22 January 1907, published in the *Englishman*, 25 January 1907.
[3] The *Englishman*, 4 January 1907.
[4] The *Bengalee*, 6, 8, 9 January 1907.
[5] The *Hindustan Review*, vol. xv, No. 89, January 1907, p. 110.

exposure of the hollowness of the Congress pretensions to speak for India, and expressed doubts whether it would make for peace, despite the pacific language of its founders.[6] The *Spectator*, while admitting that the objects of the League were excellent, did not like the 'feeling amongst Muslims that they must organise in a camp by themselves'.[7] The *Morning Post* warned the League to remain 'entirely defensive and protective,' and any deviation from its path 'will call at once for the most drastic intervention of the British rulers'.[8]

The birth of this new party, which was to split India into two parts, went unnoticed by the Government. Neither in their private letters nor in any official despatches did Minto or Morley mention it—not, at least, until the League started the campaign against Morley's proposal of electoral colleges—although the Congress, its programme and its sessions were discussed profusely.

The new party was well received by the Muslims of India. Very soon branches were set up at various places.[9] Between 1906 and 1910 the League met every year except 1909. The first of the annual sessions was held at Karachi on 29 and 30 December 1907. It was attended by prominent Muslims from all over India and presided over by Sir Adamjee Peerbhoy, a distinguished merchant from Bombay. He was one of the members of the Simla Deputation and was specially invited by Nawab Viqar-ul-Mulk to preside.[1] His address was a very moderately worded practical one. It outlined the future policy and political attitude of the Muslims. He urged the Muslims 'to be united in ourselves, to be of one mind and one purpose'. In particular he emphasized loyalty to the Government, friendly and frank relations with other Indian communities, the acquisition of higher education, and

[6] *The Times*, 2 January 1907.
[7] The *Spectator*, 5 January 1907.
[8] The *Morning Post*, 19 January 1907.
[9] The *Englishman*, 5 December 1907, the *Pioneer*, 5 December 1907, &c. One branch was opened in London, under the presidentship of Syed Ameer Ali. This branch played a very important part and will be discussed later.
[1] The *Englishman*, 23 December 1907.

an interest in industrialization. In order to allay any fears of disloyalty to the Government still lurking in the minds of some he said, 'our loyalty to Government has never yet been impeached and I trust it never will', but he warned that though 'we recognise the difficulties of the Government in adjusting conflicting claims, we must be as fearless as we are honest in our criticism, whoever and whatever they may affect'. Moderating his tone he said, 'So far as I know, the Government of India is the last to complain of criticism so long as it is fair, moderate and upright.'[2]

The League's Constitution was finally settled in this session. Its fundamental principles were not different from those of the resolution passed at the Dacca Session in 1906:

'. . . To maintain and promote loyalty towards the British Government among the Muslims; to bring before the Government their special requirements in moderate and respectful language and consistently with these objects, to promote friendly relations with other Indian communities.' A maximum of 400 members was fixed and the bulk of those who formed the Simla Deputation were amongst its first seventy members. The Central Executive Committee was to consist of forty members. Though Viqar-ul-Mulk expressed his inability to carry out the responsibilities of the League's secretaryship along with the Secretaryship of the Aligarh College (which had fallen to him after Mohsin-ul-Mulk's death on 16 October 1907), he was successfully persuaded to stay on. At its special meeting at Aligarh on 18 and 19 March 1908 the Aga Khan was elected Permanent President of the League and S. H. Bilgrami, Honorary Secretary.

The first session of the Muslim League, like its Dacca Session, was held after the conclusion of the Muslim Educational Conference, as the leaders could not afford the luxury of having political meetings separate and at different times, nor could they divorce the educational programme from their deliberations. A change had come amongst the Muslims, but it was a gradual change. Their political party was not founded overnight or by one man, but grew slowly and steadily.

[2] The *Englishman*, 7 January 1908.

The League had taken a cue from the Congress right from the beginning. It had been realized that to achieve anything substantial, it was essential to mobilize public opinion in England and the League devoted considerable attention to making its views and activities known to the public there. Fortunately Syed Ameer Ali was in London and S. H. Bilgrami had also come to London as a Member of the Council of India, so a branch of the League was founded there. The inaugural meeting of the London branch of the All-India Muslim League was held at the Caxton Hall on Wednesday 6 May 1908. It was presided over by Syed Ameer Ali. Ibni Ahmad was elected Honorary Secretary, and it had its offices at 42, Queen Anne's Chambers, Westminster. These offices and these office-bearers were to play an important part in converting Morley back to the original scheme of separate electorates from his own scheme of electoral colleges.

On 30 December 1908, the League met at Amritsar. Khan Bahadur Yusuf Shah was the Chairman of the Reception committee and Syed (later Sir) Ali Imam presided.[3] This session was important as it was then that the Constitution of the League was formally adopted.[4] By now the Government of India's reform proposals and the Secretary of State's reply had become public and from now on the League was to embark on an incessant campaign for achieving the system of separate electorates which had been promised by the Viceroy.

There has arisen a difference of opinion over the third session of the League. Maulvi Tufail Ahmed says that it was held in January 1910 and that the Aga Khan presided over it.[5] Mirza Akhtar Hasan contends that it was held in 1909 and the Prince of Arcot presided.[6] Lal Bahadur on the basis of Mazhar Ansari's *Tarikh-i-Muslim League*[7] accepts that the session was held on

[3] P. C. Ghosh, op. cit., p. 221, wrongly mentioned Yusuf Shah as President of this session.

[4] The *Civil and Military Gazette*, Lahore, 1 January 1909.

[5] Tufail Ahmad, op. cit., p. 364.

[6] Mirza Akhtar Hasan, *Tarikh-i-Muslim League* (Urdu), Bombay, 1942, p. 44.

[7] Mazhar Ansari, *Tarikh-i-Muslim League* (Urdu), pp. 61–62, quoted by Lal Bahadur.

29 January 1910 at Delhi in Sangram Theatre. He further strengthens his point by quoting a notice issued by the Secretary of the All-India Muslim League which gave the dates for the proposed assemblage of the session as 29–31 January 1910.[8] It was actually held in 1910 on 29–31 January and Sir Ghulam Muhammad Ali Khan, Prince of Arcot, presided over it. The Aga Khan, the League's Permanent President was also present. Hakim Ajmal Khan of Delhi was the Chairman of the Reception Committee.[9]

Two important changes also took place. Nawab Viqar-ul-Mulk had been originally asked to work as the Honorary Secretary of the League. On his appointment as the Secretary of the Aligarh College, he could not carry out the duties of both posts, so Major Syed Hussain Bilgrami was elected as Honorary Secretary in 1908. When Bilgrami went away to London to take up his new job, Haji Musa Khan, the Joint Secretary, performed the functions of the Honorary Secretary, but in this third session Maulvi Muhammad Aziz Mirza was appointed the Honorary Secretary, and he took charge of his office on 14 February 1910.[1] At this very session it was decided to shift the League's office from Aligarh to Lucknow, a more central place. But that was not the only reason for this change of headquarters. Sir J. P. Hewett, Lieutenant-Governor of U.P., did not like 'everything connected with Mohammedan advancement in every form concentrated at Aligarh.'[2] So he asked the Aga Khan to arrange to shift the head-quarters of the League from Aligarh. The Aga Khan obliged him by agreeing to do so.[3] Hence the change of the central office from Aligarh to Lucknow. The new Honorary Secretary opened the League's office in Lucknow on 1 March 1910. The Aga

---

[8] Lal Badadur, op. cit., p. 81.

[9] The *Pioneer*, Allahabad, 30, 31 January, 2 February 1910, the *Civil and Military Gazette*, Lahore, 30 January, 1 February 1910.

[1] *Proceedings of the All-India Muslim League*, 1910 (Allahabad, 1911), p. 38.

[2] Sir J. P. Hewett to Dunlop Smith, 25 September 1908. *M.C.*

[3] Hewett to Minto, 3 February 1910, 'The Aga Khan had managed to carry out a wish of mine that the head-quarters of the central body of the League should be removed from Aligarh.' Ibid.

Khan wanted the Government to recognize the League as the only Muslim authoritative body to be consulted on important matters. Though he did not mention it to Minto, he did ask Hewett about it. Hewett was not very favourably inclined. Minto agreed with Hewett, 'I quite agree with you that the Government of India could not agree that it is the only authority entitled to be consulted on Mahommedan matters. At the same time we should of course always accept the League as a very representative Mahommedan body to which we should naturally refer for an opinion on any question of importance.'[4]

During these early years the League met its expenses from voluntary contributions. Among its most generous contributors was the Aga Khan, who announced an annual contribution of Rs. 4,000 in the third session at Delhi. The Prince of Arcot also contributed Rs. 4,000 and Rs. 1,000 for the London branch. There were other small contributions as well.[5]

It will have become apparent that the League did not receive that sort of Government patronage which the Congress had received at its inception, yet still present-day writers call it a British organized party. Such statements reflect very poorly on the Muslim leadership and intelligentsia of the time. It is suggested that if the British had not encouraged the Muslims, they would have joined the Congress and the unity of the country would not have been shattered. Granting that the British did encourage the Muslims at this time by listening to their demands, with a few exceptions Muslims had in fact remained aloof from the Congress. They were never attracted to the Congress because of its political programme, the attitude of some of its leaders and the predominance of the Hindus in it. Furthermore they had their own special problems and interests. When, in 1906, it became necessary to embark upon a political career, they decided to have a political organization of their own rather than join the Congress. It is interesting to note how Humayun Kabir interprets the formation and aim of the League. He says,

---

[4] Minto to Hewett, 15 February 1910. *M.C.*
[5] The *Pioneer*, 31 January 1910.

'Founded in 1906 by a group of well-to-do and aristocratic Mussalmans, it was intended to keep the Moslem intelligentsia and middle class from the dangerous politics into which the Indian National Congress was just then embarking'.[6] Nothing could be further from the truth!

During all these early years of its existence the League had a difficult job. It had to counteract the disruptive activities of some of the Muslims who were backed by the Congress papers like the *Bengalee*. At least an attempt to form a rival Muslim organization was made in 1906, though its nominal President, Syed Muhammad of Madras, expressed his ignorance of such an organization.[7] It had to convince the Government of its loyalty and papers like *The Times*, who had expressed their suspicions with regard to its future policies, though they admitted the justness of the Muslim cause. It had to consolidate its forces and unify the Muslims by championing their cause and jealously guarding their interests. In all these three it succeeded. The rival Muslim organization was abortive, and it was never called into session again. The Government, after some reluctance on Morley's part at least, also agreed to concede to the League's demands, and the support which it received from *The Times* in advocating its cause shows that it had also overcome its earlier suspicion. With the aim of popularizing the League and unifying the Muslims, attempts were made to establish its branches in all important places in India. Provincial and District Leagues were established and its leaders toured the various parts of India explaining to the people the League's aims and objects.[8] Small brochures in Urdu with translations in other languages were published and through the medium of Press and platform the League was brought nearer to the people, but it could not yet become a popular mass movement.

[6] Humayun Kabir, *Muslim Politics, 1906–1942* (Calcutta, 1943), p. 2.

[7] The *Englishman*, 13 February 1907. Syed Muhammad's statement at a function at Aligarh.

[8] *Proceedings of the All-India Muslim League,* held at Nagpur, 28, 30 December 1910 (Allahabad, 1911).

# CHAPTER THREE

# MINTO AND MILITANT NATIONALISM, 1907–1909

MINTO hoped that when the extremists had walked out of the Congress and the moderates were ready to rally round the Government his task would be easier. But his difficulties were not over. There existed another group of nationalists—the terrorists. They too wanted to achieve *Swaraj*, but their methods differed from those of the moderates and the extremists. The terrorist group, which consisted mostly of young Indians, was inspired amongst other things by the writings and speeches of the extremists. With the help of ancient religious literature it had been emphasized that political assassination was justified. Whether the extremist leaders had any direct hand in the activities of the young terrorists is open to question but provocative writings were bound to influence young minds.[1] The terrorists agreed with the extremist view that constitutional methods were ineffective and believed that application of force was essential to securing their end. Thus they resorted to violent means, such as had been practised in Russia and other European countries. Some hot-headed young men from Bengal and Maharashtra organized themselves into militant groups imitating in their ways the techniques of European terrorists and anarchists. To help promote the activities of the terrorist element some potent organizations were set up even outside India. In December 1907, the *Indian Sociologist,* the organ of the revolutionary Home Rule Society started by Shyamaji Krishnavarma, observed 'the only methods which can bring the English Government to its senses are the

---

[1] J. R. McLane, op. cit., Ch. II, suggests that there is no evidence that the activities of the Chapekar brothers were inspired by Tilak's writings.

Russian methods'.[2] The terrorists hoped, as the bomb discoveries at various places suggest, that ultimately they would be able to create a revolution in India. With that view they tried to obtain as much knowledge of military matters as they could. Various *Samitis* (societies) of young men were organized where an emphasis on physical culture was made.[3]

Outside India the terrorists had their greatest inspiration and support from Shyamaji Krishnavarma and his India House at Highgate. A number of Indians were active in America as well, but they had not yet acquired great prominence. Percy Sanderson, H.M.'s Consul-General at New York, informed H.M.'s Ambassador at Washington that the Indians living in New York were busy in revolutionary activities and had been sending revolutionary literature to India for at least three years. The New York *Gaelic American* was backing them up.[4] It published a tract entitled 'Indians declare openly for Republic'.[5] It also published a description of the 'National Flag of India'. 'It is a banner of three broad horizontal bands, the uppermost green, the sacred colour of the Moslems, with a line of eight stars emblematic of the eight provinces of India; the centre band golden hue, the colour of the Sikhs and Buddists, with the words "Bande Mataram" in Sanscrit, the ancient language of India; and the lower the red of the Hindus with a radiant orb near the staff and the Mohammedan crescent near the outer edge.'[6] Sanderson's letters and extracts from the *Gaelic American* were sent to Morley by the Foreign Office and Morley sent copies of them to Minto. Minto was also informed that a person named Camille F. Saldanha, a Bombay University graduate, went to Dublin in May 1906 and

[2] *The Sedition Committee Report*, 1918, Para. 7. The *Indian Sociologist*, vol. iii., No. 12, *Political and Secret Records* (*Home Correspondence*), vol. 325, 1907.

[3] N. C. Chaudhri, op. cit., pp. 222–52.

[4] Percy Sanderson to the Ambassador, 16 October, 6 November 1906. *Political and Secret Records* (Home Department), 1906, vols. 318 and 321. See also extracts from the New York *Gaelic American,* 5, 12, 19, 26 May, 2 June and 1 December 1906. Ibid.

[5] The *Gaelic American*, 26 May 1906. Ibid.

[6] The *Gaelic American*, 27 October 1906. Ibid.

got in touch with the 'Sinn Fein'. It was reported that he was an accredited agent of 'the Swadeshi Society'[7] and had visited America as well. The Clan-na-Gael had given him financial and other support. The *Irish Independent* published a report of the 'Sinn Fein' meeting at which he spoke about India's struggle for Independence.[8] While Minto's Government showed a keen interest in Shyamaji Krishnavarma's activities, they did not take much notice of these activities of Indians in America. But these activities in America and the Irish support for the Indian cause must surely have encouraged the Indian nationalists even at that early stage.

Born on 4 October 1857, Shyamaji had a successful educational and professional career both in India and England. In 1897 he finally left India for England.[9] G. N. Singh suspects that Shyamaji Krishnavarma had some connexion with the Poona murders of Lt. C. E. Ayerst and W. C. Rand, the Plague Commissioner, who were shot dead by Damodar Chapekar.[1] Indu Lal Yajnik suggests that the Poona atrocities during Plague suppression by the Government stunned and shocked Shyamaji and after being convinced of the justification of Tilak's stand, he, instead of plunging into politics by filling the gap after Tilak's arrest, decided to go to England to carry the fight across the seas. Yajnik thinks that Shyamaji took this step because he was 'accustomed to a settled life and safe pursuits', though he had 'ceased to believe and follow Congress policies which appeared timid and futile'.[2] Yajnik's argument does not seem very convincing. Shyamaji must surely have had other reasons for leaving India at that particular time.[3] He does not seem to have indulged

---

[7] Nothing is known about this society.

[8] The *Irish Independent*, 3 December 1906. *Political and Secret Records* (Home Department), vol. 321 of 1906.

[9] Indu Lal Yajnik, *Shyamaji Krishnavarma* (Bombay, 1950), pp. 85–87.

[1] G. N. Singh, op. cit. (1933), p. 336.

[2] Indu Lal Yajnik, op. cit., pp. 101–2.

[3] Yajnik does mention Shyamaji's tussle with Col. Hunter, the British agent at the Junagadh Durbar, which led to his resignation, but does not suggest this as a reason for his leaving India for good. Ibid., pp. 84–85.

in serious political activities immediately after his arrival in England. But on 1 January 1905 he started an English monthly, the *Indian Sociologist*. It was an 'Organ of Freedom and of Political, Social and Religious Reform'. It violently criticized Government policies and encouraged the Indians to resort to revolutionary methods with a view to achieving *Swaraj*. Shyamaji Krishnavarma offered six lectureships and three travelling scholarships to young Indians to enable them to go abroad to acquire the education that would help them to struggle for national freedom. On 18 February 1905 'the Indian Home Rule Society' was formed at Shyamaji's house at Highgate. Some twenty Indians attended the meeting. Its objectives were: 'To secure Home Rule for India; to carry on propaganda in the United Kingdom with a view to attaining the same; and to spread among the people of India a knowledge of the advantages of freedom and national unity.' A hostel for Indian students, known as the 'India House', was opened at Highgate. Among one of the first arrivals on the travelling fellowships offered by Shyamaji was Vinayak Damodar Savarkar, editor of the *Vihari*, Bombay, who was to play an important part at the India House. He translated Mazzini's autobiography into Marathi and his brother Ganesh printed it in Poona. Next he wrote a history of the Mutiny entitled, *The Indian War of Independence, 1857*, which became a sort of textbook for young revolutionary Indians. Shyamaji moved to Paris, when questions were asked in Parliament about his activities, but he kept himself in touch with his headquarters in London and India. Minto referred many a time to Shyamaji's activities in his letters to Morley. These ex-India revolutionaries were sending inflammatory literature to India which the Government made haste to proscribe. The editors and printers of such journals as had the temerity to print that material were prosecuted and punished. They even succeeded in smuggling arms and ammunition into the country.[4] Thus in an organized manner the revolu-

---

[4] Pistols and other ammunition were found in the false bottom of a trunk brought by one Chatrubhuj Amin. See Indu Lal Yajnik, op. cit., pp. 285-6. Vinayak Savarkar was the organizer of this arms supply to India.

tionaries aimed to achieve *Swaraj*, and they apparently succeeded in inspiring some Indians in India, who turned to physical culture societies, to the preparation and accumulation of explosives, and to political murders.

Both Morley and Minto were of the opinion that this movement could be controlled by suppressing 'crime' sternly, and by granting political reforms in the hope that these would justify the moderates' standpoint and so prevent young men from joining the terrorists. Morley was rather reluctant to agree to repression, partly because he did not realize the real incidence of crime and partly because of the pressure exercised by the radical group in the House of Commons. There was another section in England which favoured the adoption of a policy of coercion and repression. They argued that concessions granted to the moderates would provide only new weapons of struggle in the hands of the extremists.[5] To this view, Morley replied that so long as English public opinion watched the activities of the Indian Government it would not be possible to enter upon a policy of pure repression.[6]

Minto believed that to repress sedition, it was essential to curtail to some extent the liberty of the person and the press and the holding of political meetings. In reply to Morley's remark that 'Reforms may not save the Raj, but if they don't, nothing else will', Minto replied that 'They certainly will not—though if they are thoughtfully introduced they may help to render its administration happy . . . the Raj will not disappear in India as long as the British race remains what it is, because we shall fight for the Raj as hard as we have ever fought if it comes to fighting, and we shall win as we have always won'.[7]

The Punjab was the first province to attract Minto's attention and it was there that some strict steps were taken with a view to preserving law and order. The situation in the Punjab had been

[5] Sir Austin Chamberlain's record of a conversation with Morley. *Politics from Inside: An Epistolary Chronicle, 1906–1914* (London, 1936), p. 59.

[6] Morley's speeches, 21 December 1907; Speech at the Civil Service Dinner, July 1908. *Indian Speeches, 1907–1909* (London, 1909), pp. 39, 66–67, 17 December 1908. *Hansard*, House of Commons, 4S, vol. 198, Cols. 1974–94.

[7] Minto to Morley, 27 May 1908. *M.P.*

quite calm, but early in 1907, there was some unrest particularly
due to the Punjab Colonization Bill. The Chenab Colony in the
Punjab was mostly inhabited by ex-soldiers—a majortiy of them
being Jat Sikhs. They were given lands in this rainless but
irrigated area by the Government for their services. As the size
of each holding was gradually being reduced by partition among
the heirs, the Government proposed to check their further
division by passing an Act providing for inheritance by primo-
geniture. This and other regulations in this connexion were
resented by the people as an unjustified interference in their time-
honoured practices and traditions. Numerous meetings were held
in which the Government's actions were criticized. Some of the
meetings were addressed by Lala Lajpat Rai, a prominent Punjab leader and a member of the extremist section of the Congress
party, Ajit Singh, a young man with revolutionary ideas, and
other local leaders. The meetings were attended mainly by the
peasants of the locality. The Bill was severely criticized in the
Punjab Legislative Council and numerous petitions were sent,
but the Punjab Government wanted to run the colony as a
model farm and considered the Bill essential for the better
administration of the colony. Accordingly the Bill was passed.
Later on, when the agitation grew stronger, it became a question
of prestige with the authorities. The Punjab Government
exaggerated the tension and succeeded in securing from Minto's
Government the orders for deporting Lajpat Rai and Ajit Singh.
They were arrested and deported after riots at Lahore and
Rawalpindi, in none of which they were directly involved.

In Lahore the riot started on 16 April 1907, after the Chief
Court of the Punjab had upheld the conviction and sentence
passed on K. K. Athavale, editor of the weekly (later a bi-
weekly) *Punjabee,* who was prosecuted for publishing two articles
on 11 April 1906 entitled 'How Misunderstandings Occur'
and 'A Deliberate Murder'. The first referred to two cases
of 'oppression' alleged to have occurred at Rawalpindi—the death
from exposure of two Indians who were employed to carry the
luggage of the Deputy Commissioner of Rawalpindi when on

tour. The second referred to the accidental shooting of an Indian Shikari by a European District officer which incidentally occurred also at Rawalpindi. Pindi Das, the editor and proprietor of the weekly *India*, published from Gujranwala, had also been sentenced for publishing a letter from America containing a seditious appeal to the Indian troops. It was addressed to the 'Men of the British Army' by 'The Natives of India and Afghanistan who have emigrated to America'. It urged them to rise against the British Government with a view to achieving *Swaraj*. Copies of this letter were recovered from the possession of some soldiers at Mardan.[8] The police, who were escorting Athavale and Pindi Das from the Court to the jail, were attacked by a crowd which stopped the carriage, pelted them with mud and garlanded the convicts. In Rawalpindi two meetings were held to protest against the Colonization Bill, the second of which was addressed by Ajit Singh. His speech was considered seditious. The Deputy Commissioner served a notice on the organizers, Lala Gurdas Ram, Lala Hans Raj, Lala Amlok Ram and others who were prominent local leaders, and summoned them to his court on 2 May at 11 a.m. A large crowd collected outside his court and when the Deputy Commissioner postponed the hearing, those who had gathered there rioted and damaged the Deputy Commissioner's house and other Government property.[9] Lajpat Rai was also in Rawalpindi at that time and had consented to address a meeting before it was prohibited by the Deputy Commissioner.[1]

Minto's policy was to permit the local governments to use their discretion in matters where they found any danger of disorders and to resort to the usual legal methods in prosecuting the offenders.[2] Sir Denzil Ibbetson, the Lieutenant-Governor of the Punjab, knew the Government of India's view regarding the

---

[8] *Home Progs.* Political, July–December 1907, 7590.

[9] Ibid.

[1] Lajpat Rai, *The Story of My Deportation* (Lahore, 1908), pp. 1–20.

[2] (a) See correspondence between the Government of U.P. and the Government of India, May 1907, regarding prosecution of Tahal Ram and Haider Raza for seditious speeches. *Home Progs.* Political, July–December 1907, 7590.

use of Regulation III of 1818, under which a man could be sent to prison and kept there without trial for any length of time and without being charged with an offence. He had himself written in his note on the prosecution of the five lawyers of Rawalpindi on charges of arson and riot, that 'the Government of India will be very unwilling to employ the Regulation save in the most sparing manner and in the face of grave necessity'.[3]

Officially Minto knew nothing of the political situation in the Punjab till he received Ibbetson's minute early in May 1907. Ibbetson described the situation in the Punjab as very serious and explosive because of the 'seditious activities' of Lala Lajpat Rai and his agent Ajit Singh. Lajpat Rai's private character was described as 'above reproach', but 'he is everywhere recognized as being the moving spirit of the whole agitation'. Ajit Singh was 'the most active and the most virulent of those who have spoken against the British Government'. Ibbetson based his minute on C.I.D. reports of their speeches before the peasants of Lyallpur, Multan and other places. In some of these meetings Ajit Singh was supposed to have invited the Government to prosecute him and had not hesitated to suggest that it was afraid to do so. Between 1 March and 1 May 1907, twenty-eight such meetings were held, and in most of these either Lajpat Rai or Ajit Singh or both had criticized the Government's action, particularly in relation to the Colonization Bill. Ibbetson also referred to another rumour that Lajpat Rai was in correspondence with the Amir of Afghanistan and attempts had been made to tamper with the loyalty of the army.[4] Under these circumstances Ibbetson requested Minto that the warrants for their confinement under section 2 of Regulation III of 1818 be issued.[5]

---

(b) Correspondence between the Government of the Punjab and the Government of India regarding the Rawalpindi Riot Case and the Prosecution of the lawyers. Ibid.

[3] Letter from the Government of the Punjab to the Government of India, No. 713, S.B., dated 18 June 1907. Ibid.

[4] Minute by Sir Denzil Ibbetson, 30 April 1907.

[5] Letter from the Government of the Punjab to the Government of India, No. 695, 3 May 1907. Ibid.

Minto was of the opinion that Ibbetson knew the Punjab very well and was not likely to exaggerate the situation. So, trusting Ibbetson's judgement, Minto considered his request in council and the orders were accordingly issued.[6] Lajpat Rai was arrested and deported on 9 May and Ajit Singh on 3 June 1907. Both were sent to Mandalay, Burma.[7]

Minto explained his action to Morley as 'imperatively necessary' and stated that 'the present emergency is so great that I may be forced to issue an ordinance under section 23 of the Act of 1861 to regulate public meetings, chiefly with the object of obtaining full and accurate reports of the utterances of the speakers and in extreme cases to prohibit meetings altogether'. He admitted that in the absence of shorthand reporting of vernacular languages it was impossible to obtain correct reporting of speeches. Under the circumstances it would not have been possible to obtain conviction for sedition on the basis of these reports of informers in face of the multitude of witnesses who would be brought to contradict informers.[8] And accordingly on 11 May 1907, Minto issued the Regulation of Meetings' Ordinance, limiting stringently the right of holding public meetings, and it was applied to the Punjab and Eastern Bengal and Assam at once. He wrote to Morley that, 'I believe the arrest of Lajpat Rai and the proclamation of the Ordinance have done endless good in restoring public confidence'.[9]

In Minto's view the reasons for the Punjab unrest were three— the 50th anniversary of the Mutiny (10 May 1907); the Punjab Colonization Bill, and the plague. Lajpat Rai saw the whole thing in a different light. He thought this unrest was due to the Government's unwise policies. In his view the riots in the district

---

[6] The Viceroy's Council met on Sunday. Erle Richards and Sir H. Adamson were against it, but the Viceroy, trusting Ibbetson's judgement, gave him all he had asked for. Dunlop Smith's entry, 5 May 1907, in Lady Minto's *My Indian Journal*, vol. i, 1907, p. 129.

[7] Lajput Rai, op. cit., p. 1. Minto's telegram to Morley, 3 June 1907. *M.P.*

[8] Minto to Morley, telegram, 8 May 1907. Ibid.

[9] Minto to Morley, 21 May 1907. Ibid.

of Rawalpindi, at any rate, were organized by the police with a view to arresting the popular leaders.[1]

But as later events proved and as Minto and Ibbetson subsequently admitted, the troubles in the Punjab were largely agrarian in origin.[2] Lady Minto considers the Colonization Bill 'the pretext for this new cause of trouble in the Punjab',[3] but it was no 'pretext', it was the real underlying cause. Early in May 1907 Minto disallowed the Act, notwithstanding the fact that it had been approved by the Home Department and adopted by the Executive Council. Minto disallowed the Act because he considered it 'a very faulty piece of legislation' which would 'add fuel to the justifiable discontent which has already been caused'. Ibbetson himself admitted the shortcomings of the Bill, but pressed Minto not to veto it, as it would lower the prestige of the Punjab Government and it would mean a concession to the agitators. To this Minto replied, 'I hate the argument that to refuse to sanction what we know to be wrong is a surrender to agitation and an indication of weakness. It is far weaker to my mind to persist in a wrong cause for fear of being thought weak'.[4] He further emphasized that an appearance of surrender would 'be far less dangerous than to insist on enforcing the unfortunate legislation upon a warlike and loyal section of the Indian Community'.[5] Again he wrote to Morley, 'I am always saying to you the stability of our rule here will, in my opinion, depend largely on our capability of marching with the times in a rapidly changing political atmosphere.'[6] Morley approved of Minto's action in refusing to assent to the Act, and suggested that an enquiry should be made. Minto shared the same opinion but because of

[1] Lajput Rai, op. cit., pp. 1–20.

[2] Minto to Morley, 5 June, 3 July, 26 September 1907; Government of India to the Punjab Government, 27 June 1907. M. Shafi's Memorandum to Dunlop Smith, 19 June 1907. Note by Major F. Popham Young, Offg. Settlement Commissioner, Punjab, on Administration of the Chenab Colony, 11 June 1907. *M.P.*

[3] Mary, Countess of Minto, op. cit., p. 129.

[4] Minto to Morley, 16 May 1907. *M.P.*

[5] Minto's official minute. *Home Progs.* Political, July–December 1907, 7590.

[6] Minto to Morley, 21 May 1907. *M.P.*

Ibbetson's departure on sick leave and the subsiding of agitation the matter was dropped and the contemplated enquiry abandoned. Minto's disallowance of the Act was a quick and effective step. It saved the situation in the Punjab. Minto did not want that seditious activities should spread widely in the Punjab. The Chenab Colony was inhabited by loyal Indian Army pensioners. Discontent among them ought to be avoided. Moreover the Punjab provided a considerable number of recruits for the Indian Army. In short, the Act affected not only past and future members of the Army but also present serving soldiers.[7]

Morley supported Minto's action in deporting Lajpat Rai and Ajit Singh in the beginning, but soon afterwards he became impatient. He had grave misgivings about the wisdom of the policy of deportation. As Lady Minto put it, 'the practice of deportation had always "stuck in the throat" of the Secretary of State, it outraged his Liberal conscience'.[8] Morley understood Minto's difficulties, but he was conscious of the opinions of his Radical supporters and of the fact that his 'Tory opponents will scent an inconsistency between deporting Lajpat, and my fighting of Balfour for locking up William O'Brien'.[9] Minto was, however, able to convince Morley that India being vastly different

[7] An incident that Minto mentioned in one of his letters to Morley shows that Minto was right in thinking that the matter was of political importance. It further explains that the soldiers, though ignorant of the reasons for the withdrawal of the Act, were much concerned about the episode. A story went round the Sikh regiments that Kitchener, the Commander-in-Chief, was responsible for the withdrawal of the Colonization Bill. This was due to the fact that General Barrow, Chief Staff Officer, reported to Kitchener that a certain Commanding Officer who was informed about the political situation considered that the Colonization Bill was an Act affecting Natal. In view of such hopeless ignorance, instructions were issued that Commanding Officers, if possible, be enlightened as to the true state of affairs, and it was during the course of this enlightenment that the withdrawal of the Bill was attributed to the Commander-in-Chief. Minto to Morley, 15 July 1907. *M.P.*

[8] Mary, Countess of Minto, op. cit., p. 300.

[9] Morley to Minto, 31 May 1907. See also Morley to Minto, 28 June 1907. '. . . since the deportation of Lajpat, I am often wounded in the house of my friends . . .' Mary, Countess of Minto, op. cit., p. 417. Morley was not very wrong about the impression such strict measures would create in England. W. S. Blunt, in his *My Diaries* (London, 1919), Part II, p. 177, states '10 May

from Ireland, there need not be any inconsistency if the policy pursued in India was not exactly the same as Irish policy.[1] Minto was not very fond of the policy of deportation and repression, but could see no alternative, as he wrote to Lord Roberts, who replied that, 'Morley was willing to support you in any repressive measures you may think necessary to take'. Roberts further informed Minto that 'I told Morley that we govern India by respect based on fear, remove the fear and the respect will soon disappear.'[2]

Later Minto wrote to Morley, 'I found in India in the official world a great tendency to assume all political expressions of an advanced nature to be seditious; in many cases they were very far from being so, and to judge of such expressions fairly one must recollect the position of those who give vent to them, i.e., that they belong to a conquered race, and however much they may recognise the necessity of British rule in India, it is only human that they should occasionally give signs of sympathy with their own nationality'.[3] It is not easy to say whether Minto had

1907—Morley is just the weak-kneed administrator to resort to firm measures and we shall see him using all "the resources of civilization", practised in Russia', p. 227.

20 October 1908, Nevinson 'agreed with me all the same in my estimate of Morley as a weak-backed politician, quite ignorant of India and the East, swayed by the permanent officials, and principally anxious for general praise and his social position'.

William O'Brien (1851–1928), Irish nationalist leader. He was imprisoned many times, without trial, on suspicions of treason. In 1887 he was convicted on a charge of conspiracy in order to intimidate tenants to refuse to pay their rents, and sent to Tullamore jail for six months. A. J. Balfour was Chief Secretary for Ireland in Lord Salisbury's Government. O'Brien's claim that he should be treated as a political prisoner was ignored by the Government. He declined to wear prison uniform and lay naked on his plank bed for several weeks. Morley put up a strong fight for his release. See *Hansard*, House of Commons, 3S, vol. 322, and ff.

[1] Morley's speech in the House of Commons, 6 June 1907. Morley's *Speeches*, p. 18. *Hansard*, House of Commons, 4S, vol. 175, Cols. 879–81.

[2] Lord Roberts to Minto, 17 May 1907. *M.C.*

[3] Minto to Morley, 23 December 1913. Ibid. A few years before this, the Aga Khan had put forward the same argument, 'That India is a conquered country, and, whatever her foreign Government may do, the very nature of that rule will make it unpopular . . .' 'Some Thoughts on Indian Discontent', *National Review* (London, February 1907), pp. 951–72.

always been able to analyze official opinion and distinguish between various types. But some of his actions suggest that he tried to distinguish between 'political expressions of an advanced nature' and 'seditious' expressions. It seems that he considered all those expressions and actions which led to violence as 'seditious'. He did not, however, hesitate to admit his own mistakes. The courage with which he resisted the official pressure to deport B. C. Pal in June 1907 and then his release of Lajpat Rai and Ajit Singh in the teeth of official opposition suggest that besides pressure from Morley, Minto's own inclination and understanding of the situation played a great part.

It was in June 1907 that Minto was pressed for B. C. Pal's deportation by Sir Andrew Fraser, Lieutenant-Governor of Bengal, Sir Lancelot Hare, Lieutenant-Governor of Eastern Bengal and Assam, and Sir Arthur Lawley, Governor of Madras. B. C. Pal was acting as a political missionary of Shyamaji Krishnavarma and was engaged in delivering speeches to students, for which he had received Rs. 500 in payment of the first half of his fee. Early in 1907 he delivered a number of speeches on topics of national interest—like *Swadeshi, Swaraj*, boycott and Hindu-Muslim Unity—in Madras and in Bengal. These speeches created a big stir among the students. Sir Bhashyam Aiyangar, Offg. Advocate-General, Madras, in his report to the Government of Madras, regarded Pal's speeches as of a 'most pernicious character' and thought they would 'have a peculiarly baneful influence upon the audience which consists chiefly of students'. The Madras Government suggested deportation, but Minto asked Morley's permission with the remarks that he himself liked the policy of prosecution better than deportation. Minto considered Pal's ideas as expressed in these speeches to be 'advanced' but not 'seditious'. In Morley's view there were three ways of dealing with Pal—leaving him alone, prosecution, or deportation without warning, but the last was thought to be fatal to the chances of success of the reform policy. The Government of India suggested prosecution to the Government of Madras. When the Madras Government took steps in the matter, the Secretary of State

again interfered and demanded a detailed account of the reasons
to justify the prosecution. Pal was, however, sentenced to six
months' imprisonment in October 1907, for refusing to give
evidence in a sedition case against Aurabindo Ghose.[4]

In the meanwhile the Government both at Simla and Whitehall was strongly pressed for the release of Lajpat Rai and Ajit
Singh. The Indian Press strongly condemned the Government's
action in deporting Lajpat Rai. The Congress organs were particularly vociferous and exhorted Morley 'to be himself' and
show his true liberalism by undoing these acts of repression. The
daily *Sandhya* of Calcutta, with a circulation of 7,000, even went
to the extent of suggesting that the departure of Sir D. Ibbetson
on sick leave was a curse on him of the Indian people.[5] The Congress condemnation of these deportations was equally strong.
Dr. Rash Behari Ghose, in his presidential addresses of 1907 and
1908, denounced the Regulation III of 1818. In 1908 the Congress
demanded the repeal of this Regulation and urged that the
deported persons be brought to trial. Tej Bahadur Sapru and
Syed Husain Imam, two prominent lawyers and moderate
leaders, spoke against this Regulation and declared that its spirit
was against the very first principles of English jurisprudence and
that it was opposed to all the traditions of the English Constitution.[6] Such denunciation of the Government's policy from the
Congress platform by these loyal and moderate leaders, whose
support Minto's Government intended to enlist, must have
presented the Government with a moment of worry. Gokhale
personally approached Minto for the release of Lajpat Rai. In a
letter to Dunlop Smith Gokhale stated that 'to bracket Ajit
Singh with Lajpat Rai is monstrous injustice to the latter. When
I was in Lahore in February last Ajit Singh had already begun to
denounce Lajpat Rai as a coward and a pro-Government man,
because Lajpat Rai would have nothing to do with Ajit Singh's

[4] Minto to Morley, 3, 10 July 1907. *M.P.* Secretary of State to Government of India, 1 July 1907. *Home Progs.* Public/Political, July–December 1907,
7590.

[5] *Native Newspaper Reports*, Bengal, Punjab and U.P., 1907.

[6] *Report of the I.N.C.* 1908, pp. 107–10, 115–16.

propaganda'. Gokhale had a talk with Dunlop Smith as well. The gist of this talk was that Gokhale virtually 'begged for the early release of Lajpat Rai—as for Ajit Singh he might rot in "Jehannum" [hell]'. Gokhale had again insisted that Lajpat Rai should not have been bracketed with 'that miscreant Ajit Singh who should have got transportation to the Andamans'. Gokhale also published a letter in the *Times of India* regarding Lajpat Rai's arrest, insisting on his release or some statement as to the reasons for his arrest.[7] Gokhale's anxiety was for two reasons. First, the practice of deportation was wrong on principle. Secondly, if the Government persisted in the policy, there was the risk of the extremists becoming more powerful and thus endangering the moderate cause and the Government's contemplated reform policy. Minto seems to have been greatly influenced by Gokhale in his later policy towards Lajpat Rai.

In England Morley was pressed hard. In the House of Commons questions were asked by the radical and Irish members about the reasons for the Government's action and the causes of this unrest. Dr. V. H. Rutherford, J. O'Grady, William Redmond, Sir Henry Cotton, C. J. O'Donnell, and others asked searching questions to find out the real reasons for Lajpat's deportation. They even pressed the Government to charge him and try him in a Court of Law. H. C. Lea asked 'whether there was any other place under the British flag where these *lettres de cachet* obtained as they did in India'.[8] Such questions were asked frequently and Morley first evaded direct answers, then made a statement on 6 June 1907. He justified the Government's action and based his speech on Ibbetson's minute. Though he did not enumerate the charges against Lajpat and Ajit Singh, he suggested that the unrest in the Punjab was caused more by their speeches than by any agrarian grievances. This remained the Government explanation for some time. The Government did not

[7] Gokhale to Dunlop Smith, 10 June 1907, enclosed with Minto's letter to Morley, 18 September 1907. Minto to Morley, 29 October 1907. Full text of Gokhale's letter to the *Times of India* in the *Indian Review*, June 1907, vol. viii, No. 6, pp. 463-4.

[8] *Hansard*, House of Commons, 4S, vol. 174, Col. 1634.

publicly admit that the agrarian grievances were the main cause
of unrest in the Punjab in spite of the fact that Minto vetoed the
Colonization Bill. On 18 June 1907 F. C. Mackarness then
asked whether Lajpat Rai and Ajit Singh were entitled to appeal
to the Governor-General and whether they had availed themselves of this opportunity. Morley replied in the affirmative to
the first part of the query but in the negative to the second. Thus
pestered, Morley, on his part, pressed Minto to revise his policy.[9]

Lady Minto's account of Minto's attitude towards Lajpat Rai
gives an erroneous impression.[1] She implies that Minto thought
Lajpat Rai to be 'the head and centre of the entire movement' that
excited 'discontent among the agricultural classes' and tampered
'with the loyalty of the army'. But this was Ibbetson's viewpoint
and not Minto's. Minto first took Ibbetson's views at their face
value and did not ask for more details. If he had done so, it
would have meant that he had no faith in the Lieutenant-
Governor, whom he treated as an expert on Punjab affairs. Lady
Minto by quoting his telegram of 8 May 1907 to Morley does not
make it clear whether the views expressed in it were those of
Minto or of Ibbetson.[2] Minto trusted Ibbetson's judgement so
completely that the Government of India before issuing orders
for the arrest of Lajpat Rai and Ajit Singh did not even try to find
out the whereabouts of the two. It was considered that Ibbetson
knew their whereabouts and it would be easy to arrest them.
This, however, was not the case as it took a long time before Ajit
Singh was arrested. Minto informed Morley that the Punjab
Government even made no attempt to secure all the papers connected with Lajpat Rai's arrest.[3] When all the facts became clear

[9] Morley to Minto, 23 August 1907; telegrams, 30 October, 2 November
1907. *Hansard*, 4S, vol. 174, and ff.

Lajpat Rai knew from the beginning that his imprisonment would not be
for very long; that his friends in Parliament would try to secure his release.
He wrote in his *Story of My Deportation* that he decided to petition to the
Government of India against his detention after he had learnt that a question
in Parliament had been asked as to his petition, p. 199.

[1] Mary, Countess of Minto, op. cit., p. 124.

[2] Mary, Countess of Minto, op. cit., pp. 124–5.

[3] Minto to Morley, 16 May 1907. *M.P.*

to Minto and the agitation subsided, then he admitted his true
feelings to Morley. On 5 November 1907 Minto wrote 'that we
must in common justice release them [Ajit Singh and Lajpat Rai]
and that the sooner we do so the better'. Ibbetson still objected
but Minto's reply was, 'there is nothing whatever that I know of
to justify his assertion that one of Lajpat Rai's main objects is to
tamper with the loyalty of the Indian Army. I have never seen any
evidence in support of this. Ibbetson appears to me to entirely
misunderstand the position. He appears to assume that we can
stamp out the unrest. This we can never do. It has come to stay,
in the shape of new ideas and aspirations of which everyone who
has thought seriously over the subject ought to be aware. He
confuses this with sedition which we are absolutely determined to
put down'. Minto very much regretted his action, but his only
consolation was that this drastic action had exhibited the
Government's strength at that moment. Morley's persistence in
his demand for Lajpat's release must surely have had some
influence but he was actually released when Minto himself
became convinced that 'Lajpat is undoubtedly a man of high
character and very much respected by his fellow-countrymen,
and if when I was asked to arrest him, I had known what I do
now, I should have required much more evidence before agreeing.
Ajit Singh is of much lower standing in every way and I shall
regret associating them in their release'.[4] Thus Minto admitted
that the Government's action was hasty, unjustified and based on
slender evidence. Minto's regret in bracketing Ajit Singh and
Lajpat arose from the fact that the former was definitely of lower
social standing than Lajpat Rai. Moreover there is a marked difference between the reported speeches of the two. Ajit Singh, it

[4] Minto to Morley, 5 November 1907. *M.P.* Lady Minto omitted the relevant sentences from this letter in her book. Perhaps she thought that as she
had been quoting from Minto's other letters, which were based on reports
from the local government, containing statements like Lajpat's communication with the Amir of Afghanistan &c. (p. 151), it would not do him much
credit, if this confession was also published (see p. 163). She is guilty of
creating a wrong impression. Minto had a perfectly clear conscience and
admitted frankly even the Government's mistakes.

seems, did suggest that the Government had become tyrannical and the people should rise against tyranny. But Lajpat's speeches were sober, matter of fact and less provocative.[5] On 4 November 1907, Minto informed Morley that though Ibbetson still had his objections, he was going to order Lajpat's and Ajit's release.[6] Morley immediately telegraphed the Cabinet's approval.[7] Minto specially ordered that every courtesy should be shown to Lajpat on his behalf.[8] On 18 November both were released.

The activities in India of Keir Hardie, the Socialist M.P.,[9] and H. W. Nevinson,[1] the correspondent of the *Daily Chronicle*,

[5] *Home Progs*. Public/Political, July–December 1907, 7590. Text of speeches as reported by the C.I.D. given. Lajpat's alleged communication with the Amir of Afghanistan seems to have been a rumour. No such correspondence exists in the Government records. The Punjab Government took these rumours seriously and accepted them as true without having any documentary evidence.

[6] Minto to Morley, telegram, 4 November 1907. *M.P.*

[7] Morley to Minto, telegram, 5 November 1907. Ibid.

[8] Minto to Morley, 7 November 1907. Ibid. Compare it with Lajpat Rai's account in *The Story of My Deportation*, p. 222: 'The Commissioner added a warning on behalf of the Viceroy that in case I was again found doing anything seditious, I would be arrested and immediately deported.' But he admits that he was given a First Class Compartment and the Deputy Superintendent of Police 'was generally courteous', p. 224. On subsequent pages he gives an account of the lavishness with which he was supplied with foodstuffs, &c.

Blunt, in his *My Diaries*, gives an interesting account of his interview with Gokhale and Lajpat Rai (pp. 228–30). He did not think very highly of Lajpat and thought his book, *The Story of My Deportation*, 'a naive, and in places quite childish narrative'. He thought that 'it was really preposterous that its author should have been made a national hero'. This book might have been a naive narrative, but it does present the other side of the story.

[9] *Home Progs*. Public/Political, January–December 1908, 7875.

[1] Morley recommended Nevinson to Minto and asked him to show him 'some trifle of civility'. Morley to Minto, 13 October 1907. Minto sent Morley an account of his activities from the weekly report of the Director-General of Criminal Investigation and suggested that his activities—public criticism of the Government, and public speeches suggesting that if the Indians wanted to achieve anything they must organize protest meetings, &c, to bring their grievances to the notice of the Liberal Government—were such that they would have to send him home. Minto to Morley, 12 December 1907. Nevinson in his *More Changes, More Chances* (London 1925), p. 229, admits that he did not realize then the intensity of bitterness, or the weight of solid opposi-

the *Manchester Guardian* and the *Glasgow Herald,* were not very helpful to the Government either. They attended public meetings and criticized the Government's actions. There were moments when Minto and Morley seriously thought that their activities were not conducive to good relations between the people and the Government and might lead to public disorder.[2] They very loosely used the words 'India' and 'Indians'. By 'India' they meant 'Hindu India', and by 'Indians', the 'Hindus' only. Hardie and Nevinson were chaperoned by the Congress leaders and they saw and expressed only those views which were held by the Congress leaders. Throughout the tour Hardie was accompanied by Jagesh Chaudhri, son-in-law of Surendranath Banerjea.[3] Hindu newspapers welcomed him as a Messiah for the Hindu community and the *Amrita Bazar Patrika* expressed the Hindu gratitude in a eulogistic editorial. The influence of his chaperons was shown at Mymensingh and Dacca, where he said that the Partition was the root cause of all the unrest, and that official opposition to the *Swadeshi* movement and official pat-

tion, of Morley's India Council and Anglo-Indians and the courage with which Morley faced them. He regrets some of his sayings and deeds in opposition to Morley's Indian policy.

[2](a) Minto to Morley, 16 October, 12 December 1907. *M.P.*

(b) Morley to H. Campbell-Bannerman, 2 October 1907. *Campbell-Bannerman Papers* regarding K. Hardie, 41223, vol. xviii (ff. 238). (B.M.) Morley informed Campbell-Bannerman about Keir Hardie's activities and stated that if he continued to make these seditious speeches the Government of India might have to deport him under the Regulations of 1818 and if they did not, they could not justify Lajput Rai's deportation. He hinted that the matter, being a serious one, might be discussed in the Cabinet. The song *Bande Mataram* tended to create ill-will between Hindus and Muslims in Eastern Bengal, but Keir Hardie insisted that it should be sung on the boat which took him from the steamer at Serajganj. (See report in the *Sandhya,* 28 September 1907. *B.N.N.R.,* 1907.) In 1906, Sir Gilbert Parker had asked the Under-Secretary of State for India if he intended to adopt any measure to prevent the Hindus from singing the *Bande Mataram* song in a provocative manner in the interest of communal peace in Eastern Bengal, since it was distasteful to Muslims. Sir Henry Cotton had interrupted to deny that the song was disliked by the Muslims. (See *Hansard,* House of Commons, 4S, vol. 160, 16 July 1906, Col. 1323–4.)

[3] Emrys Hughes, *Keir Hardie* (1956), pp. 149–58.

ronage of Muslims had increased it. His Indian experiences were published in 1909 under the title of *India: Impressions and Suggestions*. In this book he regretted the policy of official patronage of Muslims and warned the British people against the day when all of them in the world 'take it into their heads to try once again to win supreme power for Allah in the East'.[4] He felt sorry for the Hindus, whom he had found much maligned, though, in fact, they were well meaning, loyal and submissive.[5] Hardie asserted that 'the Government of India in its present form resembles a huge military despotism tempered somewhat by a civil bureaucracy.'[6] About Minto he wrote that 'the present Viceroy, Lord Minto, has won golden opinions for his courtesy and his kindliness of disposition, and his very evident desire to ease the strain which exists between the educated Indian gentleman and the Anglo-Indian officials'. He, however, expressed his surprise that the Viceroy had no Indian secretary and emphasized the need for one.[7] Nevinson's bias in favour of the Hindus can be gleaned through the pages of the *New Spirit in India* and *More Changes, More Chances*.[8] Such remarks, writings and activities were not meant to please the Muslims, and they only helped to widen the gulf between them and the Hindus.

On 1 November 1907, the Prevention of Seditious Meetings Act was passed.[9] This was based on the Ordinance of May 1907.

---

[4] Keir Hardie, *India: Impressions and Suggestions* (1909), pp. xv–xvi.

[5] Ibid. pp. 123–4. He said this in almost identical words in the House of Commons. See *Hansard*, House of Commons, 4S, vol. 193, 22 July 1908, Cols. 182–3.

[6] Keir Hardie, op. cit., p. 71.

[7] Keir Hardie, op. cit., pp. 77–78.

[8] Nevinson made speeches at various places to the effect that there was no sedition in India and that the Indians were unjustly persecuted because there was a national awakening among them. (*B.N.N.R.*, 1908.) In the *New Spirit in India* (pp. 191–3, 202) he states that the policy of Fuller was directed against the Hindus; they were deprived of offices, &c. Such statements were bound to create ill feeling amongst Indians. The Records, on the other hand, do not show this discrimination. Fuller did make some tactless speeches and some of his actions were also open to criticism, but this did not amount to a determined policy of the Government against the Hindus.

[9] *Home Progs*. Public/Political, July–December 1907, 7590.

It provided that no political meeting could be held in a 'pro-
claimed area' without the permission of the local authorities, who
could forbid it if they thought that it might promote sedition.
Sir Harvey Adamson, who piloted the Bill, argued that as res-
pectable law-abiding citizens of India were hesitant to help the
Government in prosecuting law-breakers by coming forward to
testify in the Courts of Law against those who preached sedition
in public meetings, the Indian law about holding meetings had
to be made more stringent than the English law.[1] Gokhale's and
Rash Behari Ghose's argument in opposing the Bill was that it
would place very great powers in the hands of the local authorities; that no parallel measure could be found in any European
country, viz., Italy, Belgium, France or Switzerland, though
Europe was 'honeycombed with secret societies of anarchists and
socialists',[2] that it was against the spirit of the British Constitution and of liberalism;[3] but most important of all, that it would
strengthen the extremists as they would attract more attention
by pointing to the Russian methods of government.[4]

Morley did not like the new Act, but on Minto's pleading,[5] he
wrote, 'the spirit in which you mean to use the powers confided
to you by the new Act, are [sic] so thoroughly remarkable that
I have no fear of being able to make a good stout defence'.[6] And
he did defend the Act in the House of Commons against the
criticisms of Dr. Rutherford and D. M. Smeaton. Morley informed them that the Act was more of a deterrent against seditious meetings and would not be used autocratically.[7]

Minto's Government was taking all possible steps to suppress
what it thought to be seditious. The liberty of the Indian Press
was to be curtailed next. During the period between June 1906

---

[1] *Proceedings of the Council of the Governor-General of India*, April 1907–
March 1908, vol. xlvi, pp. 56–65.

[2] Ibid. p. 49.

[3] Ibid. p. 50.

[4] Ibid. p. 48.

[5] Minto to Morley, 5 November 1907. *M.P.*

[6] Morley to Minto, 29 November 1907. Ibid.

[7] *Hansard*, House of Commons, 4S, vol. 183, 1908, 11 February 1908.

and July 1907, prosecutions were instituted against nine news-papers or journals and against three persons for publishing seditious pamphlets.[8] On 5 March 1907 Minto wrote, 'I am afraid we must consider seriously how we are to deal with the Native Press, for in many cases the utterances of newspapers are out-rageous. I don't know that we can afford to treat them with con-tempt'. Minto felt that these newspapers and pamphlets were not merely an expression of impossible ideas, but much of the material in them was a direct instigation to the people of India 'to get rid of British rule'. In this connexion he was able to point to the pamphlet addressed to 'Men of the British Army' by 'the Natives of India and Afghanistan who have emigrated to America', which was found in the possession of some Sikh soldiers at the headquarters of the Guides at Mardan. This circular was extremely provocative as it urged the Indian soldiers to rise against the British Government and fight for *Swaraj*. Stringent action was taken against those soldiers in whose possession the circular was found and Pindi Das, the editor of the weekly *India*, was prosecuted for publishing it in his paper. But this was not enough. Kitchener was very anxious to keep the loyalty of the Indian Army untampered. Morley had earlier sent Minto copies of letters from Sanderson, British Consul at New York, to the British Ambassador in Washington. Sanderson had given an account of the activities of the Indians in America on the lines of 'clan-na-gael'. This discovery of the circular naturally made Minto think that it might have some connexion with the activities of the Indians in America. To suppress the further dissemination of this inflammatory literature Minto emphasized the need for controlling the activities of the Press. He was aware of the fact that Morley would not readily agree to any control of the liberty of the Press. But he was of the opinion that to punish them lightly would make matters worse, as it would give the newspapers the publicity that a 'seditious editor' wanted. He was positive that 'the influence of this seditious machinery is un-doubtedly spreading', the question was 'whether we can count

[8] Minto to Morley, 7 August 1907. *M.C.*

on inflammatory writing falling flat, or whether we consider it so dangerous that we must by some means or other put a stop to it.[9] Minto admitted 'that the fault is not all on one side; some of the Anglo-Indian Press is both low and mischievous'.[1] But in his usual persuasive style he continued to emphasize the need for controlling the activities of the Press. Morley plainly told him, 'I doubt whether I could persuade the House of Commons to stand it.'[2]

Not content with private correspondence only, Minto decided to send Morley an official despatch containing the reasons for Press legislation. The list of crimes committed by the Indian Press was impressive, but Morley remained adamant. The reasons given by the Government were that deliberate attempts had been made by a number of newspapers in India, both English and vernacular, to inflame the minds of the people, to encourage enmity between classes, to promote active hostility to the Govern-

[9] Minto to Morley, 5 March 1907. *M.C.* See also letter from the Government of Eastern Bengal and Assam to the Government of India, dated 4 June 1907, complaining of the violence exhibited by the native press in Calcutta, the *Statesman*, the *Bengalee*, the *Amrita Bazar Patrika*, the *Empire*, by publishing accounts of political meetings and activities which were 'untrue and exaggerated.' *Home Progs.* Political, July–December 1907, 7590. The Calcutta press, particularly the Congress press, tended to publish coloured accounts of any incident in Eastern Bengal. For instance they published rumours that the Nawab of Dacca had ordered the Muslims to kidnap and marry the Hindu widows forcibly. They published untrue and exaggerated accounts of a 'reign of terror' by the Muslim 'goondas' in the villages of East Bengal. A comparison between the *Native Newspaper Reports*, Bengal, and the East Bengal Government's fortnightly reports will show that the local Government's letter of 4 June 1907 was justified. Such reports were bound to aggravate the already tense situation in that province.

[1] Minto to Morley, 2 April, 2 May 1907. Ibid. A clear case in this connexion was that of the daily *Civil and Military Gazette*. Lahore. This paper published certain letters which Minto thought 'disgracefully low in tone'. See H. W. Nevinson, *The New Spirit in India* (London 1908), p. 17. The Punjab Indian Association demanded prosecution of the paper, but the Punjab Government refused to allow it. Sir Henry Cotton asked Morley whether his attention had been drawn to this refusal of the Punjab Government to allow prosecution of a paper which tended to spread racial discrimination. Morley replied that he had seen the press reports and that at that time he did not think it necessary to take any special action. *Hansard*, House of Commons, 4S, vol. 170, 1907, Col. 1228.

[2] Morley to Minto, 13 June 1907. *M.P.*

ment, and to disturb the public tranquillity in many different ways, in the preaching of active rebellion against the British Government, in attempts to seduce the Indian Army from their allegiance to the Crown and so on.[3] Some papers had advised the civil population of the Punjab to combine to withhold the payment of public revenue during the Colonization Act controversy and in Bengal to employ explosive bombs for the purpose of resisting the officers of the law. It was also brought to the notice of the Secretary of State that the Government had been publicly charged with extinguishing profitable industries in the interests of foreign merchants; with instigating and abetting dacoity, sacrilege and rape; and with disseminating plague by poisoning wells and springs in order to reduce the native population and replace it by immigrants from Europe. These were very serious charges and it had not been possible to contradict or deny any of them without raising further controversy. Nor could they be ignored as there was every likelihood that such writings, if not suppressed, would influence the half-educated Indians. Hence the Government suggested some form of press legislation.[4]

Meanwhile Minto sought the opinions of the local Governments with regard to the proposed Press Act. All Governments agreed that legislation should be undertaken for the purpose of some degree of control over the newspaper press in India. Some even suggested stringent measures, i.e. 'summary trial without intervention of the courts', of the offending press,[5] some thought that to avoid any general excitement among the public, it would be wise to deal with the press in the ordinary course of law.

But a wave of crime and political murders ensued which justi-

---

[3] Selections from the *Native Newspaper Reports*, Punjab and Bengal, suggest that the Government was not very wrong in drawing these conclusions from the passionate writings of papers like the *Sandhya*, Calcutta, *Yugantar*, Calcutta, the *Punjabee*, Lahore and many others.

[4] Government of India to Secretary of State, Public letter, 11 July 1907. *Home Progs.* Political, July–December 1907, 7590.

[5] (a) Government of Burma to the Government of India, 27 August 1907.
(b) Chief Commissioner of N.W.F.P. to the Government of India, 6 September 1907. *Home Progs.* Public/Political, January–December 1908, 7875.

fied Minto's fears. On 6 December 1907 an attempt was made to blow up the train of Sir Andrew Fraser, the Lieutenant-Governor of Bengal, at Midnapur. On 23 December, B. C. Allen, a former District Magistrate of Dacca, was unsuccessfully shot at. But the crime that really resulted ultimately in the discovery of hidden bombs, dynamite and inflammable literature was the murder of Mrs. and Miss Kennedy on 30 April 1908[6] at Muzzafarpur. The bomb that killed these two ladies was actually intended for D. H. Kingsford, who as Chief Presidency Magistrate, Calcutta, had tried cases against the *Yugantar,* the *Bande Mataram,* the *Sandhya,* and the *Nabaski* newspapers and convicted persons connected with these papers, thus incurring the displeasure of the revolutionary party. He had sentenced to a whipping of fifteen stripes a boy named Shusil Kumar Sen. The Alipore organizers of the revolutionary movement sent Khudi Ram Bose and Profulla Chaki to Muzzafarpur to kill Kingsford. They mistook the carriage of Mrs. and Miss Kennedy for that of Kingsford and threw their bomb. Two days after, both of them were arrested. Profulla shot himself, but Khudi Ram made a public confession, was tried and hanged. This confession led to the discovery of some bombs, dynamite, cartridges and correspondence, in Maniktola Gardens, Calcutta, and other places, which led to the arrest of Aurobindo Ghose, his brother and others.[7] Morley immediately suggested the introduction of an Explosives Act on the lines of the English Explosives Substances Act of 1883 in India.[8] But Minto pleaded very strongly the need for a Press Act with a view 'to control the source from which all this poison has spread throughout India . . . there is nothing to be gained in prosecuting a succession of dummy editors. We must have power to seize the presses. It appears to me sheer madness to allow the continuance of public instigation to murder'.[9]

---

[6] S. N. Banerjea, op. cit., p. 248, gives the wrong date for this happening. *Report of the Indian Sedition Committee* (1918), pp. 22–50; *Summary of Lord Minto's Administration,* pp. 7–10. M.C.

[7] *Home Progs.* Political/Public, January–December 1908, 7875.

[8] Morley to Minto, 13 March 1908. *M.P.*

Morley ultimately dropped his objection because 'this villainy of the Bombs, the revelations connected with the Bombs, make a new situation for us'.[1]

He approved it but with the hope that 'the vital importance . . . of carrying English opinion with us' might not be forgotten when the Act was enforced.[2] So on 8 June 1908, the Press Act was passed.

The object of the Act was to prevent incitements to murder and other offences. Adamson, who introduced the Bill, explained that such writings, quoting from the *Yugantar*,[3] would not be considered seriously in England, because of the British frame of

[9] Minto to Morley, 13 May 1908. *M.C.* Lord Roberts expressed his grave concern at 'the discovery of this Bomb movement in Calcutta' and informed Minto that he had told Morley 'what a very serious affair it is', and that 'he will give you a free hand. But please let me know if I can help in any way in this country by bringing the matter up in Parliament.' R. C. Dutt published a letter in *The Times* (14 May 1908). While expressing detestation at the outrage, he stated that 'crimes in this or other form will increase in India until the people are admitted to some responsible share in the control and direction of the administration of their own affairs'. Lord Roberts ridiculed the idea, 'Nothing could show more clearly how unfitted the Natives are for the "share" they aim at . . .' Lord Roberts to Minto, 14 May 1908. Ibid.

[1] Morley to Minto, 7 May 1908. *M.P.*

[2] Morley to Minto, 28 May 1908. Ibid.

[3] Sir Harvey Adamson quoted from an article which appeared in the *Yugantar*, a few days after the attempt on Kingsford's life in Muzzafarpur which resulted in the death of two ladies. 'Hard-heartedness is necessary to trample the enemy under foot. An independent-spirited youth, arrested in connection with the Calcutta incident, is said to have said, "The work of the revolutionists, though progressing slowly, was very satisfactory: but two innocent women having met with violent death, all their attempts have been foiled by a curse of God". If any youth aspiring to freedom has really said so, then he has not yet become fit to obtain freedom. Hard-heartedness is necessary to trample the enemy under foot. When during the *Treta Yugu* the *Rakshasas* were perpetrating frightful oppression in the Dandaka forest, Rama extirpated the whole race of the *Rakshasas*. Laksman Thakur cut off the nose and ears of Surpanakha, the beautiful sister of Ravana, and then let her go. It is not necessary to give illustrations. If in the attempt to destroy the enemy a woman is accidentally killed, then God can have no cause of displeasure like the English. Many a female demon must be killed in the course of time, in order to extirpate the race of Asuras from the breast of the earth. There is no sin in this—no mercy, no affection'. *Proceedings of the Council of the Governor-General of India*, vol. xlvii, April 1908–March 1909, p. 10.

mind, but that had not been the case in India. The Indians were not yet prepared for constitutional agitation. They could be easily led astray and the press played an important part in doing so. The press they intended to muzzle was trying to bring into hatred or contempt or to excite disaffection towards the Government established by Law in India. It was intended to provide a more effective way than prosecution for dealing with seditious newspapers. The Bill would give powers to confiscate the printing press and to extinguish the newspaper. Minto thought it an 'exceptional' Bill 'to meet dangerous emergencies'. Nawab Syed Muhammad of Madras considered the Bill 'too wide in its scope' and complained that they were given 'no opportunity to consider the measure carefully and express any decided opinion'.[4] Gokhale accepted the Press Act as 'inevitable'[5] and Rash Behari Ghose in his presidential address to the 1908 Congress said that though he believed in the freedom of the press, under the existing conditions, such a measure 'was perhaps necessary'.[6] But it was earnestly hoped that the new Press Act would have 'only a temporary existence in the Indian Statute Book.[7]

During the discussion in the House of Lords on this Press Act of 1908, Earl Cromer, Lord Curzon and Lord Lamington, a former Governor of Bombay, expressed identical views. They thought that the working of the press in eastern countries had shown that western ideas of the freedom of the press were unsuited to Oriental conditions. The latter two speakers considered the measure even inadequate. Lord Ampthill wondered 'whether

---

The *Yugantar* (New Era), Calcutta, a daily Bengali paper, was started by Barindra Kumar Ghose with the help of two friends. It preached the gospel of revolution and carried on the political and religious instruction of the masses. It had a complete scheme of action; first to arouse hatred of servitude in the minds of educated classes by a vigorous propaganda in the Press, secondly, to instil the love of freedom and the Motherland and thirdly, to keep the enemy busy with demonstrations and agitation.

[4] *Proceedings of the Council of the Governor-General of India*, vol. xlvii, April 1908–March 1909, pp. 12, 14, 15, 22.

[5] Morley to Minto, 8 June 1908. *M.P.*

[6] *Report of the Indian National Congress*, 1908. Presidential address.

[7] Ibid. Resolution XI, p. 116.

it would not have been wiser if the Press Act had been introduced
at an earlier period'. Morley stoutly defended Minto's actions
in the House of Lords and stated that 'between no two servants
of the crown is there a better understanding and a fuller confidence than there is between the present Viceroy and the
present Secretary of State. He also admired 'the manful courage'
of Minto who had stated during the Press Act discussions in his
Council that, 'No anarchical crime will deter me from endea-
vouring to meet, as best I can, the political aspirations of honest
reformers'. Morley declared that despite these 'anarchical
crimes' to suppress which this repressive Act had been passed
the Government would 'persevere in the path of reform'.[8] Thus
during the execution and pursuance of a repressive policy,
Morley and Minto never lost sight of meeting 'the political
aspirations of honest reformers'. They aimed to suppress sedition but keep the loyal moderate Indians in good humour and
expectant. Morley's aim was to reconcile liberal opinion at home
and to save the moderates from the 'taunts and reproaches' of
the extremists. Gokhale and Dutt were in England at that time.
They had met the members of the Indian Committee of the
House of Commons. But Morley was able to convince them that
any violent criticism of the Government policies at that time
would provide 'powder and shot for revolutionaries in India'.
Thus he succeeded in preventing the formation of any group in
Parliament who might have been extremely critical of Government policies, thus hampering the administration of law and
order.[9]

The Provincial Governments were busy checking terrorism as
well. Though it existed in many provinces, Bengal was the
nucleus of the movement and it was from there that most of the
terrorist activities were directed. On 16 May 1908, the Government of Bengal proposed to the Government of India to deport

[8] *Hansard*, House of Lords, 4S, vol. 191, 1908. Debate on Indian Affairs,
30 June 1908. Curzon, Cols. 516–20; Cromer, Cols. 536–7; Ampthill, Col. 546;
Lamington, Col. 554: 'I earnestly hope the Secretary of State will consider
the desirabilities of having a more stringent Press Law'; Morley, Col. 530.

[9] Morley to Minto, 28 May 1908. *M.P.*

Aurobindo Ghose, Abinash Chandra Bhattacharji and Sailendra Kumar Bose under Regulation III of 1818, for alleged participation in various subversive activities.[1] But the Governor-General-in-Council did not find sufficient evidence to agree to deportation. It was considered that after Lajpat Rai's release, deportation would not act as a deterrent to those who sympathized with Aurobindo Ghose and his party, for they would feel confident of early release. A vigorous agitation to secure it would also be pushed on both in India and in Parliament. Moreover the moderate section of the educated population would view deportation with strong disfavour. So the Government of India did not accept the Lieutenant-Governor's proposal.[2] However, as a result of discoveries of bombs, dynamite and cartridges at Maniktola Garden in Calcutta, thirty persons were arrested and prosecuted. Aurobindo Ghose, his brother Barindra Kumar Ghose and others were amongst the arrested persons. The trial lasted till 12 February 1910, when the High Court finally sentenced four men to transportation for life, three to ten years', seven to seven years' and three to five years' rigorous imprisonment. Aurobindo Ghose and a few others were acquitted by the Sessions Court on 13 April 1909, Narendra Gosain, who had become approver, was shot dead by his companions in jail, with smuggled arms. This trial established that at least twelve persons had collected arms for the purpose of fighting the British Government. Their confessions showed that they had actually killed Mrs. and Miss Kennedy and were prepared to use explosives in order to further their purpose. Those concerned were mostly young and educated men, of strong religious conviction. They belonged to high castes and came from different parts of the province. The newspaper the *Yugantar* was 'a link of the conspiracy', as its teachings inspired them.[3]

[1] Government of Bengal to Government of India, 16 May 1908. *Home Progs*. Public/Political, January–December 1908, 7875.
[2] Government of India to Government of Bengal, 28 May 1908. *Home Progs*. Public/Political, January–December 1908, 7875.
[3] The Alipore conspiracy case judgement, *Sedition Committee Report*, Annexure I, pp. i, ii.

In Bombay, on 24 June 1908, Tilak was arrested on charges connected with the publication in the *Kesari* of articles containing inflammatory comments on the Muzzafarpur murders. In these articles the act of the Bengal revolutionary party was applauded, though he suggested that 'from the point of view of daring and skilled execution, the Chapekar brothers take a higher rank than members of the bomb party in Bengal'.[4] This could have been interpreted not only as a taunt but as an exhortation for further courage and improved skill. Mr. Justice Dawar, a Parsee Judge, thought that these articles were 'seething with sedition; they preach violence; they speak of murders with approval . . .' Tilak defended his own case for twenty-one and a half hours but the jury found him guilty and he was sentenced to six years' imprisonment. The Bombay Government conducted all these proceedings. Sir George Clarke, the Governor of Bombay, was not very willing to approach the Central Government in every matter and often kept it in the dark in many matters. Minto himself did not know of Tilak's arrest till quite late. Clarke on his own initiative ordered Tilak's arrest.[5] Morley thought the articles 'bad enough to warrant a prosecution if you wanted one on general grounds, but not at all so bad as to make a prosecution inevitable'.[6] Minto did not agree with Morley on this point. Actually he had no hand in Tilak's arrest and trial, but when Tilak was ultimately sentenced to six years' imprisonment he thought that the effect of the sentence would be 'excellent'. After

[4] These articles were published on 12 May and 9 June 1908.

[5] Sir George Clarke, Lord Sydenham, *My Working Life*, p. 222, also see Minto to Morley, 29 July 1908. *M.P.*

[6] Morley to Minto, 16 July 1908. Ibid. Morley seems to have been influenced in this, besides his own convictions, by Gokhale. Gokhale considered such prosecutions as a discouragement to the moderates. Morley's letter to Clarke, 3 July 1908. Gokhale was evidently very anxious to obliterate any suspicion from the minds of the extremists that the moderates were in league with the Government. It had been suggested that the moderates had a hand in encouraging the Government to prosecute Tilak. Clarke mentions that 'while the "moderates" gave me no public support, some of them—in private—told me they welcomed the action taken'. See Sir George Clarke, Lord Sydenham, op. cit., pp. 223, 228.

some disturbances the situation in Bombay did come under control. He had no doubt in his mind that Tilak was 'the arch-leader of sedition' and unlike Lajpat Rai, there was ample evidence to prove it. He, however, again reiterated that 'I have never advocated exaggerated measures if we can do without them, but it is the plain truth that people here are afraid for their lives, not only Europeans but Natives too . . .'[7] As later events were to prove Minto was right in one respect at least—the people were scared and a number of murders did occur very soon. Morley, though he connived at Tilak's sentence, did not in fact like these severe sentences. He was worried that, however justifiable they might be, these sentences had to be defended in Parliament. The House of Commons was most critical and he thought that after he had left for the House of Lords there was nobody who could face the criticism of Dr. Rutherford, Sir Henry Cotton and F. C. Mackarness. Minto's argument was that any criticism of Government actions would add fuel to the fire and that the House of Commons should not be allowed to meddle in this affair. This Morley would not tolerate. He plainly told Minto that these sentences would be discussed in Parliament and that if he persisted in following this policy he would not defend it. This was a serious threat and Minto had to pacify him by reiterating that he was very anxious to adopt a policy of reform but the situation at that time required a firm hand.[8]

Dr. Rutherford, Keir Hardie, A. Lupton, Mackarness, O'Grady and Cotton asked questions about Tilak's conviction in the House of Commons. Dr. Rutherford wanted the Secretary of State to recommend to the King to extend his clemency to Tilak, in view of the position he held in the Indian Nationalist movement and remit a portion of his sentence with a view to

[7] Minto to Morley, 5, 18 August 1908. *M.P.*

[8] Morley to Minto, 26 August, 7 October 1908 and Minto to Morley, 14 September 1908. See also F. A. Hirtzel's Diary, 25 February 1907. *Home Misc. 864.* I.O.L. Morley mentioned his intention of retiring or going to the House of Lords. He was tired and wanted some relief. He did not, however, intend to leave Indian affairs—'for enormous interest' in India and 'impending constitutional changes'.

allaying to some extent the present unrest in India. Buchanan, the Under-Secretary of State, replied that it was impossible for the Secretary of State to do so as Tilak had been sentenced by a Judge of the High Court after due trial, and his writings for which he was sentenced were such that the Government could not recommend any clemency. Keir Hardie wanted the publication of these articles as a Parliamentary Paper to give the House and the country an opportunity to judge these articles themselves. Cotton suggested that copies of them should be put in the Library. Lupton questioned the composition of the Jury and Mackarness enquired whether an appeal could be made against the sentence. Buchanan replied that no appeal lay against the High Court decision, but the Judicial Committee of the Privy Council might give special leave to appeal in cases where grave injustice appeared to have been done. These radical members continued their fight against Tilak's release and made J. D. Rees wonder whether expressions of sympathy in the House with notorious enemies of British rule were likely to have the effect of 'allaying to some extent the present unrest in India'.[9]

It seems that Minto was right in his reading of the situation. It was very critical. Even these arrests and prosecutions did not prevent crime. Attempts on the life of the Lieutenant-Governor of Bengal (7 November 1908) and other police officers continued. On 9 November 1908 Nando Lal Banerji, a sub-inspector of police employed in the Criminal Investigation Department, who had been instrumental in tracing one of the Muzzafarpur murders, was shot dead in the streets of Calcutta. The existence of *Samitis,* with the intention of spreading revolutionary ideas in the two Bengals, was also brought to the notice of the Government. Now there was less open agitation but there were secret organizations. The Local Government insisted on handling the situation sternly. It demanded strong action against secret societies like the *Anushilan Samiti.* This society was actually started for the promotion of culture and physical training.

[9] *Hansard,* House of Commons, 4S, vol. 193, Cols. 1216, 1217, 1218, 1483, 1747–8; vol. 194, Cols. 917, 1392.

Aurobindo Ghose's brother, Barindra Kumar Ghose, was one of its founders. Very soon its branches were established throughout Bengal. But these societies were not purely institutions of physical culture. The ultimate aim was to equip members with military training in order to raise a national army to overthrow British rule.[1] It was in these circumstances that Minto, on 11 December 1908, acting on the strong recommendation of the Governments of Bengal and Eastern Bengal and Assam, issued orders for the arrest and deportation of Subodh Chandra Mullick, Manoranjan Guha Thakurta, Kristo Kumar Mittra, Sachindra Prasad Bose, Shamsumder Chakravarti, Aswini Kumar Dutt, Satish Chandra Chatterji, Pulin Behari Das and Bupesh Chandra Nag. These orders were executed on 13 December 1908. Besides, the Indian Criminal Law Amendment Act was passed which declared such *Samitis*—like the *Anushilan Samiti*—unlawful. Again the reason for these deportations was the same—that the Government had enough evidence to show that the activities of the deported persons were revolutionary and a danger to the peace and tranquillity of the country, but that could not be proved in a Court of Law. Actually the Government wanted to curb their activities without arousing any controversy.

Morley acquiesced in these policies but was as usual apprehensive. He never liked deportation. He had expressed himself very strongly about it during Lajpat Rai's deportation. But Minto again resorted to the same method. Or more truly Minto was again forced to resort to the same method. But this time he was on surer ground. However, Morley protested against the deportations—'that is the harder nut for us to crack on this side of the water, and quite right too. I understand from your telegram that the names were decided on consultation between you, Fraser, Baker and Adamson. After all, if we press to the bottom of things, I conjecture that the active man in this chapter of business must be Stuart or Plowden or somebody of the Police; and that breed needs searching scrutiny step by step in these matters. Lawyers are not always to be trusted; still less are Police authorities'.[2]

[1] N. C. Chaudhuri, op. cit., p. 245.    [2] Morley to Minto, 6 January 1909. *M.P.*

Again, 'you may take my word for it, my dear Viceroy, that if
we do not use this harsh weapon with the utmost care and
scruple—always, where the material is dubious, giving the suspected man the benefit of the doubt—you may depend upon it, I
say, that both you and I will be called to severe account, even by
the people who are now applauding us (quite rightly) for vigour'.[3]
Godley informed Minto that though Morley had taken a 'high
line, and will not hear of any compromise or explanations in
Parliament', Buchanan, the Under-Secretary of State, was extremely nervous. To encourage Minto, he added, 'if he [Buch-
anan] shrinks from defying the lightening of Messrs. Cotton,
Mackarness, Rutherford & Co., Asquith must be invoked; and I
believe this will probably be done'.[4] This shows that at this stage
Morley was less doubtful about this policy than Buchanan. His
decision to defend it boldly in Parliament reflects that he considered that for once 'this harsh weapon' had been used with
'care and scruple'. This must have encouraged Minto.

Minto was very sure of his ground and boldly defended his
policy. 'It is easy enough for Mackarness and others to assume
that the police are corrupt and that here we are cruel dictators—
views no doubt full of the milk of human kindness—but we cannot rule this country by namby-pamby sentiment alone. No one
dislikes *lettres de cachet* more than I do. The whole essence of
them is the arrest of persons on evidence sufficient to satisfy the
Government that such persons are guilty, though not sufficient
to convict them in a Court of Law. . . . The powers conferred by
the Regulations of 1818 are not pleasant ones to wield, but their
value has been incontestably proved under certain conditions in
India. At the same time one must always bear in mind that such
powers can never be safely used unless it is absolutely clear that
the authority which puts them into force is completely trusted
to do so judiciously, and is perfectly free from the risk of enquiry
into its action, or from the necessity to justify it.'[5]

[3] Morley to Minto, 13 January 1909. Ibid.
[4] Godley to Minto, 15 January 1909. *M.C.*
[5] Minto to Morley, 4 February 1909. *M.C.*

In the House of Commons, the Radicals, however, strongly criticized these deportations. Mackarness said in April 1909 that the power of deporting without trial was clearly unconstitutional if Magna Carta had any meaning.[6] J. C. Wedgwood asserted that the principle of the Regulations of 1818 'is the principle of the Bastille. It is the principle of *lettres de cachet* under Louis XIV'.[7] J. D. Rees, on the other hand, while admitting that the power of deporting without trial was an autocratic one, thought that the Government had not used this method as much as was necessary for suppressing sedition. He hoped that the Government would deport Aurobindo Ghose, as he excited youths by calling them cowards. He opined that in order to make the people of the East realize that their rulers had power, it was essential to use it autocratically in grave and critical situations.[8]

Apart from a few isolated bomb explosions, the political situation in the two Bengals showed a considerable improvement in the beginning of 1909. But on 10 February 1909, Asutosh Biswas, who was public prosecutor in the Alipore Sessions Court and was engaged in the prosecution of the Calcutta prisoners, was murdered. In March certain letters, which were discovered in a house in Nasik, revealed the existence of two secret revolutionary societies in Gwalior and one in the Deccan with branches in a large number of towns. This evidence led to the conviction by the Sessions Judge of Nasik of Ganesh. D. Savarkar, the brother of the famous Vinayak Savarkar of Shyamaji Krishnavarma's India House, London. Thirty-nine persons were convicted in Gwalior. On 1 July 1909 in London, Sir William Curzon Wyllie, the Political A.D.C. at the India Office, was shot dead by Madan Lal Dhingra, again of the India House. On 13 November 1909, an attempt was made on the Viceroy's life at Ahmedabad. On 21 December 1909 A. M. T. Jackson, the District Magistrate,

---

[6] *Hansard*, House of Commons, vol. iii, 1909 (29 March 1909–23 April 1909), 19 April 1909, Col. 1270.

[7] Ibid. House of Commons, vol. xix, 1910 (11 July–3 August, 1910), 26 July 1910, Col. 2036.

[8] Ibid. House of Commons, vol. viii, 1,909 (19 July–6 August, 1909), 5 August 1909, Cols. 2051–4.

who had committed Ganesh Savarkar for trial, was murdered. On 28 December 1909, a bomb was found at the house of the Deputy Commissioner of Ambala. On 24 January 1910, Khan Bahadur Shams-ul-Alam, the Deputy Superintendent of Police, who was engaged in instructing the Counsel for the Crown in the Alipore Conspiracy case appeal, was murdered. There were numerous instances of dacoity in the two Bengals as well.[9]

All these acts of violence horrified Morley but he continued to insist on the policy of reform and the release of the deportees.[1] Minto remained adamant. He emphasized that 'my first duty is to look after the necessities of the charge committed to me irrespective of public opinion at home'[2]; that 'it is impossible to convey to you in letters or despatches the knowledge the Government of India possesses, and which I possess more than anyone else from a wide correspondence and intimacy with many Natives, of the risks we daily run, or of our acquaintance with underground machinations. . . . And it is quite impossible to convey to you a just impression of the everyday life of India'.[3] He even mentioned that the ruling princes had supported him in his actions.[4] It seems quite natural that Morley's pride of intellect should have induced him to believe that he knew better than the man on the spot, while Minto, despite doing his best, was unable to translate the intricacies of the situation on paper. The apparent changes of view, in the case of Morley particularly, were presumably due to advisers near at hand.

Surendranath Banerjea suggests that the bomb was the result of repression. 'Bureaucracy was alarmed, startled at the result of its own blunders.'[5] While G. N. Singh arrives at a different

[9] *Home Progs.* Political, January–July 1910, 8430.

[1] See Morley's telegram, 30 August, 8, 10, 14 September and 20, 27, 31 October 1909 &c. and letters.

[2] Minto to Morley, 21 June 1908. *M.C.*

[3] Minto to Morley, 21 October 1909. Ibid.

[4] See *Correspondence between H.E. Lord Minto and certain Ruling Chiefs.* **Ibid.** Minto sought suggestions from Chiefs such as the Nizam, the Gaekwad, and others, with regard to the suppression of sedition. All of them suggested a stringent policy.

[5] S. N. Banerjea, op. cit., p. 249.

conclusion. To him 'It appears that the terrorist crime had unnerved the Bureaucracy and the Anglo-Indian having given way
under the strain they began to advocate a policy of revenge and
unmitigated repression'.[6] But who was actually responsible for
that state of affairs in India—terrorists or bureaucracy? Morley
blames the bureaucracy. 'It is not you or I who are responsible
for "unrest", but the over confident and over-worked Tchinoviks
who have had India in their hands for fifty years past.'[7] Minto,
on the other hand, went deep into the problem. The very fact
that India was ruled by an alien people was enough to arouse
Indian antipathy towards that rule. Practically every British
move in every field of life had been resented. That resentment
turned into open resistance in Curzon's time. Minto found India
up in arms against British rule. Bureaucracy seemed to have lost
its nerve and was willing to resort to repressive measures to suppress 'sedition'. In that mêlée it was difficult to distinguish
between genuine Indian aspirations for reform and terrorism.
In the eyes of certain Local Governments Surendranath Banerjea
was as big a disturber of peace as Tilak or Pal. Minto's only
contribution was to make a distinction between the two. He
aimed to secure and achieved, to a great extent, the sympathies
of the moderate leaders of the Congress, particularly Hindus.
As for the Muslims they had not involved themselves in any
revolutionary activity. He was able to keep 'sedition' bound to
its narrowest limits. Whenever he found necessary he never
hesitated to suppress it sternly. The fact is that the Local Governments were out to suppress every movement against the Government—like the Punjab Government's actions against agitation in
opposition to the Colonization Bill—but it was Minto who
checked them. He resisted the bureaucratic pressure for repression not only because he knew that Morley would not agree to it
but because he knew that most of it was not based on solid
evidence. He resisted Morley's pressure equally boldly because
in his view Morley was at times ignorant of the real situation.

[6] G. N. Singh, op. cit. (1933), p. 361.
[7] Morley to Minto, 17 June 1908. See Morley's *Recollections*, vol. ii, p. 265.

He had his own convictions. After the mistake he committed in deporting Lajpat Rai at the insistence of the Punjab Government, he ceased to place categorical reliance on the judgement of Local Governments. On most occasions he required much greater evidence than they provided for deportation or any such act, before agreeing to it, and many a time he refused to sanction it.[8]

[8] In 1910 he disallowed the deportation of fifty-three persons as suggested by the Government of Bengal—Government of Bengal's letters to Government of India, I, 28 February 1910 and Government of India's letter to Government of Bengal, 7 March 1910. *Home Progs*. Political, January–July 1910 (8430).

# CHAPTER FOUR

# INTRODUCTION OF THE REFORMS

As we have seen, when Minto arrived in India the political atmosphere was very tense. He was not inhibited by any pre-conceived ideas about Indian affairs. But immediately on his arrival in India he started discussion with members of his Council and other prominent officials to find an amicable way of meeting the demands of the educated Indians.[1] The emergence of a separate Muslim political party in 1906 introduced another factor into Indian politics. Besides the Congress and the League, there were the Anglo-Indians. Theirs was a powerful voice in Indian affairs. They had an effective and vociferous press. There were certain other interests, like the landlords, the merchants and the Indian chiefs, who could not be ignored in the event of any administrative changes in the Government of India.

Morley, though very sympathetic towards Indian aspirations, was sceptical in the beginning about the Congress aims. Minto was soon able to convince him that the moderate Congress was an important factor and that these demands for the increased representation in Indian administration should be considered sympathetically. While the Congress demand had grown from increased representation to the attainment of *Swaraj*, the League desired separate representation and weightage as it distrusted the Hindu majority. Minto and Morley were to work out a policy which should meet these demands.

Minto was willing to recognize the genuine wish of educated Indians, but he felt like Curzon, that 'it was not so much political reform or political ambitions that, in the present stage of Indian history, we ought to look to, but the means of giving most happiness and prosperity to the everyday lives of its teeming

[1] John Buchan, op. cit. (London, 1924), p. 231. See also Lady Minto, *My Indian Journal*.

millions'.[2] This happiness and prosperity would come, he thought, not by granting political demands of the extremist element in the Congress, but by the continuance of the *Raj*. The *Raj* would continue only if the educated Indians were given a share in the administration of the country. The problem was how this should be done? Minto thought that a large number of Indian interests should be represented on Indian Councils. This representation of interests would not only satisfy a greater number of people, but also act as a counterpoise to the extreme Congress aims. He dismissed the ideal of self-government as 'an impossibility'[3] and in his opinion a constitutional autocracy was the best form of government for India. Minto was fully conscious that by its very nature the Government of India was autocratic and would remain so for some time. But it could be made liberal by introducing the spirit of British democratic institutions and liberalizing its policies. Thus a constitutional autocracy combining the principles of autocracy of Mughal Emperors and Hindu Rajas and British constitutionalism seemed to him a possible solution. Both Minto and Morley would have satisfied themselves, if they could 'hatch some plan and policy for half a generation'.[4]

The idea of representation of interests in the Indian Councils was not new; for such a vast country, with its numerous races and interests, the only suitable form by which the Government could know the opinions of its people was through the representation of various interests on its Councils, and this was the accepted cornerstone of the British policy. The Aitchison Committee appointed by Dufferin in 1888 specifically mentioned these various interests, which it required to be represented on Provincial Legislative Councils. These were (a) 'the interests of the hereditary nobility and landed classes, who have a great permanent stake in the country; (b) the interests of the trading,

[2] Minto to Morley, 4 November 1906. *M.P.*

[3] Minto to Morley, 13 May 1909. Ibid.

[4] 'If we can hatch some plan and policy for half a generation that will be something: and if for a whole generation, that will be better. Only I am bent, as you assuredly are, on doing nothing to loosen the bolts.' Morley to Minto, 17 April 1907. Ibid.

professional and agricultural classes; (c) the interests of the planting and commercial European Community, and (d) the interests of stable and effective administration'.[5] Dufferin emphasized this point in his despatch to the Secretary of State on 6 November 1888.[6] It was discussed in Parliament and Lord Northbrook, Lord Salisbury and others supported it.[7] The Act of 1892 recognized the principle of representation of interests on the Legislative Councils. By the time Minto reached India the Muslims had become conscious that their interests had not been properly represented on these Councils. They asked Minto for safeguards for their interests in any new set-up of Indian administration.

With a view to meeting the demands of educated Indians and after having been convinced that Minto was thinking on the same lines, Morley asked him to make a 'start in the way of reform in the popular direction'. Amongst the things he suggested were—the extension of the native element in the Viceroy's and Provincial Legislative Councils, 'full time for discussing the budget in the Legislative Councils instead of four or five skimpy hours' and the right of moving amendments. However, he wanted the official majority to be kept. He wondered whether there was any scope for an Indian on the Viceroy's Executive Council as it would frighten that 'nervous animal—the European Indian'. Morley pointed out that from Minto's letters he had guessed that he had no disposition whatever to look on such changes as these in a hostile spirit.[8] Morley wanted Minto's opinion as he expected to announce his policy in Parliament to silence 'the Indian Com-

[5] *Public Letters from India, 1888*, vol. ix. The Committee consisted of three members of his Executive Council—General Chesney, Sir Charles Aitchison, and J. Westland. Sir Anthony MacDonnell was its secretary. As Home Secretary MacDonnell had chalked out a scheme of reform which formed the basis of their discussion. The Committee completed its work on 10 October 1888.

[6] Ibid., vol. ix, p. 1,190.

[7] *Hansard*, 6 March 1890, 3S, vol. 342, Col. 98. 15 February 1892, 4S, vol. i, Col. 416. For a detailed discussion see: S. Chakravarty, *The Evolution of Representative Government in India, 1884–1909, with reference to Central and Provincial Legislative Councils*, Ph.D. Thesis (London University, 1954), Chs. II, III, IV, V.

[8] Morley to Minto, 15 June 1906. *M.P.*

mittee of the House of Commons', and before the demands of the Indians became greater. To avoid any appearance of forcing the Indian Government's hands, he wished 'the move to be directly and closely associated with yourself [with Minto]'.[9]

Minto liked Morley's suggestion of reform in the popular direction. But he suggested that before bringing the matter up in Council it would be better if they both put their ideas into shape as far as possible. Then after discussion in the Council, he would send Morley these proposals in the shape of an official despatch. Minto emphasized that he attached great importance to the 'official initiative being taken by the Government of India'. 'It is better in every respect, both for the present and for the future, that the Government of India should appear to recognize all that is in the air here, the necessity of meeting new conditions, and that they should not run the risk of being assumed to have at least taken tardy action out of respect to instructions from home.'[1] This suggestion of Minto was based on the fear that in the contrary case the Government of India would come into disrepute which would not be beneficial for the future administration of the country. Morley had no objection. He himself wanted the Government of India to take the initiative. He would, then, be able to steer through the reform scheme in Parliament by saying that the Government of India desired these reforms. Even the Conservative House of Lords would have some hesitation in attacking the Government of India's reform policy.

Commenting on Morley's proposals Minto asserted that there was no difference between them: but difference between them there was. While Morley put the suggestion of an Indian on the Viceroy's Executive Council last of all and in a most casual way, Minto gave it priority and thought it most important. He informed Morley that he had thought of suggesting the appointment of an Indian on his Council, but dropped the idea as being

[9] Morley to Minto, 22 June 1906. *M.P.*
[1] Minto to Morley, 11 July 1906. *M.C.* In a telegram on 14 July 1906, Minto repeated the above and stated that these were his points and that his colleagues in the Council knew nothing about them.

premature.[2] Being still under the influence of official opinion he
thought that there was a risk of leakage of secrets in the event of an
Indian appointment. He even expressed some doubts as to the
possibility of finding an able Indian 'with a stake in the country',
as (again echoing official opinion), one was 'not to promote anyone of the purely Gokhale type'.[3] Still his inclination was to have
an Indian as 'Minister without portfolio'. The possibility of an
Indian member on his Council appealed to Minto strongly.
Though doubts lurked in his mind, he did not feel sure 'that we
are not exaggerating the risk'. He agreed with Morley's suggestion of an increase in native representation on the Imperial and
Provincial Legislative Councils and the prolongation of the
budget debate with greater liberty for discussion. In addition to
these he suggested a Council of Princes as well, which Morley
had thought useless.[4] Minto was also in favour of giving greater
powers and greater encouragement to the native element on
district councils and municipalities.[5]

Meanwhile Morley, in a telegram, stated that he was much
inclined to mention the notion of putting an Indian Judge on the
India Council and asked Minto's opinion.[6] Minto immediately

[2] It has been mentioned before that Minto did discuss the appointment of
an Indian and other matters with some important officials of the Government
of India. The suggestion for an Indian on the Viceroy's Council was not new.
It was once made to Curzon by R. C. Dutt, President of the Congress, 1899.
In a letter to Hamilton, Curzon wrote that 'I told him [Dutt] frankly that the
idea was, in my opinion, quite out of the question. The notion that the so-
called "woes of India" are likely to be met by placing one or two natives who
would be always in a minority in a cabinet of Europeans, quite apart from its
political absurdity, suggested to me Sidney Smith's reply to the little girl
whom he saw stroking the back of a tortoise that you might as well expect to
gratify the Dean and Chapter by tickling the dome of St. Paul's'. Curzon to
Hamilton, 11 January 1900. *Hamilton Papers*, vol. xvi, p. 61.

[3] Everyone admired Gokhale's ability, but as he was a member of the Congress, the officials hesitated to trust him with State secrets. Minto himself would
have had no objections in appointing him to his Council as he did write to Morley that 'I am also considering the advisability of Gokhale as a member. There is
a good deal to be said in his favour'. Minto to Morley, 12 September 1907. *M.P.*

[4] Morley to Minto, 22 June 1906. Ibid.

[5] Minto to Morley, 5 July 1906. Ibid.

[6] Morley to Minto, telegram, 13 July 1906. Ibid.

replied that though the suggestion was good, it would at once raise questions as to an Indian member on his Council. Minto was anxious that no step should be taken until the Anglo-Indian opinion in India had been softened. Minto, therefore, suggested that it would be better not to raise the point at that moment, but to consider such points later on. For the moment Morley should make a general statement that the 'Government of India are in thorough sympathy with the necessities of the hour'.[7] Morley agreed with Minto—'I have hung up the notion of a native on my Council, as you wished—quite prudently, I think, until you know how things go on with your people.'[8] Three days later Minto informed Morley that Sir E. Baker, the Finance Member, was in favour of an Indian on the Council and thought that Law Port-folio was the best for him. Others, though first taken aback at the novelty of the suggestion, seemed quite inclined to consider it. Minto thought that though there was something in the argu-ments—i.e., susceptibilities of the European population; differences between Hindus and Muslims—against the Indian member, much more was due to racial prejudice. For a detailed study of this proposal, as well as others, he proposed to appoint a small committee of his Executive Council. He informed Morley that if he thought it fit he could announce this appointment of the committee to consider the possibility of reforms generally in Parliament.[9] Morley accordingly made an announcement in Parliament to that effect, and acknowledged that Minto had authorized him to make it.[1] 'I owe you more, for if I had not been able to make the practical announcement so seasonably authorized by you, the thing would have been an affair of sounding brass and tinkling cymbals.' Gokhale was in the Gallery in the House of Commons and he wrote to Morley that he left the House 'with a load removed from his heart.'[2]

[7] Minto to Morley, telegram, 14 July 1906. *M.P.*
[8] Morley to Minto, 27 July 1906. Ibid.
[9] Minto to Morley, telegram, 17 July 1906. Ibid.
[1] *Hansard*, 20 July 1906, 4S, vol. 161, Col. 588.
[2] Morley to Minto, 27 July 1906. Ibid.

Morley mentioned in the House of Commons the proposed appointment of the Viceroy's Committee and generally hinted that the questions which could be discussed were 'the extension of representative element in the Legislative Council—not the Executive Council, but the Legislative Council', longer discussion of the Budget and powers to move amendments. He scrupulously avoided any hint of an appointment of an Indian member to the Viceroy's Executive Council or to the India Council.[3] Earl Percy congratulated the Secretary of State for this announcement and stated that the House 'would await with great interest the recommendations of the Committee'.[4]

The Committee of the Executive Council, which was appointed by Minto on 16 August 1906, consisted of Sir A. Arundel, chairman; Sir D. Ibbetson, E. N. Baker, Erle Richards, members; and H. H. Risley, secretary. For their guidance Minto wrote a minute. His main emphasis was that now the time had come when the changing conditions in India should be seriously considered and an effort be made to meet the Indian demands. It is interesting to note that in this minute he referred to those very four important interests, which the Aitchison Committee had emphasized, as worth special protection. The Muslim deputation had not met him yet and he had not been made aware of the Muslim interests. This suggests that Minto had no preconceived notions about safeguarding Muslim interests. He desired to secure the representation of interests other than those represented by the Congress, but he would not create any of these interests himself. When the problem was presented to him, he certainly gave his careful consideration to it and forwarded the Muslim demands to the Committee. The appointment of an Indian member to the Executive Council was one of the subjects for the Committee's consideration.[5]

He was, however, not very hopeful of 'very grand results',

---

[3] *Hansard*, House of Commons, 20 July 1906, 4S, vol. 161, Col. 588.
[4] Ibid. Col. 589.
[5] Minto's Minute to his Committee, 15 August 1906. *M.P.* Minto to Morley, 15 August 1906; telegram, 20 August 1906. Ibid.

because of the adverse Anglo-Indian opinion towards any reforms, though he realized that 'it would be disastrous for any
Government to attempt to ignore the signs of the times.'[6] The
points of reference to the Committee were kept secret. But
Morley, being a cautious politician, did not want any expression
to be used which might appear to suggest any 'possibility of
administrative reform' or 'likely to excite larger expectations that
you will find yourself generally [not] able to satisfy'.[7] Because
sooner or later the terms of reference, the Committee's report,
along with the Government of India's recommendations, were to
be presented to Parliament. So the press communiqué was
diplomatically worded. It only informed the public that the
Viceroy had appointed a Committee of his Executive Council in
consequence of the Secretary of State's statement in the House of
Commons in July 1906.

The Committee started its work in earnest, and Minto was
kept informed of the views of its members. Arundel described
them to him: Ibbetson represented the old Tory, Baker the
advanced Liberal and he himself the Liberal-Unionist view,
while Erle Richards was sitting on the fence. While the Committee was busy, Minto was making up his own mind. He
admitted that 'the more I think of it, the more inclined I am for a
Native member on the Viceroy's Executive Council' as 'it would
answer much of the accusation against the narrow character of
Indian bureaucracy, for whilst recognizing that India is unfit for
popular government it would be the admission of one of her
people to a direct share in the executive authority of Imperial
administration. It would be an immense move forward.'[8]

The Arundel Committee, even to Minto's surprise, completed
and submitted its report on 12 October 1906.[1] With regard to an
Indian member of the Viceroy's Executive Council, the Com-

---

[6] Minto to Morley, 15 August 1906. *M.P.*

[7] Morley to Minto, telegram, 21 August 1906. Ibid.

[8] Minto to Morley, 12 September 1906. Ibid.

[1] Minto to Morley, 4 and 28 October 1906. Ibid. The Arundel Committee's
Report. *Public Letters from India*, 1907, No. XXXV.

mittee was not unanimous. The members, however, were agreed as to the great importance of the measure, and as to the significance which would attach to it in the eyes of all classes of the people. Arundel and Baker were of the opinion that the step both could and ought to be taken at once, Ibbetson and Erle Richards considered that the objections to it outweighed its advantages. The objections were that the presence of an Indian would impose some restraint on the freedom with which Members of the Government expressed their views on cases which came before them[2]; that there was a danger of a leakage of confidential matters; that 'at some future time an unsuitable selection for the appointment might be made, in which case the Indian Member might conceivably use his official influence to advance improperly the interest of the class to which he belonged'; that such an appointment to the Viceroy's Council would lead to the addition of an Indian member to the Councils of Provincial Governors. Arundel and Baker did not consider these very solid objections. They stated that 'we regard the admission of a native of India to the inner Counsels of Government not as the introduction into the citadel of an enemy to be feared, but as the addition to the garrison of an ally whose advice will be highly valued, and whose mere presence will insure the confidence and enhance the loyalty of his fellow-countrymen'. The Committee was thus divided in halves on this question.[3]

This divergence of opinion amongst the members of the Committee disappointed Minto. He thought that a 'native member' was by far the best answer that could be made in reply to Indian demands for increased representation in the Government of India, but 'British feeling in this country is not yet ripe for such

---

[2] Kitchener was against such an appointment. Minto wrote to Morley, 'I found K. decidedly opposed to it, the reason he gives me being very amusing. That he had heard Curzon say such appalling things about H.M.'s Government and individual members of the Cabinet at Council meetings that it had made his hair stand on end, and that it would have been too terrible in the presence of a native member', 29 August 1906. See also P. Magnus, *Kitchener, Portrait of an Imperialist* (London, 1958), p. 234.

[3] The Arundel Committee's Report. *Public Letters from India*, 1907, No. 35.

an advance in our methods of administration, and we cannot disregard this feeling'.[4] Morley also felt strongly. He considered that it was the cheapest concession they could make. He told Minto that in the event of a majority of the Viceroy's Council being adverse to this idea, it would be awkward to put pressure on him. The question was whether it was better to have an Indian on the Viceroy's Council or the Secretary of State's Council? Morley throughout was trying to emphasize that it would be much better if an Indian were put on the Viceroy's Council. Godley had also in an earlier letter to Minto written 'that the thing that ought to be done *last* is—what is sure to come in time—the putting of a Native on to our Council here'.[5]

Minto's views and anxieties were similar. He knew that British feeling in India was against such a move and people suspected that it would arouse the same sort of controversy as the Ilbert Bill did.[6] But, in his opinion, it was wrong to compare it with the Ilbert Bill case. 'The Ilbert Bill affected the individual rights of Europeans, which the appointment of an Indian to the Viceroy's Council would not in any way do' and 'the Executive could not possibly be weakened with his presence.' He thought that if 'out of anxiety and respect to British sensitiveness' this chance was missed, the opportunity of meeting demands for reform, 'which we shall be obliged to deal with sooner or later', would be lost.[7] Arundel was no more the member of his Council and of all the others, he knew that only Baker supported him. Even then he was inclined to advocate the appointment of an Indian member to his Council and suggested the name of Dr. Asutosh Mukerji, Vice-Chancellor of the Calcutta University and a High Court Judge.

---

[4] Minto to Morley, 28 October 1906. *M.P.*

[5] Morley to Minto, 23 November 1906. Ibid. Godley to Minto, 20 July 1906. *M.C.*

[6] In 1883 Sir Courtney Ilbert, the Law Member, introduced a Bill in the Legislative Council to remove judicial disqualifications based on race distinctions. It aroused vehement opposition and had substantially to be withdrawn.

[7] Minto to Morley, 12 December 1906. *M.P.*

But he indicated that he was opposed to moving in a hurry and it would take some time before Morley could receive the Government of India's despatch.[8] The mention of delay annoyed Morley and he insisted on an early despatch.[9]

Minto again became influenced by the opinions of the members of his Council, who were strongly opposed to the Indian member. He began to have doubts as to the advisability of such an appointment, even if it was right in principle. His main worry was how would British public opinion in India take this step.[1] He remained in this state of mind for about a fortnight, but by 26 February 1907, he made up his mind to advise the appointment, but asked Morley not to make public the views of the members of the Council against it as they were 'based almost entirely on supposed untrustworthiness and possible disloyalty of the Native'; and public knowledge of such views might endanger the future career of the present members in India.[2]

On 6 March 1907, Minto's Council met and discussed the proposed draft of the despatch. The much argued proposal was the appointment of an Indian, and besides the arguments, which had been already discussed at length, a new argument was raised that a membership of the Council was a perquisite of Indian Civil Servants, and that 'such an appointment would practically be

[8] Minto to Morley, 2, 23 January 1907. Telegram, 17 February 1907. *M.P.*
[9] Morley to Minto, telegram, 18 February 1907; letter, 22 February 1907. In a letter dated 1 March 1907 Godley explained to Minto that in case of a majority of his Council being against the proposal of an Indian member, he must remember the case when, in 1882-3, Ripon sent a despatch about the Ecclesiastical Establishment in India and he was in a minority of three, with five against him. The Secretary of State informed Ripon that that would not do, he could have over-ruled the majority decision. Ripon was asked to send another despatch. Thus Minto was warned that in case a majority of his Council were against him, would he be able to over-rule it? Godley further warned him that if a majority of his Council members and those of Morley's Council were against the proposal, Morley would be reluctant to accept it. *M.C.*
[1] Minto to Morley, 14 and 18 February 1907. Morley knew that his Council would also be against the Indian member. Morley to Minto, 28 February 1907. Ibid.
[2] Minto to Morley, telegram, 26 February 1907, letter, 27 February 1907. Ibid.

taking the bread out of their mouths'. One member[3] was of the view that 'he would not object to a native if he was a Civil Servant, whilst others maintained that the employment of natives in official capacities had already militated against the supply of candidates for the Civil Service whose parents did not approve of their coming to India on the chance of their having to serve under natives'; that India did not provide a young British officer with the type of society such an officer used to have, now that he had to associate with natives. Minto considered all these arguments 'narrow' and they produced a 'really melancholy' effect on his mind.[4] He tried to convince them of the changed times. The very fact that those members, who bitterly criticized the proposal, were anxious to remain anonymous suggests that in their heart of hearts they were convinced that they could not stem the tide of change, but they made their last effort to cling to the old traditions. This further shows how far advanced Minto was in his thinking as compared to the members of his Council. Morley wanted to have minutes of members for his secret personal guidance,[5] but Minto refused to comply with his request on the ground that the members did not want them to be conveyed to the Secretary of State. They did not want the Secretary of State to form an adverse opinion about them which might affect their careers.[6]

The members of the Viceroy's Council were not alone in opposing an Indian member, for some Indians did not look favourably upon the idea. Dunlop Smith in one of his notes narrates an interview with Babu Moti Lal Ghose, editor of the *Amrita Bazar Patrika,* who told him that he had heard a rumour

[3] Names of the members who objected could not be traced. These were not even divulged to Morley.

[4] See H. Adamson's letters to Minto, 12, 13 March 1907. Minto to Morley, 19 March 1907. M.C. Morley thought the argument that a native would diminish the 'perquisites' of the Civil Service 'disgusting, but thoroughly characteristic of all bureaucracies and Tchins all the world over'. Morley to Minto, 28 March 1907. Ibid.

[5] Morley to Minto, telegram, 27 March 1907. Ibid.

[6] Minto to Morley, telegrams, 29 March, 1 April 1907; letter, 28 March 1907. Ibid.

about an Indian's appointment to the Viceroy's Council. 'He [Ghose] said . . . that the agitators had never asked for this particular appointment, that they did not want it, that it would only result in friction, and that any Indian appointed to the post would have the life of a dog. He said he would be the subject of most terrific pressure from all sides and would make bitter enemies either of his own friends or of persons belonging to other religions. He said that the Indian newspapers would all say that this was a mere clever device to stop all agitation, as if Government brought in an unpopular measure they could always turn round and say it had been approved by their Indian colleague. He said the thing would be a sham, and he devoutly hoped it would not be carried out.'[7] Looking at this statement of Moti Lal Ghose, it seems that though some of his fears were justified most of them were based on misunderstanding of the proposal. But coming from a person of his calibre and standing, these views must have influenced Minto as well. The very fact that he passed this note to Morley suggests that Minto was conscious of public opinion in India with regard to his reform policy and was willing to give due consideration to the opinions of all shades of thought.

But the official opinion was gradually changing. Sir Andrew Fraser, the Lieutenant-Governor of Bengal, first thought the proposal for an Indian member premature, then agreed. Harcourt Butler, the Commissioner of Lucknow, wrote to Dunlop Smith, 'At this crisis a bold policy is usually the safest policy. You cannot say—there never shall be an Indian Member of the Council. The concession will be squeezed out if it is not given, and that soon. I would give it now while you have the opportunity of making many friends by doing so.'[8] Minto liked this argument and specially pointed it out to Morley. Other important officials were also beginning to think seriously of the matter.

Though only Minto and Baker supported the appointment of

---

[7] Note by Dunlop Smith, 15 March 1907. Attached with Minto's letter to Morley, 19 March 1907. *M.P.*

[8] Harcourt Butler to Dunlop Smith, 24 March 1907. Ibid.

an Indian member to the Viceroy's Council as yet, the Government of India suggested this proposal in their despatch of 21 March 1907 to the Secretary of State.[9] Minto also thought it advisable to inform the Legislative Council that a despatch explaining his views and those of his colleagues with regard to possible changes had been sent to the Secretary of State. He emphasized that he had thought it imperative that the 'initiative of possible reforms should emanate from us' to avoid any misunderstanding that the Government of India had failed to recognize 'the signs of the times' and that its hands had been forced by the Home Government. The Government of India had acted on their own conviction and it meant no submission to agitation either.[1]

While the Indian Press welcomed Minto's announcement of the Government despatch with regard to reform proposals being sent to Morley, the Anglo-Indian Press naturally showed some nervousness. A correspondent in a letter to the *Englishman* expressed the fear that the 'Great Possibilities' were nothing but 'to hand us up to the tender mercies of those English-speaking Babus' and he appealed to 'the English Press, the Anglo-Indian Defence Association and such other public bodies to stir themselves to protect us before it is too late'.[2] Minto thought it 'the first shot in the campaign and a good indication of the sort of thing we may expect,' but he had decided to brave the storm.[3]

Now it was Morley's turn to gather public opinion in England with regard to the reform scheme. Like Minto he consulted important members of his Council and other Anglo-Indians.

[9] Government of India to the Secretary of State. Public Letter No. 7 of 1907, 21 March 1907. *India Public Letters*, 1907, vol. xxxv. The proposal of an Indian member was opposed by Ibbetson, the Lt.-Governor of the Punjab; Sir J. Hewett, Lt.-Governor of U.P.; Lord Lamington, Governor of Bombay, and Sir Arthur Lawley, Governor of Madras; Kitchener, H. Erle Richards, Major-General Scott, H. Adamson, J. F. Finlay and J. O. Miller—all members of the Viceroy's Council.

[1] Minto's speech in the Legislative Council, 27 March 1907. *Speeches by Earl Minto* (Calcutta, 1911), p. 124.

[2] The *Englishman*, 1 April 1907. See also *Native Newspaper Reports*, 1907.

[3] Minto to Morley, 2 April 1907. *M.P.*

Sir Henry Fowler, Theodore Morison and Lord Lansdowne were opposed to the idea of an Indian member. Sir Bampfylde Fuller, Sir James La Touche and Sir Courtney Ilbert were in favour of the reforms and the Indian member.[4] Lord Lansdowne was strongly opposed to the Indian member and he even wrote to Minto that 'I am a little perturbed by a rumour which reaches me that you have some idea of admitting a native or natives to the Executive Council. That seems to me a formidable innovation.' According to him the proposal had two serious objections. First, such an appointment would satisfy only the community to whom the member would belong; second, it might be difficult to find a trustworthy Indian to whom the secrets could be confined. His suggestion, therefore, was that instead of an Indian member of the Council, there should be appointed some Committees on whom more prominence should be given to Indians.[5]

Morley appointed a small committee of his Council to consider the Government of India's proposals. The Committee rejected the proposal of an Indian member, but hoped that eventually an Indian member of the Indian Civil Service might be appointed. Even Ripon and Elgin objected to the Indian member for secrecy reasons. This opposition to the Indian member really worried Morley and he asked Minto whether it would be possible to keep secret that that proposal had ever been made and that Minto supported it and if not, what effects would it have.[6]

Minto rejected the suggestion that an Indian member of the Indian Civil Service might eventually be appointed. This, he thought, was 'the very worst reasoning of the opposition'. It meant that only members of the Civil Service could qualify for that appointment. This contention would be angrily attacked by non-official English as well as by the Indians. 'Moreover the Indian of the Civil Service is not the man we want and no one knows it better than the Service itself. The class of Indian that should be useful to us would not join the Civil Service and the

[4] Morley to Minto, 17, 26 April 1907. *M.P.*
[5] Lord Lansdowne to Minto, 21 April 1907. *M.C.*
[6] Morley to Minto, telegram, 16 April 1907; letters, 12, 26 April 1907. Ibid.

Europeanizing effect of its early training and the home political associations it seems likely to encourage will not tend to produce the high-class Indian gentleman whose assistance we should I think enlist.' He made it clear as well that it would not be possible to keep it a secret that such a proposal had been made or that he supported it. He realized that now he had made up his mind to recommend the appointment of an Indian to his Council, it would be impolitic to go back on it. A large number of people had already known it and if he shrank from it now, it would be considered a weakness on his part. It might weaken his position before Indian eyes. He, however, felt that if he insisted Morley would come round to his proposal. The effect of all this on his position, Minto wrote, would be that 'Anglo-Indian opinion would be divided into two camps agreeing and disagreeing with me and that I should be violently attacked by the latter both here and at home.' If the Indian was appointed the opposition would die down, otherwise there would be a tremendous revival of agitation which would be joined by moderate Indians. His view was that 'notwithstanding the forces ranged against us I think we must fight.'[7] He was willing 'to stand the shot'; and emphatically said that 'it is time to overrule bureaucracy, and that though we shall be bitterly attacked at first, feeling would subside before long, whilst British administration would gain in strength and in popular confidence.'[8]

Minto had to clear away another misunderstanding. Morison and others, whose opinions Morley had communicated to him, thought that it was a concession to the Congress demands. Minto made it clear that 'we do not want a Congress wallah or leader of opposition, but a representative of moderate Indian thought, who would assist us in dealing with extremists and in many native questions, as to which we are now dangerously out of touch.'[9] He was more emphatic in his letter, 'Really the ideas people get into their heads are marvellous. Scarcely anyone seems

[7] Minto to Morley, 17, 25 April 1907. *M.P.*
[8] Minto to Morley, telegram, 19 April 1907. Ibid.
[9] Minto to Morley, telegram, 29 April 1907. Ibid.

to suppose that the very object of suggesting a Native Member is as a counterpoise to extreme Congress doctrines. Scarcely anyone seems to imagine that there is such a thing as an Indian of moderate political views loyal to British rule. Mere possession of political views at all is apparently assumed to indicate disloyalty.'[1] Minto clearly explained that his aim in insisting on an Indian for his Council or Constitutional reforms was not a concession to Congress demands. He genuinely felt that the legitimate demands of moderate Indians must be sympathetically considered and met. He believed firmly that India was perfectly unfit for representative government and must be autocratically ruled for many years to come, yet 'that ought not, in my opinion, to prevent her best men from sharing more largely than they do at present in the executive administration of the country'.[2]

Minto strongly repudiated the objection with regard to secrecy. These arguments never seemed to him to hold water. 'This very letter I am writing you will pass through many Native hands in my office before it reaches you, and so does every State secret in India that is once committed in print. The Government Printing Presses are full of Natives. I am far from saying secrets do not get out. The issue of the warrant for the arrest of Lajpat Rai is said to have been known in the bazaar here long before it was executed,[3] and one cannot reasonably doubt that any State secret would be far more likely to be kept by a Native Member of Council whose known integrity would be one of his first qualifications than by the numerous irresponsible Native Clerks through whose hands State papers of the greatest importance pass.'[4]

Minto fully recognized the weight of the opposition to the Indian Member; but he had made up his mind to face it.[5] And

[1] Minto to Morley, 2 May 1907. *M.P.*

[2] Minto to Morley, 8 May 1907, telegram, 6 May 1907. Ibid.

[3] Lajpat Rai, in his *The Story of My Deportation* (Lahore, 1908), pp. 22–30, testifies that he himself knew about his warrant of arrest before it was executed.

[4] Minto to Morley, 21 May 1907. *M.P.*

[5] Minto to Morley, 8 May 1907. Ibid.

even Morley's announcement that the Cabinet also did not like it[6] did not deter him from the decision he had taken. Yet Morley thought 'the possible gain' was 'not worth the risk', though he admitted that the policy was 'wholly defensible'. He was sure that 'if European opinion would have stood it, the effect on Indian opinion would be in the highest degree and sense conciliatory'. But he was afraid that the Government would have found difficulty in legislation of which most of Minto's Council and all of his would have strongly disapproved. He further regarded the risk of an Ilbert Bill explosion as too grave to be faced.[7] Moreover there were no legal limitations of appointing any Indian to the Viceroy's Executive Council, if there arose any need of it. Since it was not essential to pass an Act of Parliament for appointing an Indian to the Viceroy's Council, this proposal was dropped from the Secretary of State's Despatch.[8]

Morley's assurance that there was no legal bar to the appointment of an Indian and it was not essential to pass an Act calmed Minto but did not satisfy him. With a view to showing how intensely he felt about it, Minto wrote to Morley that he agreed with him in his doubts that 'with the combined forces here and at home against us and certainly in the conditions of the present movement I doubt if we should have been justified in giving battle. At the same time I hope my suggestion will let in a ray of light, and that before very long India may recognize the dawn of a new day.'[9]

While this correspondence was going on the situation in the

[6] (a) Morley to Minto, telegram, 3 May 1907; letter, 3 May 1907. *M.P.*
(b) In a letter to Lady Minto, Minto wrote that Morley was 'doubtful as to over-ruling the opposition' to the Indian member. He expressed the fear that if Morley did not overrule the opposition, 'then I shall be in a position of having been overruled, and I shall be "overruled" and "abused" simultaneously'. Mary, Countess of Minto, op. cit. p. 119.
[7] Morley to Minto, 16, 17 May 1907. *M.P.*
[8] Secretary of State to the Government of India, 17 May 1907. Public Despatch No. 71, paras. 17–18. *Public Despatches*, 1907, vol. xxviii. 'This proposal in its purpose involves no material innovation either in law or principle.'
[9] Minto to Morley, 21 May 1907. *M.P.*

Punjab and Eastern Bengal and Assam worsened. There were riots and the Government had to take strict measures. This 'crisis' could have affected Minto's zeal for reform, but he became more emphatic. His opinions remained the same. Though he admitted recent events, that had accentuated 'European nervousness in respect to the possible aggrandizement of native political power'; and the impressions he had formed from the various letters from home, had made people in England more apprehensive than in India. He stuck to his point that opposition to the Indian member in India would be confined to the official ranks and there was no fear of a revival of the excitement that prevailed at the time of the Ilbert Bill. He frankly told Morley that 'the retired Viceroys in England and Members of your Council, though in a less degree, cannot keep pace with the general move forward of Indian public opinion.'[1]

The correspondence between these two shows that Minto had more courage and persistence than Morley. Minto it was who would have faced the real storm of Anglo-Indian opposition in India against this proposal for an Indian member. Similarly, Morley, right from the beginning, knew that the Conservative forces in England were quite powerful: the House of Lords, the Anglo-Indians and above all the King, who opposed the appointment till the last minute, were against such a step. He genuinely wanted to do something, but he had to consider his own position: but his position despite these handicaps was not as serious as that of Minto. Minto had to face the consequences of the new policy. Morley had only to learn it from the despatches, newspaper reports and private letters. Morley admitted to Lady Minto that though he meant to support Minto's suggestion manfully he was worried concerning its reception by the country. He could have dropped the idea altogether but then there was the fear of the House of Commons, who would have said, 'Here is a Liberal Secretary of State refusing to go as far as the Viceroy who is not a pronounced Liberal.' He was afraid that the radical members of the House of Commons as well as the members of the Indian

[1] Minto to Morley, 5 June 1907. *M.P.*

Committee of the House would be critical of his policy. That was why he enquired from Minto if the proposal and that the Viceroy had supported it could be kept a secret. He, however, declared that 'before I retire this measure will have to be brought forward for good or ill', and in his usual way, said, 'Mind you, it might lead to incurable evils.'[2] Minto's courage and boldness to stand up to it put heart into Morley and the policy was ultimately carried out. Slackness on Minto's part might have changed the course of events.

On 6 June 1907 Morley briefly announced in the House of Commons the Government of India's proposals and his reply to them. Though he did mention that he intended to appoint one or more Indians to his Council, he omitted any reference to an Indian on the Viceroy's Council.[3] Morley stated that the Secretary of State 'may safely, wisely and justly nominate one, and it may be two, Indian members to his Council'. But he did not secure a favourable reception for this proposal either. Earl Percy thought that this proposal had some advantages as the Secretary of State would have 'a readier access to the opinions of those who would look at Indian questions from a somewhat different standpoint from those who form the large majority of his Council'. But he saw two practical difficulties. First the present number of the Council did not permit any addition and second it might not be possible to induce the right type of men to abandon their professional career in India to serve on the Council in England for five or ten years.[4] Dr. V. H. Rutherford thought the policy of reform was a step in the right direction. India had been waiting for it for a long time. His objection was that 'it was neither wide nor extensive'. However, he saw in it 'the opening of the door to better things'.[5] There were a number of people in England who were extremely critical of Morley's decision to appoint an Indian to his Council. Sir Austen Chamberlain had many an argument

[2] Mary, Countess of Minto, op. cit., p. 116.
[3] *Hansard*, House of Commons, 4S, vol. 175 (30 May–13 June 1907), 6 June 1907, Cols. 883–5.
[4] Ibid. Cols. 892–3.
[5] Ibid. Col. 913.

with Morley.[6] Minto, who had at one time been sceptical, on the other hand, welcomed the idea. When Morley informed him of his decision to appoint K. G. Gupta, I.C.S., of the Revenue Department, and S. H. Bilgrami, at that time in the Nizam of Hyderabad's service, to his Council, he immediately sent his approval.[7] In order to implement this decision Morley introduced a bill in Parliament to amend the constitution of the India Council, which became an Act on 28 August 1907. Gupta and Bilgrami were nominated to the Council.[8] While Morley thought these appointments 'a great move',[9] his choice of persons was not approved by even the moderate Congress newspapers. It was thought that both these gentlemen would adopt the civil service point of view.[1] The *Hindustan Review* suggested that these appointments were no encouragement to the Congress and that the aim of the Government was to rally the bureaucrats and thus hoodwink the real Indian representatives. It was like giving with the right hand and taking with the left. Surprise was also expressed at the necessity for passing an Act for such appointments. It was suggested that the Act was passed so that no Anglo-Indian might be called upon to surrender his seat to an Indian.[2] R. C. Dutt did not like the choice of these two, as he told Morley later on. Morley, however, remarked that 'I could only rejoice that other people, and very likely himself [Dutt] also, would have said just the same thing of any other Indian brace on whom I might have laid my hands.'[3] Minto reported that the Muslims

---

[6] Sir Austen Chamberlain, *Politics from Inside: An Epistolary Chronicle, 1906-1914* (London, 1936).

[7] Minto to Morley, 31 July 1907. *M.P.*

[8] Bilgrami took up his appointment on 11 November 1907 and Gupta on 9 March 1908.

[9] Morley to Minto, 18 July 1907. *M.P.* See also Morley's *Recollections,* vol. ii, p. 228.

[1] The *Behari,* Calcutta, 23 August 1907; the *Bengalee,* 31 August, 1 September 1907; the *Indian Mirror,* 1 September 1907; the *Indian Empire,* 1 September 1907; the *Hindu Patriot,* 3 September 1907; the *Amrita Bazar Patrika,* 4 September 1907. See *B.N.N.R.,* 1907.

[2] The *Hindustan Review,* September 1907, pp. 285-6.

[3] Morley to Minto, 21 May 1908. *M.P.*

had welcomed the appointment of Bilgrami and that he had received numerous telegrams from them, but that the Hindus had not done so.[4]

It was on Minto's suggestion that the Government of India made public the circular issued to the Local Governments on 24 August 1907 for their views and comments. Minto was very anxious to take the Indian public into their confidence.[5] He considered 'the criticism on our reforms', which had begun to appear in the newspapers, 'on the whole very satisfactory'.[6]

Minto had not forgotten the possibility of appointing an Indian to his Council. He again wrote to Morley about the importance of such an appointment and stated that he was not afraid of the personal criticism with which he would have been attacked if such a step had been taken. But he could wait and recollected an old racing motto—'wait in front'—meaning that one should not do too much running, but always be in the place from which one could win if one wanted to.[7] Morley replied, 'you refer to an Indian Member on your Council, by way of a case where you were bold, and I was less bold. The illustration is perfectly fair . . . I do believe if a vacancy should occur on your Council when I am in office, you shall have an Indian. I am in excellent hopes of turning out well on the Council here.'[8] But the matter remained hanging till Minto again wrote on 29 January 1908 and praised Dr. A. Mukerji. On 26 March 1908, Morley enquired from Minto if there was any Indian to fill the post of Finance Member. He admitted that 'I sometimes blame myself for defect of energy in carrying on this part of our policy—the promotion of Natives. *You* cleared yourself of any such defect by the fight you made for an Indian Member in the first draft of your Reforms, though I still hold that, at that period, neither you nor I was strong enough in public confidence to face the popular

[4] A large number of telegrams were received by the Governor-General from the Muslims. See *Public Letters from India*, 1908, vol. xxxvi.

[5] Minto to Morley, 12 June 1907. *M.P.*

[6] Minto to Morley, 29 August, 4 September 1907. Ibid.

[7] Minto to Morley, 9 October 1907. Ibid.

[8] Morley to Minto, 31 October 1907. Ibid.

outcry either in India or from the Tory opposition here. Now things are different. People have learned that we both of us know what we are about; and, without saying that we can do what we like, I am persuaded that anything we like to do, will stand a very good chance of securing all the assent we need.'[9] Despite all these expressions of confidence, the position, as later events were to show, was not as favourable as to secure 'all the assent we need.' Morley was conscious of it. His policy was to mark time and wait for the opportune moment. Minto's insistence continued. On 17 June 1908, he informed Morley that in his discussions with H. H. Risley 'a possible candidate occurred to us in Sinha, the new Advocate-General . . .' and in his subsequent letters he continued his pressure on Morley. Harvey Adamson, the Home Member, had been converted to a belief in the advantages of an Indian member on the Council. Now was the chance to appoint somebody to succeed Erle Richards, the retiring Law Member. Minto thought that either Sinha or Mukerji would do.[1] On 10 August 1908 Morley wrote, 'you need not fear that I shall be deterred from putting an Indian on to your Council, by anything that may be said or done *here*. I shrank from seeking a *bill* last year, because a *bill* against a man in Lansdowne's position, might have proved an awkward and tiresome affair. But my executive competence to fill a vacancy by an Indian will be undisputed, because law gives that power clearly.'[2] Morley, nevertheless, remained unsure and indecisive. On 3 September 1908, he wrote that he had been thinking about the possibility of a law member. There was one advantage. It would not take 'the bread out of the mouth of the Indian Civil Service', but the Congress might object to this exclusive appointment. Why should he not be given some other department, Finance, Commerce or Home?[3] Minto informed Morley that it would be a flimsy objection, for all departments were open to Indians. What they were trying to

[9] Morley to Minto, 26 March 1908. *M.P.*
[1] Minto to Morley, 17 June, 1, 14, 21 July, 12 August 1908. Ibid.
[2] Morley to Minto, 10 August 1908. Ibid.
[3] Morley to Minto, 3 September 1908. Ibid.

do at the moment was to appoint an Indian to the department he was best suited to handle. It was not supposed to be a racial appointment, but the inauguration of a principle that an Indian might not be debarred from holding an office, for which he was suitable, simply because he was an Indian. Under the Queen's Declaration of 1858 all offices were open to Indians, but in practice they were deprived of most of these offices. In the past years they had acquired great prominence in the legal profession. So in Minto's opinion Law Membership was the most suitable post for an Indian.[4]

Since all these points pertaining to the reform scheme were discussed in their private correspondence, Minto thought it advisable to send Morley privately a brief outline of the reforms he would like before the Government of India's Reform Despatch reached him. In this outline, which was purely for Morley, he mentioned the appointment of an Indian to his Executive Council,[5] though such a suggestion was not made in the despatch. On the receipt of the Government of India's despatch of 1 October 1908, Morley appointed a committee of his Council to consider the proposals. It consisted of Sir David Barr, chairman, and Lord MacDonnell, Sir James La Touche, Sir James Thomson, Sir Lawrence Jenkins, K. G. Gupta, Sir Walter Lawrence and S. H. Bilgrami. His committee was, as he himself said, 'a very strong one'. MacDonnell and La Touche had had uncommonly wide experience of provincial administration. Jenkins had 'a well-trained judicial mind'; Bilgrami and Gupta were Muslim and Hindu representatives, Lawrence had had 'an inside view of Simla' and Sir James Thomson was a Madras man.[6] He was also conscious that the subject was grave and that it was important to keep in step with Minto. Moreover 'to present a front that won't offend the Bureaucracy; nor the non-official Anglo-Indian, nor the Mohammedans, nor the right wing of the Congressmen, is no joke'.[7] But the committee submitted its report on 5 October

[4] Minto to Morley, 24 September 1908 and subsequent letters. *M.P.*
[5] Minto to Morley, 12 August 1908. Ibid.
[6] Morley to Minto, 1 October 1908. Ibid.
[7] Morley to Minto, 5 November 1908. Ibid.

1908. The India Council deliberated on it and the proposals were passed by the Cabinet, which 'took the thing on trust, having rather urgent business of much domestic moment on their hands'.[8]

The committee had rejected by five votes to three the proposal for an Indian member on the Viceroy's Council. Bilgrami voted against and Gupta in favour of the proposal.[9] Minto objected to this reference to Morley's committee. It had long been assumed that there was no need to pass any law and the matter rested with the Secretary of State and the Viceroy to find and appoint any Indian capable of holding such office. Morley's reference to his committee, thus, was most surprising.[1] But Morley was trying to get moral support for his subsequent announcement in Parliament.[2] On 27 November 1908 the Secretary of State's despatch was on its way to India.

On 17 December 1908 Morley announced in Parliament his intention to appoint an Indian to the Viceroy's Executive Council in the event of a vacancy. He admitted that 'if it were on my own authority only I might hesitate to take that step, because I am not very fond of innovations in dark and obscure ground, but here I have the absolute and the zealous approval and concurrence of Lord Minto himself.'[3] But this announcement was met with opposition both inside and outside the House of Lords. The Marquess of Lansdowne opposed it and stated that it was 'a tremendous innovation' and 'ought not to be introduced until Parliament had had full opportunity of discussing the Government scheme in all its completeness'. He was not convinced with the argument that it would be advantageous to have on the

[8] Morley to Minto, 27 November 1908. *M.P.*

[9] Morley to Minto, 14, 16 October 1908. *M.C.*

[1] Minto to Morley, 29 October 1908. Ibid.

[2] Morley to Minto, 19 November 1908. '... you speak about the Indian member for your Council. I only put it to my council, because I like to collect as many opinions as possible, without feeling myself in any degree *bound* by them. It will fortify me against hostile views in London. About the thing itself, I am quite fixed. Here my two Indians have made far less indifference, either way, than I used to expect ...' Ibid.

[3] *Hansard*, House of Lords, 4S, vol. 198, 1908, Cols. 1985–6.

Viceroy's Council a member who knew the country. He asked Morley 'what country? There are a great many countries in India. If the noble Viscount could discover a native gentleman who knew the whole of the Indian Empire, and could speak authoritatively on behalf of all the different races and creeds concerned, I should say by all means give him a place on the Viceroy's Council . . .'[4] Lord MacDonnell, who was a member of Morley's Reform Committee, agreed with Lansdowne and pointed out the vastness of the Empire and racial differences.[5] This presented Morley with the situation he feared, but by now he had built up enough courage to face the storm as he wrote to Minto, 'It is lucky that my appointment of an Indian member on your Executive Council does not need parliamentary sanction, for I don't believe the House of Lords would agree'.[6]

The Government's intentions were now clear. An Indian would soon be appointed to the Executive Council. Who could that be? A Hindu or a Muslim? Ameer Ali, President of the London Branch of the League met Morley to find it out and put forward the League's point of view. A deputation of the League's London Branch also waited upon Morley in January 1909 and demanded an equal share for the Muslims. But Morley refused their plea and explained that no other qualification but personal fitness would be considered in appointing an Indian to the Executive Council.[7]

There was another reason for Morley's concern. He had an audience with King Edward, who expressed his anxiety over Morley's proposed appointment of an Indian to the Viceroy's

[4] Ibid. Cols. 1995-6. Minto exerted all his influence in pleading for an Indian member with Lansdowne—Minto to Lansdowne, 21 January 1909. M.C.

[5] *Hansard*, House of Lords, 4S, vol. 198, 1908, Col. 1997.

[6] Morley to Minto, 21 January 1909. M.P. Morley respected Sir Alfred Lyall's suggestions and always sought refuge in his advice: '. . . the one man to whom I must look for counsel in decisions of real moment—Alfred Lyall, the friend of a lifetime—entirely approves, though characteristically his eyes are wide open to drawbacks. So are mine, but it has to be done.' See also Sir Mortimer Durand, *Life of the Right Hon. Sir Alfred Comyn Lyall* (London, 1913), p. 428.

[7] Address of the deputation and Morley's reply. M.P.

Council. Morley thought that MacDonnell had influenced the King.[8] In the beginning Morley had very friendly relations with MacDonnell and it was he who influenced Morley to insert the Electoral Colleges scheme into his despatch, but soon they fell apart, so much so that he called MacDonnell 'a hard-mouthed brute'.[9] Moreover Godley suggested another influence on the King. Sir Walter Lawrence had wanted to join the P. & O. as director, but Morley had not permitted him to do so. He resigned from the Indian Council and stated that he did not agree with Morley's policy with regard to the Native member. Since he was a frequent visitor to Marlborough House, he might have influenced the King against the scheme.[1] Minto tried to encourage Morley by saying that all those people who were opposing this appointment were old Anglo-Indians with no knowledge of the present condition in India, and even pleaded with the King who, when the time came, gave his sanction 'reluctantly'.[2]

Though the appointment of an Indian had almost become certain,[3] irrespective of the opposition by the Lords and the King's dislike, some of the members of the Viceroy's Council still opposed it. Lord Kitchener kept silent, but General Scott, Military Member, opposed it on grounds of secrecy. But it was Fleetwood Wilson who 'with a fine old British obstinacy'

[8] Morley to Minto, 12 January 1909. *M.P.* See also Morley to Minto, 12 March 1909. *Recollections*, vol. ii, p. 302.

[9] Sir Arthur Bigge to Minto, 11 March 1909. *M.C.* Morley to Minto, 18 December 1908. *M.P.*

[1] Morley to Minto, 5 March 1909; Godley to Minto, 5 March 1909, see Minto's reply, 25 March 1909. *M.C.*

[2] See Minto's letters to Morley and to the King. Minto assured the King that the appointment would really mean the removal of racial disability in case of an Indian possessing the necessary qualifications and it was in no way intended to satisfy a claim for racial representation. These letters must have done tremendous good to allay the King's fears. Ibid. The Prince of Wales also expressed his fears to Minto with regard to the appointment of an Indian —26 January 1909. Minto assured him as well. Ibid.

[3] Godley to Minto, 22 January 1909. Ibid. '. . . his [Morley's] performance on this particular subject [appointment of an Indian to the Viceroy's Executive Council] was so clear and decided that any one who heard, or had read, his speech, must know that it is a settled thing.'

declared 'that an Indian Colleague would be the admission of the thin end of the wedge which is to bring about the downfall of British administration'.[4]

It is interesting to note how the candidate was ultimately chosen. Minto personally liked Dr. A. Mukerji and pressed for his appointment to his Council; but when Sinha's name was proposed to him, it was impressed upon him that Sinha stood high in public estimation because of his professional skill and ability. Besides, Sinha and his family were more in touch with European society. Being a barrister, his appointment to the Council would require no legislation, and the upward step from Advocate-General would not seem unnatural. Minto wanted to take the line of least resistance in making this great change. 'Moreover please do not think me terribly narrow but Sinha is comparatively white, whilst Mukherji is as black as my hat! and opposition in the official world would not be regardless of mere shades of colour,' Minto wrote to Morley.[5] Hence Sinha was appointed on 23 March 1909. His appointment was generally welcomed; even the Muslim League did not object much, though it was disappointed that a Muslim had not been appointed. But the Muslims had been assured that a Muslim's turn would come in due course, and Sinha's successor was actually a Muslim, Syed Ali Imam. Minto and Morley were surprised that there was no voice raised against Sinha's appointment.[6] The surprise is

[4] Minto to Morley, 4 March 1909. *M.C.*

[5] Minto to Morley, 9 November 1908. *M.P.*

[6] Morley to Minto, 25 March 1909: 'So far,—that is to say, twenty-four hours after the event—the launch of the Indian member had produced no shock. *The Times* . . . shakes it head a little solemnly, but without scare . . .' Morley to Minto, 15 April 1909: 'It rejoices me that Sinha has produced no Anglo-Indian storm. You were evidently most right in declining to believe that the fuss would be violent; so much is certain, and is to be counted to your credit. You ask whether the King said anything about your letter to him. No, he did not. And I half gather that you suppose his "approval" meant that he approved in other than a formal sense. Not in the least. His last word was a definite "protest" to me against the whole thing, coupled with a pious hope that the Almighty might perhaps prevent mischief—with the pretty plain implication that the divine powers would do nothing of the sort. Whether my last letter, enclosing the formal submission, melted the spirit of "protest" away, I have

understandable because they had entertained enormous fears. Minto had had a tough fight in securing the appointment and Morley had encountered bitter opposition from the Conservative section in British political life and the old Anglo-Indians.[7]

But the appointment of an Indian to the Executive Council was not the only proposal which Minto had asked the Arundel Committee to consider to meet the nationalist demands. They had to consider advisability of a Council of Princes, increased Indian representation on the Viceroy's and Provincial Legislative Councils, prolongation of the budget debates and procedure as to presentation of the budget and powers of moving amendments.[8] The Committee realized the advantages of a Council of Princes, but was not prepared to recommend a formal constitution or any definite public pronouncement at that stage. It was not a new proposal. Lord Lytton in 1877 had thought of a Privy Council of Ruling Princes. Though the scheme was rejected by the Secretary of State, titular Counsellors from amongst the Chiefs were appointed. Curzon also wanted a Council of Princes—which, in the Committee's eyes, was 'too narrow and would prove ineffectual in practice'. Its suggestion, therefore, was that 'it would be desirable for the Viceroy to summon for purposes of consultation selected chiefs from time to time to discuss particular subjects, and on occasions to associate with them leading landholders from British territory, whose high status would justify their

---

no means of knowing for the submissions come back with no word beyond the single talismanic sign inscribed upon it.' But to Minto the King wrote: 'I unwillingly assent, but wish that my protest should remain on record.' King Edward VII to Minto, 22 March 1909. *M.C.*

[7] Morley never forgot this opposition. When Sinha wanted to resign from the post for private reasons, he refused to grant him permission as he thought that his resignation would be misunderstood and dubbed as the failure of their policy. When Sinha ultimately did resign, Morley refused to put his name on the list of honour which Minto had sent, because he was very angry with Sinha. Minto even approached Sir A. Bigge, the King's private secretary, to get Sinha's name included in the list. Minto to Sir A. Bigge, 20 December 1910. Ibid.

[8] Minto's Minute to the Arundel Committee. *M.P.*

admission'. Ibbetson did not concur wholly in this recommendation. He realized the importance of enlisting on the side of the
Government the conservative elements as a counterpoise to the
advanced party, and he accepted the idea of an Advisory Council,
but not a Council of Chiefs. He would make it a Council selected
from among the Indian aristocracy and great landowners of
India, on which the chiefs would be represented in some such
proportion, say, as six chiefs in a Council of thirty. He thought a
Council of Chiefs would be politically dangerous as very soon
they would exhaust the topics for discussion and their bringing
together might lead to their political union.[9]

The Government of India, however, suggested a Council of
Princes to the Secretary of State, though the members of the
Viceroy's Executive Council were not unanimous on points of
detail. They were at one in holding that the idea of associating
the Indian aristocracy with the Government of India was one
that contained great promise and ought not to be abandoned.[1]
Morley did not like this proposal and informed Minto that Lord
Ripon and Sir A. Lyall were 'provisionally' adverse to the scheme
and Sir Charles Elliot, ex-Lieutenant-Governor of Bengal,
'pretty entirely adverse'.[2] But Morley's reform committee agreed
with the suggestion of a Council of Notables with an increased
number of territorial magnates. Morley, however, did not much
appreciate the idea of a Council of Princes. The main purpose of
setting up any Council was to elicit public opinion on administrative measures, and also to afford the Government adequate
facilities to explain their measures and policies to the people.
For that purpose a Council of Princes was not enough. Morley,
however, concurred in the general line of the scheme and considered the Advisory Councils more advantageous. But he was
doubtful about the utility of the Councils, as proposed by the
Government of India, because much weight was cast in the direc-

[9] The Arundel Committee's Report, op. cit.
[1] Government of India to the Secretary of State. Public Letter No. 7, 21
March 1907. *India Public Letters*, 1907, vol. xxxv.
[2] Morley to Minto, 28 March, 4 April 1907. *M.P.*

tion of enlisting the advice of the nobles and great landholders. Nevertheless he left the matter open for further discussions with the Local Governments.[3]

The Government of India in their circular letter to the Local Governments dropped the proposal of a Council of Princes but instead asked their opinion on Imperial and Provincial Advisory Councils.[4] Minto, like Morley, was doubtful as to the reaction of the ruling chiefs towards the idea of sitting with other representatives. The opinions of the Local Governments were not due till 1 March 1908, and were actually received even later than that. Minto, in the meanwhile, started collecting information regarding the views of the Indian Princes. The Nizam of Hyderabad and the Gaekwad of Baroda had already refused to sit with minor princes, while the Maharaja of Mysore was lukewarm.[5] The general attitude of the ruling chiefs towards this proposal, which Minto had ascertained, gave him a feeling that they did not want anybody else besides themselves on such an assembly. Minto also suspected that the political officers were prompting these Ruling Chiefs, because in the event of their coming together and having a direct contact with the Viceroy, the importance of the political officers would be diminished.[6]

Morley, in his despatch of 27 May 1907, had hinted that he was willing to consider the proposal of Advisory Councils for the Central and Provincial Governments. The Local Governments did not like it; nor did Minto like it. 'I have never liked Advisory Councils, but swallowed them in the shape we have submitted them to you for the sake of showing a united front here, which I considered very important.'[7] The opinions of Local Governments on the advantages of an Advisory Council were divided. The Lieutenant-Governors of Bengal, the United Provinces, Burma

---

[3] Secretary of State to Government of India. Despatch No. 71, 17 May 1907. *Public Despatches,* 1907, vol. xxviii, paras. 8–12.

[4] Government of India to Local Governments, circular letters nos. 2310–17, dated 24 August 1907. *Public Letters from India,* 1908, vol. xxxvii, paras. 4–7.

[5] Minto to Morley, 14 November 1907. *M.P.*

[6] Minto to Morley, 26 December 1907. Ibid.

[7] Minto to Morley, 14 October 1908. Ibid.

and Eastern Bengal and Assam generally approved the scheme. The Lieutenant-Governor of the Punjab was opposed to a mixed Council and so was the Chief Commissioner of the Central Provinces. The Governor of Madras was wholly adverse; the Governor of Bombay agreed with the principle involved but demurred to the combination of chiefs and territorial magnates. The main objections were that Ruling Chiefs would not sit with subjects of the British Government; that they had no knowledge of the conditions of British India and so would be useless in either advising the Government or diffusing information to the people. Territorial magnates were out of touch with the people and their interests were adverse to those of the great body of agriculturists. Thus their association would also serve no purpose. There were objections as to the powers and functions of this Council. Since it would have no legal recognition and formal powers, the Government would be under no obligation to consult it or be guided by its advice. It was also doubtful if its views would command the same respect as that commanded by the views of the elected members of the Legislative Council.[8] Thus the Government of India suggested the abandonment of the idea of the Imperial Advisory Council, but substituted for it that of the Council of Princes.[9]

[8] Replies of the Local Governments:
Government of E.B. & A. to Government of India, No. 9460, dated 14 March 1908, para. 13.
Government of Bengal to Government of India, No. 1746A, dated 29 February 1908, paras. 3–11.
Government of U.P. to Government of India, No. 447, dated 16 March 1908, paras. 4–9.
Government of Burma to Government of India, No. 860, dated 24 February 1908, paras. 4–5.
Government of Punjab to Government of India, No. 40, dated 6 July 1908, paras. 6–20.
Government of Madras to Government of India, No. 222, dated 13 March 1908, para. 5.
Government of Bombay to Government of India, No. 1768, dated 28 March 1908, paras. 5–10. *Public Letters from India*, 1908, vol. xxxvii.
[9] Government of India to the Secretary of State, 1 October 1908, paras. 6–8. Ibid.

Minto personally and the Government of India generally seem to have been influenced in dropping the proposal of an Imperial Advisory Council by the opinions of the Local Governments, prominent Indians and Indian associations. They had invariably expressed their doubts and suspicions with regard to its composition, functions and powers.[1] So he reverted to his original proposal of 'a Council of Princes, small in number to begin with, to deal with questions affecting Native States and their relations with British India, for the express purpose of recognizing the loyalty of Ruling Chiefs and enlisting their interest in Imperial affairs'.[2]

Morley accepted the rejection of the proposal of an Imperial Advisory Council, but doubted the necessity of a Council of Princes. This proposal was also full of insurmountable difficulties and though he refrained from placing 'any obstacle in the way of a full and fair trial' he was not very sympathetic to it, because he thought a Council of Princes would serve no useful purpose. He explained to Minto that the matter had been left open in deference to his views.[3] Minto, however, soon made up his mind and wrote to Morley that 'I think after all it is wiser to drop it [Council of Chiefs]'.[4]

Similarly after careful consideration the proposal of the Advisory Councils for Provinces was dropped. Because Morley thought that the creation of Provincial Advisory Councils was not 'likely to prove an experiment of any marked actual value'. There was also the risk of a rivalry between these Councils and Legislative Councils and their creation might be suspected 'as designed to be a check upon the old'.[5]

---

[1] *Public Letters from India*, 1908, vol. xxxvii.

[2] Mary, Countess of Minto, op. cit., p. 214. Minto to Morley, 12 August 1908. *M.P.*

[3] Morley to Minto, telegram, 27 November 1908. Ibid. See also Secretary of State to the Government of India, No. 193, 27 November 1908. *Public Despatches*, 1908, vol. xxix.

[4] Minto to Morley, 5 December 1908. *M.P.*

[5] Secretary of State to the Government of India, 27 November 1908. *Public Despatches*, 1908, vol. xxix.

Along with the creation of new Advisory Councils, Minto and Morley were thinking of extending the existing Legislative Councils with an increase in members' powers. The Arundel Committee had suggested that between 1893 and 1906 the working of the elective principle had not justified the expectations that all the more important classes and interests should as far as possible be represented and that it had given a prominence to the legal profession to which it was not entitled. Its suggestion, therefore, was that special interests should be represented on the Viceroy's Legislative Council.[6] This suggestion was very near to Minto's heart. Quite early Minto had made up his mind that 'the only representation for which India is at present fitted is a representation of Communities, . . . and only to a very small extent in that direction'.[7] Morley did not disagree.

When in 1893 the Councils were enlarged and the elective principle was introduced it was recognized that territorial representation was not suitable to India, and an endeavour should be made to secure on them the representation of all the more important classes and interests. But the results had not justified the expectations, at least in two cases—the landholders and the Muslims.[8] Out of fifty-four members elected by the District Boards to the Provincial Councils only ten had been landholders while thirty-six had been barristers and pleaders. Similarly out of forty-three members elected by the District Municipalities forty had been barristers or pleaders and only two landholders. The Government had made an attempt to remedy the deficiency by nomination but out of the 338 non-official members who had been appointed, whether by election or nomination, to the Provincial Councils since 1893 as many as 123 or 36 per cent. had been lawyers and only 77 or 22 per cent. landowners. Thus it was clear that the elective system had given to the legal profession a great prominence in the Provincial Councils. The

[6] The Arundel Committee Report, op. cit.

[7] Minto to Morley, 23 January 1907. *M.P.* See also Mary, Countess of Minto, op. cit., p. 102.

[8] Questions relating to the representation of the Muslims have been discussed in Chapter 5.

Government was naturally concerned because 'the more stable elements of the community' had not been able to secure proper representation on its Councils. The landholders had shown their dislike for standing against anyone lower than them in social position for election because of their pride and prestige. The Government of India, therefore, suggested to Morley that without denying the due share to the professional classes, they intended to create an additional electorate for the landed and moneyed classes. The reason for this suggestion was that though the number of these professional classes was small, their influence was large and the Government was not willing to allow them a virtual monopoly of the power exercised by the Councils. Thus the creation of this additional electorate was thought to be 'the soundest solution of the problem' as it would supply 'the requisite counterpoise' to the excessive influence of the professional classes.[9]

Morley agreed with the Government of India's views that the Legislative Councils in India should be enlarged and so constituted in respect of non-official members as to give due and ample representation to the different classes and interests of the community. With regard to the creation of an electorate for the landholders Morley stated that 'I have no difficulty in accepting your conclusion that the member elected to represent this class must himself belong to it.'[1] The matter was accordingly referred to the local Governments for further consideration.[2]

The Local Governments did not oppose the representation of the landed classes. The Government of Bengal, however, pointed out that it was wrong to assume that the lawyers did not at all represent the landed interests. On the contrary, many of them were themselves fairly large landowners. Some had intimate connexions with the landholders and owed their election largely to

[9] Government of India to the Secretary of State. Public Letter No. 7 of 1907, 21 March 1907, para. 43. *Public Letters, 1907*, vol. xxxv.
[1] Secretary of State to Government of India. Despatch No. 71, 17 May 1907, paras. 21–26. *Public Despatches, 1907*, vol. xxviii.
[2] Government of India's circular to Local Governments, 24 August 1907, paras. 9–14.

the support of that class.[3] The Government of the U.P. stated that in the U.P. far from the local bodies being dominated by the lawyers, the representatives elected by the district boards in the course of the last fourteen years had invariably been landholders. Similarly half of those elected by the municipalities had a substantial stake in the land. But it was also pointed out that the representation of the Muslims and the commercial interests other than those of the Upper India Chamber of Commerce had been inadequate.[4] On the whole the Local Governments agreed that the interests of the landed classes should be safeguarded in the new set-up.

The Bombay Presidency Association deplored the underlying policy—one of 'counterpoise' against the influence of the professional classes. It was thought a retrograde step in many respects as it betrayed 'a prejudice against the professional classes'. They suggested to the Government that 'the aim of the reforms should not be cleavage or counterpoise but the re-adjustment and expansion of the proportionate representation of the different communities so as . . . to enable the Government to secure the benefit of the knowledge, experience, advice and co-operation of the most capable and the best trusted representation of all classes and interests'.[5] The landholders, on the other hand, welcomed the separate representation of their interests. The Government of India, encouraged by the replies of the Local Governments and the response of the landholders, incorporated the proposal of separate representation of the landowning classes in their scheme.[6] Morley agreed with the Government of India in principle. But he differed from Minto on the method through which the representation of interests should be secured to the Legislative Councils. Though the details had yet to be worked out in accordance with the local conditions, Minto wanted through election

[3] Government of Bengal to Government of India, No. 1746A, dated 29 February 1908, para. 14. *Public Letters from India*, 1908, vol. xxxvii.
[4] Government of U.P. to Government of India, No. 447 of 1908, dated 16 March 1908, para. 12. Ibid.
[5] Bombay Presidency Association to the Government of Bombay, 24 February 1908, paras. 51–53. Ibid.
[6] Government of India to Secretary of State,1 October 1908,paras. 27–29. Ibid.

and nomination to secure representation of the landholders and the Muslims; Morley, on the other hand, suggested joint electoral colleges.[7] The Muslims took strong exception to Morley's suggestion and vigorously fought for separate representation for themselves.[8]

What were Minto's intentions in suggesting the separate representation of the interests of the landholders and Muslims on the Legislative Councils? Was it really intended to find a 'counterpoise' to the influence of the professional classes? It has been explained that he genuinely felt the need for meeting the demands of the educated Indians, but he did not think that they were the only people in India whose demands should be met. There were other communities and interests who were perfectly loyal and equally important, but their views had not been adequately represented in the Legislative Councils. But he never underrated the significance of the Congress either and always thought it an important factor in Indian political life. But for the betterment and continuation of the *Raj*, it was essential to give other communities and interests their proper share in the administration and representation on the Legislative Councils. 'Counterpoise' was perhaps the wrong word used by him. His policy was more of recognition of other interests without prejudicing the existing ones for consultation on Government affairs. His policy could have been a policy of 'counterpose' if he had been thinking of any other form of government than a constitutional autocracy. For a constitutional autocracy, a semblance of the support of all classes and interests was not only essential but was by far the best policy. He never tired of declaring that 'We are ready to accept Indian assistance, to share our administration with Indians, to recognize their natural ambitions, but, for their own sakes, the supreme guidance must be British . . .'[9]

The Arundel Committee had unanimously recommended that there should be more opportunity to discuss the Budget and that

[7] Secretary of State to Government of India, 27 November 1908. *Public Despatches, 1908*, vol. xxix, paras. 8–14.
[8] For detailed discussion see Chapter 5.
[9] Minto to Morley, 17 June 1909. *M.P.*

the discussion should be more real than at present. But there was difference of opinion as to the number of non-official members on the Legislative Councils. Baker saw no objections to a non-official majority in the Legislative Councils.[1] This alarmed even Minto. He thought that this would mean the frequent use of the veto by the Viceroy or the Secretary of State and hindrance to administration.[2] Under the Indian Councils Act of 1892 an official majority had been maintained in the Provincial Councils, except that in the Bombay Legislative Council, for some years, the Government was run with a non-official majority and quite smoothly. The Government of India was conscious of the fact, yet they suggested that the official majority should be maintained in these Councils. They, however, recommended that it could be reduced to its narrowest limit by making the number of officials and non-officials (excluding the head of the Government) equal. In the event of the full Council being equally divided, the vote of the head of the Government would turn the scale.[3] Morley, on the other hand, decided that an official majority in Provincial Councils might be dispensed with, provided that a substantial official majority could be permanently maintained in the Imperial Legislative Council. With a view to alleviating any fears that might be entertained by the Government of India, Morley suggested a number of safeguards. He pointed out that the first safeguard for the smooth running of the administration would be the power of the Head of the Government to withhold assent from legislation he disapproved. Secondly, there already existed certain important restrictions on the power of local councils to legislate; thirdly, if the Council was sufficiently representative, it was unlikely that some non-official votes would not be cast on the side of the Government. If, however, all the non-officials opposed a measure it would probably be open to grave objection, but if absolutely necessary, it could be carried by means of an official majority in the Imperial

[1] The Arundel Committee Report, op. cit.
[2] Minto to Morley, 12 September 1906. *M.P.*
[3] Government of India to Secretary of State, 1 October 1908. *Public Letters from India*, 1908, vol. xxxvii, para. 34.

Legislative Council.[4] Thus in his view there was no need to have an official majority in the Provincial Councils. Minto whole-heartedly agreed with Morley's suggestion.[5]

Morley approved of the Government of India's proposal for increased discussion of the budget and an extension of the right of members to ask questions. He also suggested an increase in the Executive Councils of Madras and Bombay with the addition of two more members of whom one at least should always by usage be an Indian, though this need not be provided by Statute; and that power should be acquired for creating Executive Councils for Lieutenant-Governors, not immediately, but when it might be considered desirable in any particular case.[6] Morley, again, in making this suggestion showed how cautious he was. He realized the significance of the Executive Councils for provinces and the presence of an Indian on them, but was not in any hurry to provide them, at least to the Lieutenant-Governor's provinces, immediately. Personally Minto liked the idea and agreed with Morley[7] but when it was discussed in his Council, the members were unanimous that there should be an addition of one member instead of two in the Executive Councils of Madras and Bombay. Both Madras and Bombay strongly opposed the obligatory appointment of an Indian to their Councils. Lawley, Governor of Madras, informed Minto that he could not possibly find a suitable man. Clarke, Governor of Bombay, opposed the recognition of race representation instead of individual efficiency and personal suitability, and Minto agreed with him in that regard.[8] Morley kept these objections in his mind while incorporating the suggestion of Executive Councils for the Provinces in his Bill.

Thus after careful consideration and wide consultation the reform scheme was ready for presentation to Parliament.

[4] Secretary of State to Government of India, 27 November 1908. *Public Despatches*, 1908, vol. xxix, para. 19.

[5] Minto to Morley, telegram, 22 November 1908. *M.P.*

[6] Secretary of State to Government of India, 27 November 1908. *Public Despatches*, 1908, vol. xxix, paras. 39–41.

[7] Minto to Morley, telegram, 22 November 1908. *M.P.*

[8] Minto to Morley, 9 February 1909. Ibid.

# CHAPTER FIVE

# THE MUSLIMS SECURE SEPARATE REPRESENTATION, 1906–1910

MINTO in reply to the Simla deputation said, 'The pith of your address, as I understand it, is a claim that, in any system of representation, . . . in which it is proposed to introduce or increase an electoral organisation, the Mahommedan Community should be represented as a Community . . . I am entirely in accord with you. Please do not misunderstand; I make no attempt to indicate by what means the representation of communities can be obtained, but I am as firmly convinced as I believe you to be, that any electoral representation in India would be doomed to mischievous failure which aimed at granting a personal enfranchisement regardless of the beliefs and traditions of the communities composing the population of this continent . . .'[1]

It was an explicit endorsement of the principles of representation of communities laid down in the address. Morley approved of Minto's commitment and the press, with few exceptions, both in India and in England, applauded Minto's statesmanship and thought the Muslim demands just, moderate and practicable. Minto's reply was no departure from his general policy. It has earlier been explained that he firmly believed that the best method to secure Indian representation on Indian Councils was through representation of interests and communities. Minto accordingly forwarded the address and his reply to the Arundel Committee which was, at that time, sitting to consider the impending changes in the Government of India.

The Arundel Committee finished its work early in 1907 and its recommendations were discussed by the Viceroy's Executive Council and later on incorporated in the Government of India's

[1] Minto's reply to the Deputation, 1 October 1906. *M.P.*

despatch of 21 March 1907. The Government of India concurred with the presenters of the address that neither on the Provincial nor the Imperial Legislative Councils had the Muslim community hitherto received the measure of representation to which its numbers and its political importance entitled it. It agreed with the Viceroy that 'any electoral representation in India would be doomed to mischievous failure which aimed at granting a personal enfranchisement regardless of the beliefs and traditions of the communities composing the population of this continent'. It further stated that under the systems of election hitherto in force, Hindus had largely predominated in all or almost all the electorates, with the result that the few Muslim members that had been elected were not true representatives of the Muslims. The Government had supplemented them by nomination. But the total representation thus effected had not been commensurate with the weight to which the Muslim community was entitled. It further recognized the strength of the argument that even the system of nomination had frequently failed to secure the appointment of the type of Muslims whom the community desired to represent their cause.[2]

Its suggestions, therefore, were firstly, in addition to the small number of Muslims who might be able to secure election in the ordinary manner . . . a certain number of seats be filled exclusively by Muslims. Secondly, for the purpose of filling the latter, or a proportion of them, a special Muslim electorate might be constituted. While any recommendation as to the precise number of seats to be assigned specially to Muslims in the Provincial Councils was deferred pending the fixation of the total strength of each of the Councils, for the Viceroy's Council four seats for the Muslims were suggested to be set apart, two of which were to be filled by nomination by the Viceroy and the other two by election by rotation by Bengal, Eastern Bengal and Assam, the United Provinces, the Punjab, Bombay and Madras.[3]

[2] Government of India to the Secretary of State, 21 March 1907, para. 52. *Public Letters from India*, 1907, vol. xxxv.
[3] Ibid. Paras. 52-55.

Morley received the despatch early in April.[4] Sir Arthur Godley informed Minto that Morley had taken ten to twelve days' complete holiday to think about it. He had made arrangements that no one should see the despatch or learn its contents until he had thought over it. Though Godley suspected that some of the Government of India's suggestions, like that for the appointment of a Native member to the Viceroy's Executive Council, went 'somewhat beyond what Mr. Morley expected of you',[5] none at the India Office foresaw the complications that would arise with regard to Muslim representation. The Secretary of State accepted the principle of separate representation, but with regard to the details he stated 'that your proposals on this head afforded a sufficient basis for discussion'.[6]

After the Secretary of State's approval the reform scheme was circulated amongst the Local Governments for their views.[7] With a view to avoiding giving any prominence to this recognition of Muslim interests the word 'Mahomedan' was cut out 'wherever its omission did not affect the spirit of the draft'.[8] The Local Governments thoroughly considered the whole scheme and gathered the opinions of their officials, prominent members of the public and public associations.

All Local Governments approved of the proposals for the special representation of the Muslims. No Government disputed the principle, though there was a difference of opinion regarding the method of selecting the Muslim representative. This difference was mainly due to local conditions. While some of the provinces wanted to form Muslim electoral colleges,[9] others

[4] Morley to Minto, 4 April 1907. *M.P.*

[5] Godley to Minto, 5 April 1907. *M.C.*

[6] Secretary of State's despatch, 17 May 1907, para. 26. In the Minto Collection in the National Library of Scotland, Edinburgh, there is a scheme for representation of the principal communities of India by Sir W. Lee Warner with a note by Theodore Morison dated 18 April 1907. Both agreed with the Government of India's view. This seems to have influenced Morley as well.

[7] Circular letter to Local Governments, 24 August 1907.

[8] Minto to Morley, 21 August 1907. *M.P.*

[9] Government of Bengal to Government of India, No. 1746A, dated 29 February 1908, para. 19. Government of U.P. to Government of India,

preferred to use the recognized Muslim associations.[1] Madras and Bombay preferred simple nominations.[2] The Government of India in their despatch of 1 October 1908, however, explained that the Hindus adversely criticized the proposals as they regarded them 'as an attempt to set one religion against the other, and thus create a counterpoise to the influence of the educated middle class. Some Hindus, however, recognize the expediency of giving special representation to the Muhammedan community, and the Bombay Presidency Association, while they object strongly to the creation of a special Muhammedan electorate, make provision in their scheme of a Council for the election of two members by the Muhammedan community.'[3]

Progress had hitherto been smooth, though, of course, none amongst the Indians except a few officials knew much about the details. Many Hindus had indeed expressed nervousness at the Viceroy's acceptance of the principle of separate representation, but a few enlightened ones amongst them did not much resent it.[4] Many Muslims had expressed great pleasure.[5] But now Morley changed his mind under the influence of Lord MacDonnell and

No. 447 of 1908, dated 16 March 1908, para. 16. Government of Punjab to Government of India, No. 40, dated 6 July 1908, para 38. *Public Letters from India*, 1908, vol. xxxvii.

[1] Government of E.B. & A. to Government of India, No. 946C, dated 14 March 1908, para. 9. Ibid.

[2] Government of Bombay to Government of India, No. 1768, dated 26 March 1908, para. 13. Government of Madras to Government of India, No. 222, dated 13 March 1908, para 8. Ibid.

[3] Government of India's despatch, 1 October 1908, para. 30. Ibid.

[4] Minto to Morley, 5 November 1907. Gokhale recognized the Muslim claims. In an address delivered in Marathi under the auspices of the Deccan Sabha on the Hindu-Muslim question Gokhale stated that he 'had all along been in favour of special separate electorate for important minorities' . . . The *Indian World*, August 1909, pp. 610–13. See also Gokhale's letter to Sir H. Risley, 12 January 1909. *Home Progs*. Public, pp. 1909, 8150–8151. But the *Hindustan Review*, September 1907, pp. 279–85, criticized the idea of special Muslim representation and said that 'every honest and intelligent Indian, who earnestly cares for the future prosperity of his country, must utter an emphatic protest against this new-fangled policy, and not rest content till the idea of caste representation is given up', p. 283.

[5] Minto to Morley, 3 October 1907. *M.C.*

some Hindu pressure.[6] Morley had appointed a Reform Committee of his Council consisting of Sir David Barr, chairman, Lord MacDonnell, Sir James La Touche, Sir James Thomson, Sir Lawrence Jenkins, K. G. Gupta, Sir Walter Lawrence and S. H. Bilgrami. It unanimously passed the following resolution regarding Muslim representation—'The Committee think that the best plan for securing the representation of the Mahommedan Community (as of all other communities) in the various Councils would be by a system of electoral colleges, and cumulative voting in case of minor minorities, whereby the representation of each great division of the population in accordance with its proportion to the whole population would be preserved; such system to be supplemented, when necessary, by nomination'.[7] A scheme for the formation of electoral colleges was presented by Lord MacDonnell and it was supported amongst others by Bilgrami, who opposed it bitterly later on.[8] In his despatch of 27 November 1908 Morley suggested that 'the object [representation of important Indian classes like the Muslims] in view might be better secured, at any rate in the more advanced provinces in India, by a modification of a popular electorate, founded upon the principle of electoral colleges'.[9]

This was a complete departure from the Government of India's proposal for separate electorates, to which the Secretary of State

[6] Minto to Morley, 9 February 1909, 27 May 1909. *M.C.* The electoral colleges scheme as formulated by Lord MacDonnell is in the Minto Collection at Edinburgh.

[7] Morley to Minto, 14, 16 October 1908. Ibid.

[8] Bilgrami had never been able to present Muslim views properly to the Secretary of State. It was Morison who championed the Muslim cause and helped to safeguard Muslim interests. The Minto-Morley correspondence contains ample evidence to this effect. Bilgrami's work on the India Council was praised by the *Hindustan Review*, December 1909, vol. xx, No. 124, p. 732. 'That during the two years that he has served as Councillor, Mr. Bilgrami never betrayed his trust as an Indian, and never took advantage of his great position to press the claims of his own community, at the expense of those of his non-Muslim fellow-subjects.' Gupta, on the other hand, forcefully presented the Hindu point of view in his minutes.

[9] Secretary of State to Government of India, 27 November 1908, para. 12. *Public Despatches*, 1908, vol. xxix.

had agreed in principle. The new proposal threw overboard the Government of India's scheme for the representation of communities and replaced it with joint electoral colleges to which would be returned a fixed proportion of Muslims and Hindus in the ratio of population, and these would later on elect to the Legislature of the province representatives for the two communities in like proportion. Morley did not think the introduction of this system would be a novelty as it already existed in the groups of District Boards and of Municipalities which in several provinces returned members to Provincial Councils. Moreover, he thought, it had certain advantages; it would meet the Hindu objections by bringing the classes together; it would eliminate any danger of further claims for representation by classes; it would create a healthy interest in local self-government by linking up local bodies; 'it would ensure the person chosen being actually drawn from the locality that the electoral college represents'. He, of course, realized that the system was not a simple one and that the primary vote would be removed by more than one stage from the ultimate choice.[1]

The scheme was not, however, welcomed either by the Government of India or by the Muslims. It produced great controversy and the Muslims both in India and in London lodged vigorous protests when the despatches of the Government of India and the Secretary of State were published on 17 December 1908. In India the Muslim press expressed concern and took it as a political abandonment of the Muslims in favour of the Hindus. The *Paisa Akhbar*, Lahore, stated that Morley had tried to please the advocates of *Swaraj* at the expense of minorities and the Muslims had not been considered worthy of attention on account, perhaps, of their being a peaceful people and keeping themselves aloof from the prevailing agitation and crime. It, however, expressed complete faith 'in the sense of justice of [the] British Government' and felt confident that 'Lord Minto's vigilant Government will not fail to do justice to

[1] Secretary of State to Government of India, 27 November 1908, paras. 11–14. *Public Despatches*, 1908, vol. xxix.

them.'[2] The *Watan*, Lahore, also thought that Morley had been influenced by the Hindus, and feared that the Muslims 'being in a minority will not fare well at the elections'.[3] The *Zamindar*, Karamabad, congratulated the 'Congress wallah' for Morley's scheme. In its opinion 'while the opposition of Muhammadans to the National Congress has had the effect of creating estrangement between them and Hindus Lord Morley's reform scheme has alienated them from Government also (*Government ki taraf ka bhi na chhora*) and has dispelled all their dreams of English help and protection, of which they had been assured by Sir Syed Ahmed, Mr. Amir Ali and other leaders of their community, as also by Anglo-Indians and their organs'. It suspected that perhaps Morley did not know of the faith which the Muslims reposed in the British Government and on the strength of which they had offended their Hindu fellow-countrymen by not joining their agitation against the Government.[4] The *Observer*, Lahore, also bitterly criticized Morley's scheme.[5] M. Shafi, a prominent Punjab leader, also wrote a series of letters to Dunlop Smith expressing his own views and conveying the Muslim concern over Morley's reform scheme. In his opinion Morley's scheme had created dissatisfaction amongst Muslims and was contrary to the promise made by Minto.[6]

At its Amritsar Session, the Muslim League viewed the electoral college scheme with great alarm and announced that its implementation would 'mark the first breakdown of that implicit faith which Muslims have for so long placed in the care and solicitude of the Government'.[7] Syed Ali Imam, the President of the Amritsar Session, denounced the scheme as dangerous to the

---

[2] The *Paisa Akhbar*, Lahore, 25 December 1908; 3, 15, 27 February 1909. P.N.N.R., 1909.

[3] The *Watan*, Lahore, 8 January 1909. Ibid.

[4] The *Zamindar*, Karamabad, 8 January 1909. Ibid.

[5] The *Observer*, Lahore, 23 December 1908, 14 April 1909. Ibid.

[6] M. Shafi to Dunlop Smith, 8, 10, 13, 18, 26 January 1909. *M.C.*

[7] Resolution 3, The All-India Muslim League Session, Amritsar, 1908. Letter from Offg. Hon. Secretary of A.I.M.L. to the Viceroy's Private Secretary, 22 January 1909. *Home Progs.* Public, 1909, 8151.

vital interests of the Muslims and contrary to the suggestions made by Minto, who, as the man on the spot, knew the situation better than Morley. He urged the Muslims to protest strongly against Morley's scheme.[8] In the following months numerous protest meetings were held throughout India and many resolutions and petitions were sent to the Government of India; but the most vigorous campaign was carried on in London, where Ameer Ali was very active. The London Branch of the League published various pamphlets explaining the Muslim demands and the promise given to them by the Viceroy. A number of letters for and against the scheme were published in *The Times*, Lord MacDonnell supporting it, Ameer Ali, Bilgrami, A. C. Murray, Liberal M.P., opposing it.[9] *The Times* supported the Muslim viewpoint and agreed with their fears that under this scheme the Muslim representation would be illusory. 'The type of Muslim who secures Hindu support secures it by virtue of his utility to Hindu rather than Muslim interests; yet this is the type most likely to be elected under the provision of Lord Morley's scheme.'[1]

The Congress, which was meeting at Madras when the scheme was announced, expressed its approval of it and hoped 'that details of the proposed scheme will be worked out in the same liberal spirit in which its main provisions as outlined in the Secretary of State's despatch have been conceived'.[2] Malaviya suggested that 'we should leave Lord Morley's proposals as they stand in this matter and not ask that any different principle of representation should be introduced'.[3] Gokhale, being more realistic, admitted that there were acute differences amongst Indians and stated that for the promotion of 'unity in the country', any scheme of representation which secured to important classes proper representation should be welcomed. His view was that in

[8] Speech by S. Ali Imam, 31 December 1908. *Public Letters from India,* 1909, vol. xxxviii.
[9] *The Times,* 26 December 1908, 4, 5 January 1909.
[1] Ibid. 29 December 1908.
[2] *Report of the I.N.C.,* 1908, Resolution II, p. 46.
[3] Ibid. p. 56.

order to alleviate the 'unjust fear' of the Muslims that 'they would be swamped by Hindus', they should be allowed to elect their own representatives themselves.[4]

Minto was doubtful whether this scheme would work and he informed Morley that there was a fear 'that the cleverness of the pleader class may enable them to manipulate the machinery of the Electoral College so that whenever representatives of minorities are elected they will be, whether Mahommedan or otherwise, as a matter of fact representatives of the pleader political section'. There was also some suspicion that Gokhale by some means, possibly through Lord MacDonnell, had suggested the scheme, thus making it all the more unpalatable for the Muslims.[5] Minto was definite that the Muslim objections to the scheme were perfectly sound and that any attempt to introduce it would increase the Muslim storm that was already raging. He informed Morley 'that though the Mahommedan is silent he is very strong.'[6] Minto's intense dislike of Morley's scheme is apparent from what he wrote to Lansdowne, 'The electoral colleges are absolutely impossible—mad and distinctly contrary to pledges I had given to the Mahommedans and of which the Government of India approved. We simply can't have them.'[7]

Minto was not the only person who disliked the electoral college scheme. Arundel considered this suggestion for electoral colleges 'the weak point in the whole Despatch', as it destroyed the Viceroy's promise to the Muslims; he thought it would be 'a thousand pities to disgust and alienate the Mahommedan community by deviating a hair's breadth from the promise given

[4] *Report of the I.N.C.,* 1908, p. 137.

[5] Minto to Morley, 24 December 1908. *M.P.*

[6] (a) Minto to Morley, 31 December 1908; 12 January 1909. Morley did not like Minto's admission of the just claims of Muslims. 'Your language to the Islamites about their "just claim to something more than numerical strength" was perhaps a trifle less guarded than it might have been if you will allow me to say so . . .' Morley to Minto, 21 January 1909. Ibid.

(b) See also Minto to Arthur Elliott, 24 May 1909. *M.C.*

[7] Minto to Lansdowne, 21 January 1909. Ibid.

to them in 1906 . . .'[8] The Prince of Wales thought Morley's reforms 'on the whole sound' but saw 'considerable difficulties' in settling the question of Muslim representation.[9] Sir A. H. Fraser discussed at length the electoral colleges scheme with Morley. Later on he informed Minto that Morley had shown 'no disposition to stand strongly by the idea of the Electoral College'. Fraser, therefore, suggested to Minto 'that the direct representation of Mahommedans, apart from all interference by Hindus, must be insisted on'.[1]

Morley, too, realized that his suggestion had not been well-received. Of the various objections to it, two were most prominently put forward by the critics of Morley's scheme. Firstly, that proportional representation on a purely numerical basis violated the assurance given to the Simla Deputation in 1906. Secondly, that in electoral colleges Hindus might run an opposition Muslim candidate of their own and carry his election. Minto thought both objections 'perfectly sound'.[2] When Morley was pressed to receive a deputation from the League's London Branch, he sought Minto's advice.[3] Minto saw no objection to his meeting the deputation and explaining the Government's policy. He, however, asked Morley to make it clear that the scheme was merely a suggestion. Being convinced of the fact that the scheme was unworkable, Minto impressed upon Morley that all Local Governments would unanimously oppose it. Sir George Clarke, Bombay's Governor, who was not favourably inclined towards Muslims, also opposed it, and even Gokhale saw no justification in insisting on its introduction in the face of Muslim opposition.[4]

[8] Sir A. T. Arundel from Woking to Minto, 8 January 1909. *M.C.* See also Sir A. T. Arundel, 'The New Reforms in India', *National Review*, February 1909, pp. 1032–3, and Sir A. C. Elliott's 'Lord Morley's Indian Reforms', *Ninteenth Century*, February 1909, p. 190.

[9] Prince of Wales to Minto, 26 January 1909. *M.C.*

[1] Sir A. H. L. Fraser to Minto, 29 January 1909. Ibid.

[2] Viceroy to Secretary of State, telegram, 8 January 1909. Ibid.

[3] Secretary of State to Viceroy, telegram, 14 January 1909. Ibid.

[4] Minto to Morley, telegram, 15 January 1909. Minto to Morley, 14 September 1909: 'Clarke is somewhat anti-Mahommedan'. Ibid.

On 27 January 1909, Morley received a deputation of the London Branch of the League. Ameer Ali led it and Bilgrami was one of the members. Morley, in the company of T. R. Buchanan, Sir A. Godley and Sir C. Lyall, received them. Ameer Ali and Bilgrami spoke on behalf of the deputation. Their demands were simple. All they wanted was that the interests of the Hindus and Muslims should be co-ordinated; that neither the one nor the other should be in a position to say that its interests were either sacrificed or subordinated to the interests of the other. The best way to safeguard their interests was the introduction of the principle of separate representation—of Muslims by Muslims.

Morley's reply was cautiously worded. It is very difficult to pick out any sentences which may be looked upon as constituting a definite pledge[5]: the reason was that 'in picking up the Mussulman', he did not want 'to drop our Hindu parcels'.[6] But he did explain that his 'electoral scheme' 'was merely a suggestion thrown out for the Government of India, not a direction of the Medes and Persians stamp'; and he made use of a number of phrases which indicated a disposition to accede to their requests. 'It would be no departure in substance from the principle of our suggestion that there should be a separate Mahommedan electorate—an electorate exclusively Mahommedan; and in view of the wide and remote distances and difficulties in organization, in consequence of those distances in the area constituting a large province, I am not sure that this is not one of those cases where election by two stages would not be in the highest degree convenient, and there might be a separate electoral college exclusively Mahommedan'; and 'I repeat, I see no harm, from the

---

[5] In a letter to Minto, Morley wrote, 'the honest Moslems went away decidedly disappointed. I never expected that it would be otherwise. How could I satisfy them by a straight declaration off my own bat?' 28 January 1909. *M.P.*

[6] Morley to Minto, 28 January 1909. As early as June 13 1908, Dunlop Smith wrote from England to Minto that Morley was obsessed with the idea that the promises to Muslims 'might look as if we wished to set race against race'. This obsession led Morley to make many changes in his scheme. Ibid.

point of view of a practical working compromise, in the principle that population, numerical strength, should be the main factor in determining how many representatives should sit for this or the other community; but modifying influences may be taken into account in allotting the numbers of such representatives.'[7]

The Muslims were naturally not satisfied, nor was *The Times*, with the expressions used by Morley in his reply to the deputation. *The Times* pleaded that no reforms which left the Muslims with a just cause of grievances could possibly work for the good of India as a whole.[8]

A number of articles supporting the Muslim views were published in English journals. Amongst those who favoured the Muslim cause were Sir Charles Bruce,[9] A. H. L. Fraser,[1] A. E. Duchesne,[2] J. D. Rees,[3] Sir V. Chirol,[4] R. A. L. Moore,[5] and Sir T. W. Holderness.[6] These writers were almost all agreed that because Hindus and Muslims differed in their attitudes to life and religion, the Muslim demand for separate representation was justified, for without it the Muslim minority would be swamped by the Hindu majority. The electoral colleges' scheme would not solve the problem but aggravate it. Chirol forecast that 'the more we delegate our authority in India to the natives of India on the principles which we associate with self-government, the more we must necessarily in practice delegate it to the Hindus',[7] but Muslims were afraid of this.

Sir Henry Cotton, Lord MacDonnell, Charles O'Donnell, K. Hardie, Ramsay MacDonald, and the *Manchester Guardian*

---

[7] Morley's reply to the deputation, 27 January 1909. *M.P.*

[8] *The Times*, 28 January 1909, 9 February 1909.

[9] Sir Charles Bruce, 'Crown and Congress in India', *Empire Review*, February 1907.

[1] A. H. L. Fraser, 'Lord Morley's Indian Reforms', Ibid. March 1909.

[2] A. E. Duchesne, 'The Indian Muhammadans and the Reforms', Ibid. May 1909.

[3] J. D. Rees, *Modern India*, 1910, pp. 184-5.

[4] V. Chirol, *Indian Unrest*, 1910.

[5] R. A. L. Moore, *Imperial and Asiatic Quarterly Review*, January 1911.

[6] T. W. Holderness, *People and Problems of India*, 1911, pp. 127-8.

[7] V. Chirol, op. cit., p. 128.

opposed these views and thought that the recognition of separate Muslim electorates would offend the Hindus.

In the correspondence that followed Minto and Morley discussed the scheme thoroughly. Minto explained that the scheme had been disliked by all the Local Governments and the Government of India and that 'their [Muslims] reasoning as to their own representation cannot in fairness be disregarded'.[8] Morley pointed out that 'this scheme of obtaining Muhammedan representation by means of exclusively Muhammedan electoral colleges I described to the deputation as not outside the terms of my Despatch'.[9]

The result of all this agitation by the Muslims and controversy in the press[1] was that Morley had to make a much more definite statement and gave an unequivocal pledge, when moving the second reading of the Indian Councils Bill. 'The Mahommedans demand three things. I had the pleasure of receiving a deputation from them and I know very well what is in their minds. They demand the election of their own representatives to these Councils in all the stages, just as in Cyprus, where, I think, the Mahommedans vote by themselves. They have nine votes and the non-Mahommedans have three, or the other way about. So in Bohemia, where the Germans vote alone and have their own register. Therefore we are not without a precedent and a parallel for the idea of a separate register. Secondly they want a number of seats in excess of their numerical strength. Those two demands we are quite ready and intend to meet in full.'[2] The third demand was for a Muslim member of the Viceroy's Executive Council, if

---

[8] Minto to Morley, 4 February 1909, 4 March 1909, telegram, 8 February 1909. Minto even suggested dropping the word 'colleges' to avoid misunderstanding by a population ignorant of electoral terms (9 February 1909). *M.P.*

[9] Morley to Minto, telegram, 2 February 1909. Ibid.

[1] *Native Newspaper Reports*, 1909, Punjab; U.P., Bengal; Eastern Bengal and Assam; Bombay, are full of selections from the papers which discussed the whole scheme exhaustively.

[2] *Hansard*, House of Lords, vol. i (6 February–26 May 1909), Col. 125. Morley's Speech, 23 February 1909. P. Mukherji, *Indian Constitutional Documents* (1600–1918), vol. i (Calcutta, 1918), pp. 336–7. He, however, gives '4th March 1909' as the date of the speech on p. 333. It is incorrect.

a Hindu was appointed. This Morley rejected outright, because this appointment was not supposed to be a racial one. It would go to a suitable Indian whoever he might be.

The reference to the deputation is important, because it meant that when Morley promised 'to meet' the Muslim demands 'in full', he had in his mind the demands which the Muslim deputation had made to him. Thus Morley had conceded that the Muslims were to have more representatives than they were entitled to upon a calculation of their numerical strength, and that all those representatives were to be returned by separate Muslim electorates 'in all the stages'.

The pledge was reiterated by Buchanan while moving the second reading in the House of Commons on 1 April 1909. He said, 'And more than that, particularly with regard to the Mahommedans, they have a special and overwhelming claim upon us, namely, the solemn promises, given by those who are entitled with full responsibility to speak for us, that they would get adequate representation to the amount and of [the] kind they want— a promise given to them by Lord Minto specifically in October 1906, repeated in a Despatch by the Secretary of State in 1907, and again repeated by the Secretary of State to a deputation here and in a speech in another place. From that promise we cannot go back, ought not to go back, and we will not go back.'[3] The Prime Minister also emphatically said that 'undoubtedly there will be a separate register for Mahommedans'.[4] Privately Minto, too, emphasized that 'Mahomedan electorates are absolutely necessary—if we retreat at all from that view, we shall have an infinitely worse trouble than anything that can arise from Hindu opposition'.[5]

Morley's statement in the House of Lords was received with much relief by a number of Muslims, but some Hindus denounced it. Surendranath Banerjea, Madan Mohan Malaviya and others disapproved of the 'innovations' and declared them

[3] *Hansard*, House of Commons, vol. iii (29 March–23 April 1909), Buchanan's Speech, 1 April 1909, Col. 500.
[4] Ibid. Asquith's Speech, 1 April 1909, Col. 533.
[5] Minto to Morley, 7 April 1909. *M.P.*

to be dangerous.[6] Malaviya had earlier expressed his strong disapproval of separate representation of the Muslims in a telegram
to the Government of the United Provinces.[7] In Parliament
C. J. O'Donnell tabled an amendment, though it was not moved,
asking the House not to approve of 'legislation by which it is
intended to establish sectarian discrimination, and to apply
sectarian tests both to members of Legislative Councils and the
voters who will elect them'.[8]

But the real controversy started when, after making that statement regarding the abandonment of the electoral college scheme
and the fulfilment of 'solemn promises', Buchanan unfolded the
details of the scheme based on the Government of India's despatch of 1 October 1908. According to that the Muslim representation would be obtained in different ways in different
provinces. 'In some by a system of Mahommedan electorates
specially constructed; in other cases by asking Mahommedan
associations to name representatives; in other cases, at any rate,
for a time, by nomination.' Earl Percy, Lord Ronaldshay and
Balfour pointed out the inconsistency between the scheme and
the promises so far given, as according to it the number of Muslim representatives would fall far below the number they had
been promised.[9] On 19 April 1909, Hobhouse, who was speaking
for Buchanan who had been taken ill, made another statement

[6] *The Indian Mahommedans and the Government,* issued by the London
Branch of A.I.M.L. *M.P.*

[7] Telegram, 23 January 1909. From M. M. Malaviya to the Chief Sect. to
the Govt. of U.P.

[8] *The Indian Mahommedans and the Government,* issued by the London
Branch of A.I.M.L. *M.P.*

[9] No definite number of Muslim representatives had been promised but
they were assured that they would be given adequate representation in the new
Councils to enable them to safeguard their interests. When the details were
announced the number of Muslims proposed for various Councils was far
below their percentage to the population. For example, for the Viceroy's
Council twenty-eight elected members were proposed, of whom six would be
Muslims, their percentage being 21·4, while their percentage to total population
was twenty-three. This was thought to be a betrayal of promises. The Government of India was of the view that the Muslims would win some seats in the
general electorate as well. But the Muslim leaders were not thinking in terms

reiterating the promises and hiding behind a telegram from Minto which further confused the issue. It said, 'the method proposed is simply that in general electorates such as municipalities, district boards and members of provincial Councils, all sects and classes, including Mahommedan, will vote together. By this means some, but not sufficient, representation will be obtained for Mahommedans. In addition a certain number of seats will be reserved for Mahommedans, and none but Mahommedans will have a voice in filling these.' These seats would be filled differently in different provinces.[1] Minto himself admitted in another telegram that 'the telegram puts the cart before the horse and is badly worded, inasmuch as it would lead any one not acquainted with the whole history to assume that Mahommedans must depend upon the general electorates in the first place, and that their own electorates would only give them a sort of second chance.' The Government of India's recommendations were, on the other hand, as Minto put it, 'separate Mahommedan electorates in the first place, which were to secure for them their proper proportion of representation, and beyond that again was their chance of winning seats in the general electorates, and also nomination'.[2] For some obscure reason this second telegram was not read before the House.

Realizing the Government's predicament, the opposition in the House made capital out of it. Hobhouse was pressed hard and he had to admit that there was some divergence between the pledges given by the Viceroy and the Secretary of State and the views expressed in the telegram of 12 April 1909 from the Government of India. But in order to avoid further embarrassment he added that 'that does not mean that the telegram necessarily closes discussion' and emphatically said, 'Before I sit down I would add one sentence, and it is that where ever elections are

of the general electorate. The India Office did not probe into the details of the Government of India's scheme, and so were unable to satisfy the opposition. The discussion in Parliament further aroused Muslim fears.

[1] Minto to Morley, telegram, 12 April 1909. *M.P.*
[2] Minto to Morley, telegram, 20 May 1909. *M.C.*

found possible they shall be conducted on the basis of separate representation of the Mahommedan community'.[3]

In their nervousness the Government made another mistake when they presented to the House another telegram from Minto in which he stated, 'I do not understand any Muhammadan here to claim concession suggested by Hobhouse, namely, that where ever elections are found possible they should be conducted on basis of separate representation of the Muhammadan community. If interpreted literally that would involve having separate Muhammadan electorates within the various electorates proposed, such as presidency corporations, district boards and municipalities, universities, landholders, and the commercial community. This is manifestly impracticable and has never been suggested.'[4] Minto sent this telegram in reply to a charge by Morley that the Muslims had all along been considering the Government of India's proposals as worse than the electoral college scheme.[5]

The publication of these conflicting and contradictory telegrams and statements re-kindled the Muslim agitation. Ameer Ali in London, particularly, became very uneasy and the London Branch of the League produced many pamphlets in which they clamoured for fulfilment of promises. The confusion arose simply because neither the Muslims nor the India Office had really understood the Government of India's scheme. To agree to a principle may have been easy, but to work it out in detail the Government of India had to take into consideration many other administrative difficulties. The Viceroy had promised separate representation and weightage to the Muslims, but had not committed himself as to the form it would take. The Government of India's scheme, while giving the Muslims separate representation, did not debar them from taking part in the general electorate. However, the Muslims never seem to have cared much about

---

[3] *Hansard*, House of Commons, vol iv (26 April–14 May 1909), 26 April 1909, Col. 5.

[4] Minto to Morley, telegram, 2 May 1909. *M.P.*

[5] Minto to Morley, 27 April 1909. Ibid.

that. But Morley's scheme of electoral colleges aroused the
Muslim fears anew. Morley, who had earlier agreed to separate
Muslim representation, seems to have felt that too much had
been promised to them; that if that promise had to be fulfilled it
would annoy the Hindus and would appear as setting race against
race. When the Muslims started their agitation and Minto kept
firmly to his promise, Morley, too, reverted to the old position
and even went a little further by promising separate electorates
'in all stages'. Now this was contrary to the Government of
India's policy. Some Muslim leaders, particularly of the London
Branch of the League, thought that the Government of India's
scheme did not give the Muslims the right of exclusive Muslim
representation and was not compatible with Morley's promises.
In the beginning the India Office did not attach much importance
to the whole problem and never tried to understand it.[6] Morley,
though he liked Gokhale, did not have a good opinion either of
Ameer Ali or of the Aga Khan.[7] The India Office did not take
much notice of the Muslim protests and thought that 'like most
people they were asking for more'. The opposition was, on the
other hand, properly coached by the London Branch of the
League and made the Government 'look rather foolish'[8] when
the inconsistency in their pledges and in the scheme for the
actual implementation was pointed out. The mere mention of
the words 'pledges' and 'promises' later annoyed both Morley
and Minto.[9] Morley put the blame on Minto for starting 'the

[6] Sir Charles Lyall was the India Office expert, who dealt with the question
of separate representation. He was responsible for all the confusion as he
could not advise Morley properly. Hirtzel, Private Secretary to Morley, wrote
to Dunlop Smith. 'The real fact is that the man here whose business it was to
keep us straight failed to do so . . .' That is why Morley asked Morison to look
into the problem. Hirtzel to Dunlop Smith, 30 April 1909. *M.C.*

[7] Morley called Ameer Ali a 'windbag' and a 'conceited egotist'. Morley to
Minto, 21 May 1909. See Morley to Minto, 18 February 1909. 'He [the
Aga Khan] does not really attract me'. *M.P.*

[8] (a) Hirtzel to Dunlop Smith, 30 April 1909. *M.C.*
   (b) Morley to Minto, 28 April 1909. Ibid.

[9] (a) Morley to Minto, 6 August 1909. Ibid.
   (b) Minto to Morley, 9 September 1909. Ibid.

Muslim hare'.[1] But the position was that promises had been given and pledges had been made. Ronaldshay impressed upon the Government that unless they were able to clear up the mess created by the telegram two beliefs of very serious import would arise in India—first, that the only way to obtain the ear of, or satisfaction from, the Government was to adopt the method of agitation; secondly, that the word of the British Government was no longer its bond which was incapable of violation.[2]

Many Hindus viewed the whole agitation as an Anglo-Indian move which had its support in *The Times,* the *Times of India,* and the *Statesman* with men like Lovat Fraser at their back. It was suggested that these Anglo-Indians made use of the Muslims 'because they found the Mussulman name eminently fit to do duty for (a) a good stick to beat the Hindus with, (b) a good factor to work the principle of *divide et impera,* and (c) a sound rock upon which to wreck the good ship of Lord Morley'.[3] Even K. G. Gupta, commenting on Morison's note on the 'pledges',[4] stated that 'to take advantage of the loose language that may have been used in and out of Parliament in order to magnify the Muhammedan claim may be the work of partisanship, but true statesmanship requires that no *undue* favour is shown to one community at the *expense* of another.'[5]

Morley was on the horns of a dilemma. On the one side was the Muslim agitation and on the other the fear of dropping 'our Hindu parcels'. What could be done? He again sought Minto's help to pacify the Muslims in India[6] and asked Morison to look into the whole problem at the India Office.

Morison in his note pointed out that the scheme under con-

[1] Morley to Minto, 6 December 1909. *M.C.*

[2] *Hansard,* House of Commons, vol. viii (19 July to 6 August 1909). Ronaldshay, speech, 5 August 1909, Col. 2068.

[3] *The Indian World,* vol. ix, Nos. 47 and 48, February and March 1909.

[4] 'Note upon the Pledges given to the Mahommedans', by T. Morison. *M.P.*

[5] Note by K. G. Gupta, 10 August 1909. Ibid.

[6] Morley to Minto, 28 April 1909. 'The thing is no doubt horribly difficult to manage. I am sure of that . . . I can only ask you to make what you can of the Sphinx's riddle.' Morley to Minto, 20 July 1909. Ibid.

sideration would not give the Muslims the type of representation that had been promised to them. Confusion had arisen over the details of the scheme that had caused grave misunderstanding. Now that the Muslims had been aroused nothing would satisfy them except complete fulfilment of the promises given them.[7] This produced a severely critical note by K. G. Gupta who believed that 'the proposals of the Government of India not only amply redeem whatever pledges may have been given, but in so far as they keep the mixed electorates open to Mahommedans, they give an additional advantage to that community which the other peoples have a right to resent'.[8] These notes instead of easing increased Morley's nervousness.[9]

Despite Morley's wavering, Muslim protests for and Hindu expressions against separate representation, Minto all along remained sure of the stand he had earlier taken in this controversy. He was convinced that the Muslim claims were just, but that they had misunderstood the details of the scheme and the policy of the Government,[1] that they appeared to have 'got hold of the wrong end of the stick',[2] that the whole agitation was the work of Ameer Ali, a frustrated man for not being knighted,[3] and that Lord MacDonnell's scheme had much to do in giving it a start.[4] In the beginning he did not think much of this agitation,[5] but with its growth grew Morley's nervousness which resulted in enormous correspondence between the two. Minto knew that the best way of escape from this dilemma was to parley with the Muslims, but there was the risk of 'Hindu dissatisfaction' with

[7] 'Note upon the Pledges given to the Mahommedans', by T. Morison. *M.P.*

[8] 'Mahommedan Representation', Note by Mr. Gupta, 3 August 1909. Ibid.

[9] Sir H. Adamson to Dunlop Smith, 24 September 1909. *M.C.*

[1] Minto to Godley, 29 April 1909. Ibid.

[2] Minto to Morley, 29 April 1909. *M.P.*

[3] Minto to Morley, 28 June 1909. See also Minto to Lawley, Governor of Madras, 28 June 1909. Minto was, however, wrong in this observation, because the Muslims were genuinely worried as to their future as is apparent from the enormous number of public meetings held throughout India. Ibid.

[4] Minto to Morley, 28 June 1909. Ibid.

[5] Minto to Morley, 29 April 1909. Ibid.

him for doing so.[6] He was, however, obliged to call some prominent Muslim leaders to Simla and discuss with them the
details of the proposed scheme. In May 1909, letters were sent to
all Local Governments asking them to suggest the names of
prominent Muslim leaders and out of the suggested names seven
were called, the Nawab of Dacca, Ali Imam, the Raja of Mahmu-
dabad, Abdul Majid, a barrister of Allahabad, M. Shafi of
Lahore, Ibrahim Rahimtoola of Bombay, and Abdul Aziz. The
selection of the names is also significant as only those who were
expected to be moderate in their views were called for this
meeting. Minto and Sir H. Adamson, a Member of the Viceroy's
Council and of the Committee for Rules and Regulations, decided
to be firm with the Muslims and 'not to go beyond the increase
in Mohammedan representatives the Committee now thinks
possible', as it was impossible to give the Muslims 'an entirely
separate communal representation.'[7]

During their stay at Simla they called on Kitchener, who
pleaded their case in the Viceroy's Council without much success.
Minto thought he knew nothing of the problem.[8]

The Congress-owned or inspired press strongly resented these
consultations with the Muslims. The *Tribune* of Lahore, amongst
numerous others, considered this whole movement 'a childish
scramble for Council seats irrespective of the justice or righteous-
ness of the demand, and regardless of the rights of other and far
more important classes of His Majesty's subjects'.[9]

The discussion centred round three proposals—first the electoral college scheme; secondly separate electorates conferring
exclusive representation, the Muslims not voting in any mixed
electorates; and thirdly separate electorates, supplemented to the
full extent of their legitimate claims by further representation
either through mixed electorates, or by nomination where they
failed to obtain a fair share of the elective seats. The first one had

[6] Minto to Morley, 23 June 1909. *M.P.*
[7] Minto to Adamson, 20 June 1909, and Adamson to Minto, 19 June 1909.
*M.C.*
[8] Minto to Morley, 22 July 1909. Ibid.
[9] The *Tribune*, 2 July 1909. *P.N.N.R.*, 1909, p. 612.

been dropped, for the second a majority of Muslims were insisting, but the third was the proposal of the Government of India.

Minto was able to convince these handpicked Muslim leaders that their insistence on exclusive Muslim representation would mean their complete separation from political life. This perpetuation of rigid exclusiveness would be detrimental to their interests. He was of the opinion that 'whilst they [the Muslims] certainly must have a certain number of seats guaranteed as a community, it would be suicidal for their political future to be rated on a lower standard than Hindus and to be completely debarred from competing with them.'[1] These Muslim leaders went away agreed that the principle of entire Muslim separation would not be pressed for, if they were given six fixed seats on the Imperial Council instead of five.[2] But when Ali Imam called a special meeting of the League at Lucknow to endorse the decisions reached at Simla, he failed because the elder leaders like Viqar-ul-Mulk did not think the suggested solution a right one.[3] Minto, however, stuck to his decision that it was in Muslim interests not to be divided into a 'watertight compartment', 'no matter what Ameer Ali says'.[4]

The Government of India's despatch of 22 July 1909 discussed the whole problem and practically guaranteed eight seats to the Muslims, i.e. six fixed seats and two by nomination, if they failed to gain that number in general electorates. The despatch, however, purposely avoided the appearance of such a guarantee with a view to disarming Hindu accusations of favouritism to Muslims.[5]

In the meanwhile Ali Imam went to London to persuade Ameer Ali and the Aga Khan to come round to his views. Morison was entrusted to brief him before seeing Ameer Ali.[6]

---

[1] Minto to Kitchener, 28 June 1909. *M.C.*
[2] Minto to Morley, 1 July 1909. *M.P.*
[3] (a) Off. Hon. Secretary of the A.I.M.L. to Dunlop Smith, 15 July 1909. *M.C.*
(b) Ali Imam to Dunlop Smith, 14 July 1909. Ibid.
[4] Minto to Morley, 15 July 1909. Ibid.
[5] Minto to Morley, telegram, 24 July 1909. *M.P.*
[6] Morley to Minto, 26 August 1909. Ibid.

The Aga Khan was won round[7] but Ameer Ali remained adamant.[8] Since Sir V. Chirol of *The Times* was advocating the Muslim cause, Morley thought it necessary to bring him round as well. He was invited to a luncheon, along with Adamson, and Morley hoped that 'the friendly meal will do good, and at all events keep *The Times* from being over-ferocious, when the Regulations come out for discussions in the open.'[9]

Along with these manœuvres Minto also suggested that it was time for the Government to put its foot down[1] and stop listening to the Muslim demands, as there was the fear of the growth of Hindu hostility which the Government could not risk any longer. The result of all this activity was that Sir Richmond Ritchie (the new Permanent Under-Secretary of State for India) gleefully wrote to Minto, 'An outbreak of "Ghazi" [*sic*] on the part of the Mahommedan sympathizers on the staff of *The Times* and in Parliament, which at one time seemed imminent, has been averted.'[2]

The Rules and Regulations were published in November,[3] and were well received by the Muslims. The Aga Khan claimed that they were accepted not because they contained 'all that we could have desired, or that they constitute an ideal solution of the problem', but because 'of our readiness to co-operate with our rulers and to help them in their difficult task of introducing the principle of constitutional government in so diversified a country as India, and also as exhibiting our cordial goodwill towards other communities'.[4] *The Times,* which had fought the Muslim battle, welcomed them as well.[5] There is no denying the

[7] Adamson to Dunlop Smith, 28 October 1909. Morley to Minto, 29 October 1909. *M.C.*

[8] Adamson to Dunlop Smith, 24 September 1909. Morley to Minto, 17 September 1909. Ibid.

[9] Morley to Minto, 7 October 1909. *M.P.*

[1] Minto to Morley, telegram 24 July 1909. Ibid.

[2] Ritchie to Minto, 12 November 1909. *M.C.*

[3] *East India (Executive and Legislative Councils) Regulations, etc., for giving effect to the Indian Councils Act, 1909* (1909), Cd. 4987.

[4] The Aga Khan, Letter to *The Times*, 18 November 1909.

[5] *The Times*, 16 November 1909.

fact that these Rules and Regulations fulfilled to a great extent Minto's promise to the Simla Deputation. Morley wrote to Minto, 'I am very sure of one thing, and this is that, if we had not satisfied the Muhammedans, we should have had opinion here which is now with us—dead against us,' and that 'nothing has been sacrificed for their sake that is of real importance'.[6]

But the Congress did not like this grant of separate representation to the Muslims. In 1909, it recorded 'its strong sense of disapproval of the creation of separate electorates on the basis of religion . . .' It objected to 'the excessive and unfairly preponderant share of representation given to the followers of one particular religion; the unjust, invidious, and humiliating distinctions made between Moslem and non-Moslem subjects of His Majesty in the matter of the electorates, the franchise and the qualifications of candidate . . .'[7] Speaker after speaker condemned the provision of separate representation for Muslims. The number of Muslim delegates in this session was five out of 243.

Thus ended the controversy which occupied and agitated the minds of the officials and Muslims for more than a year. The reasons for this controversy were three. There was, first, Morley's electoral college scheme. Morley in one of his letters blamed Minto for starting 'the Muslim hare',[8] but it was Morley who was responsible for turning the Muslims from a loyal, slow-moving, politically immature community into an agitating one. G. N. Singh is surprised 'that a sapling of hardly two years should have succeeded in browbeating one of the most powerful and experienced among the modern Secretaries of State.'[9] Surprising though it does seem, yet it happened perhaps because Morley refused to listen to Minto's warning that 'though the Mahom-

[6] Morley to Minto, 18 November 1909. *M.P.* In the new edition of the *Cambridge History of India*, vol. vi (Delhi, 1958), p. 618, it is stated that Minto was 'the real father of communal electorates'. V. Chirol, *India, Old and New* (London, 1921), states that 'Morley yielded to a pressure'.

[7] *Report of the I.N.C.*, 1909. Resolution IV, p. 47.

[8] Morley to Minto, 6 December 1909. *M.C.*

[9] G. N. Singh, op. cit. (1950 edn.), p. 211.

medan is silent he is very strong'.[1] Secondly, there was the confusion created at the India Office by the experts who did not understand the Government of India's scheme. Conflicting and contradictory statements and schemes infuriated the Muslims who were beginning to think that for the satisfaction of their claims the promises and pledges given by the Viceroy and the Secretary of State were not enough. Thirdly, the Muslim leadership, being extremely immature, was unable to grasp the significance of what it was demanding. These Muslim leaders interpreted 'separate representation' differently. The London Branch of the League led by Ameer Ali wanted exclusive Muslim representation, to which Morley had committed himself. A large number of Muslim leaders in India supported this view. Minto and some moderate leaders like Ali Imam were of the opinion that while the Muslims should be given special representation as a community, they must not be deprived of the right to vote in general electorates in competition with the Hindus. While a number of moderate Hindu leaders were willing to accept the Muslim claim for larger and better representation, they did not like the principle which, they thought, would create more problems.[2] Nevertheless Minto's view prevailed over all others ultimately.

[1] Minto to Morley, 31 December 1908. *M.P.*
[2] See *Proceedings of the I.N.C.*, 1909–10.

CHAPTER SIX

# ENACTMENT AND ENFORCEMENT OF THE INDIAN COUNCILS ACT OF 1909

On 17 December 1908 Morley announced the reform scheme in the House of Lords with the remark that 'If I were attempting to set up a Parliamentary system in India, or if it could be said that this chapter of reforms led directly or necessarily up to the establishment of a Parliamentary system in India, I for one would have nothing at all to do with it.' As he was speaking in the Conservative House of Lords, he naturally emphasized that the reform scheme was a 'well-guarded expansion of principles that were recognized in 1861' and stated that he had no wish 'to set up some sort of Parliamentary system in India, it is no ambition of mine, at all events, to have any share in beginning that operation. If my existence, either officially or corporeally, were prolonged twenty times longer than either of them is likely to be, a Parliamentary system in India is not the goal to which I would for one moment aspire'.[1] On the other hand Buchanan in explaining the reform proposals in the House of Commons stated, 'the proposals are a real step forward, and go a long way to meet in Lord Minto's words "the political aspirations of honest reformers". They are intended to associate a much larger body of Indians in the work of government to throw greater responsibility upon them, both in the higher and in the lower ranges of government, to maintain British supremacy clear and unchallenged at the top, but to endeavour to secure that under our guiding, directing, and restraining hand, the Indians shall learn the work

[1] *Hansard*, House of Lords, 4S, vol. 198 (7 December–21 December 1908). Morley's Speech, 17 December 1908, Cols. 991–1001.

of administration and government in the only school worth anything, the school of experience.'[2]

The Congress's first reaction to Morley's announcement of
reforms was one of overwhelming satisfaction. The moderates
were generally jubilant.[3] The Congress leaders were in close
touch with the Government officials, particularly Dunlop Smith.
Through him Minto was kept informed of the views of the Congress leaders. Dr. Rash Behari Ghose went to consult Dunlop
Smith about his opening speech at the Madras Congress of 1908
and told him that possibly reforms might even win over the
extremists. Rash Behari Ghose in that speech welcomed the
reforms while remarking that some people thought that a fair
share in the government of the country for the people of India was
impossible. This was a taunt at the extremist view that the
moderate constitutional methods would achieve nothing. He
hoped that relations between India and Great Britain would
improve because Morley's declaration had opened 'a chapter of
constitutional reform which promises to unite the two countries
together in closer bonds than ever'. India was 'on the threshold
of a new era', he declared. He boasted that this 'grant of representative government' was a step 'for which the Congress had
been crying for years', and hoped that the extension to India of a
Colonial type of government would not be far away. In the
opinion of Dewan Bahadur K. Krishnaswami Rao, the Chairman
of the Reception Committee, the reforms were a substantial step
towards *Swaraj*. Surendranath Banerjea considered them 'the
crowning triumph of constitutional agitation', and he urged the
audience to rise to its feet to express their 'deep gratitude to
the Government of India for what it proposes to do.'[4]

---

[2] *Hansard*, House of Commons, 4S, Vol. 198 (7 December–21 December
1908), Col. 2160.

[3] Minto to Morley, 29 October 1908. Earlier in a talk with Erle Richards
Rash Behari Ghose had asked him earnestly 'not to go in too much for
election as my people are quite unfit for that'. This coming from 'the great
Congress leader!' amused Minto very much. Minto to Morley, 14 July 1908.
*M.P.*

[4] *Report of the I.N.C.*, 1908, p. 48.

The Congress passed the following resolution, 'This Congress desires to give expression to the deep and general satisfaction with which the Reform proposals formulated in Lord Morley's despatch have been received throughout the country; it places on record its sense of the high statesmanship which has dictated the action of the Government in the matter and it tenders to Lord Morley and Lord Minto its most sincere and grateful thanks for their proposals.' The proposals contained in the Reform scheme 'constitute a large and liberal instalment of the reforms needed to give the people of this country a substantial share in the management of their affairs and to bring the administration into closer touch with their wants and feelings.' The Congress also hoped 'that details of the proposed scheme will be worked out in the same liberal spirit in which its main provisions as outlined in the Secretary of State's despatch have been conceived.'[5] Surendranath Banerjea proposed the resolution and Malaviya seconded it. It was supported by many delegates, including M. A. Jinnah from Bombay, who spoke very briefly and hoped that more Muslims would join the Hindus in this struggle. While neither the President nor any other delegate thought it wise to touch on the delicate topic of the representation of various interests, Malaviya did mention this 'important question'. He thought that the interests of Hindus, Muslims, landholders and merchants did not conflict with each other and were alike and he saw no need of 'having such class representation as has been given a prominent place in the reform scheme'. When 'a voice' reminded him that 'there are certain questions', he said 'there are questions; it is perfectly right, but these questions do not come before the Legislative Council either of the Viceroy or of the Local Governments'. The President did not want him to go on in order to avoid controversy at that time, so under the pretext of shortage of time, he was asked to terminate his speech. Being aware of the delicate nature of Morley's proposal for electoral colleges, Malaviya suggested that 'we should leave Lord Morley's proposals as they stand in this matter and not ask

[5] *Report of the I.N.C.*, 1908, Resolution II, p. 46.

that any different principle of representation should be introduced'.[6]

Gokhale was more realistic. He admitted that there were acute
differences amongst Indians and for the promotion of 'Unity in
the Country', any scheme of representation should be welcomed.
In his view the aim of both Hindus and Muslims was the same,
but the methods of approach were different. He moved a resolution of thanks to Hume, Wedderburn and the British Committee
of the Congress, for the work they had done during the past
years.[7] Gokhale had an interview with Dunlop Smith and Minto
informed Morley that 'the pith of it was that he had prevented
the discussion of the boycott, deportation, and the Partition at the
Madras Congress, and that he is now about to start on a tour
with the object of preaching co-operation with the Government
in the furtherance of our reforms . . .'[8]

The same enthusiasm was shown by other important members
of the Congress. Dr. G. B. Clarke, a former M.P. and a supporter
of the resolution on the Reform Scheme, remarked that 'one
could not fail to be struck with the warm appreciation accorded
to the Secretary of State and to the Viceroy.'[9] Morley appreciated
this feeling of the Congress. 'The Congress has done all that we
had a right to expect, and will do a good deal to justify our policy,
both in persevering with Reforms and in making them liberal.'[1]
In a letter to Godley, Minto also wrote, 'Dr. Ghose, Gokhale and
other leaders will, I know, do all they can now to support the
Government, whether Cotton & Co. will have the sense to follow
their lead of course I don't know.'[2]

The Reforms were generally welcomed. The *Englishman,* an
Anglo-Indian paper, which was very doubtful in the beginning
about the reform policy, published a favourable editorial regard-

[6] Report of the I.N.C., 1908, p. 56.
[7] Ibid. p. 137.
[8] Minto to Morley, 7 January 1909. *M.P.*
[9] G. B. Clarke, 'Impressions of the Madras Congress', *The Indian Review,*
January 1909, pp. 20–21.
[1] Morley to Minto, 31 December 1908. *M.P.*
[2] Minto to Godley, 7 January 1909. *M.C.*

ing the proposed appointment of 'the Legal Member' on 24 December 1908. Minto was pleased with the reception of the Reforms. He received a deputation of about 100 prominent Hindus and Muslims, representing various shades of thought, which presented him with a congratulatory address on the Reforms. He wrote to Morley, 'After all I have not been too sanguine as to the reception our reforms would meet with. The welcome they have received is far better than anything we were at all entitled to expect.'[3] Morley was very satisfied with the reception of the Reforms. He wrote to Minto, 'I never have had, and I never shall have, a more splendid Xmas box than when I opened *The Times* on Christmas morning, and read about the famous deputation to you about Reforms.'[4] Morley proudly stated in the House of Lords that the Reforms had received a wonderful welcome in India.[5]

The Reforms were well received in England as well. In Morley's words, 'Here the chorus of approval has been very satisfactory indeed. The pig-headed section of the Ultra-Radicals pretend to think that our chances were ruined by deportation; that the Congress counts for little because it excluded the Extremists; that Chandra Pal is the live man, not Gokhale; that without the release of Tilak, etc., and the undoing of Partition, all the Reforms are no good. But the croaks of these few sour-blooded critics count for nothing.'[6]

Only the Muslim League did not approve of the Reform Scheme. It was not satisfied with Morley's scheme of electoral colleges and started a vigorous campaign against it.[7]

Morley presented the Indian Councils Bill in the House of Lords on 17 February 1909. He moved for the second reading of the Bill on 23 February 1909. It was sent to Committee on 24 February and the debate continued on 4 and 9 March. It was read

[3] Minto to Morley, 24 December 1908. *M.C.*
[4] Morley to Minto, 31 December 1908. Ibid.
[5] *Hansard*, House of Lords, vol. i (16 February–26 May 1909), 23 February 1909, Cols. 117–18.
[6] Morley to Minto, 31 December 1908. *M.C.*
[7] See Chapter V.

for the third time on 11 March and passed as amended on the same day.[8] Explaining the necessity for introducing the Bill, Morley stated that there were two schools of thought regarding the Government in India. One school, represented by Curzon, believed that better government depended on efficiency of administration. The other, with which he associated himself and Minto, not ignoring the cause of efficiency, 'looks also to what is called political concessions'. In his view, without political concessions, 'true, solid endurable efficiency' could not be ensured. He admitted that he was aware of the risks dependent on a policy of political concessions. But once occidental education had been introduced in India, occidental machinery must follow.[9] His claim was that the Bill did not make any violent departure. It was a modest attempt to extend the principles embedded in the Indian Councils Act of 1892. Morley evidently did not want to arouse suspicions in a Conservative House, 'to whom of course the very word "reform" is of evil savour',[1] by declaring that this Bill was a revolutionary step.

The debate in the House of Lords was quite lively. Godley was surprised at the number of peers able, 'both by understanding and by personal knowledge and experience, to make speeches about Indian administration'.[2] While MacDonnell, Ampthill, Midleton, Reay and Cromer agreed with Morley that Western education had inspired Indians 'with the idea of political activity' and the political demands were 'the natural and inevitable result.' Most of the speakers did not think that the Bill was an extension of the Act of 1892.[3] Lansdowne stated that it was 'not

[8] *Hansard*, House of Lords, vol. i (16 February–26 May 1909), Cols. 70; 117–216; 255–304; 409–28.

[9] Ibid. Cols. 122–3.

[1] Morley to Minto, 25 February 1909. *M.P.*

[2] Godley to Minto, 26 February 1909. *M.C.* The following took part in the debate: Lord Ampthill, Courtney of Penwith, Lord Crewe, Earl Cromer, Viscount Cross, Lord Curzon, Lord Harris, Lord Lansdowne, Lord Mac-Donnell, Viscount Midleton, Lord Northcote, Lord Reay, Lord Ripon, Lord Sandhurst, Lord Wenlock and Lord Wolverhampton.

[3] *Hansard*, House of Lords, vol. i (16 February–26 May 1909), Cols. 149, 157, 170, 178, 185.

merely a step forward, it is a plunge forward, and a plunge which will lead us we cannot tell where'.[4] Midleton thought that the Bill introduced 'some of the very worst features of our own Parliamentary practice' despite Morley's denial of any intention of introducing parliamentary government in India.[5] In Curzon's opinion there was 'a great difference' between the Act of 1892 and the new Bill, which created 'almost representative government'. It introduced some of 'the features inseparably attached to a parliamentary system', which system would 'inevitably be the consequence' of the new measure. He strongly objected to the enlargement of the Legislative Councils, which in his opinion was a 'revolutionary change'.[6] 'Thus in the words of Godley, the Conservative Lords criticized the bill 'as a rash and revolutionary measure'.[7] The impression that these speeches created in the India Office is worth noting. Godley wrote to Minto that Curzon's speech was 'full of knowledge, and very able, though not lively reading; Broderick's excellent—so everyone says, including Lord Morley'. In his opinion Curzon did 'show himself off' and narrated his own Indian achievements and experiences, but the Government was able to carry the day. Wolverhampton, though very old and knowing nothing, made a 'useless' speech. Crewe stood up many times, said 'a few graceful words', made 'a good point' against the opposition but did not understand the Bill, nor pretended to do so. According to Godley there were twenty other Liberal peers who knew nothing and cared little about the matter. The Archbishop of Canterbury told Godley that there were about sixteen peers who were qualified to speak on Indian matters and all of them except four or five were Unionists. Morley was handicapped because he was not very familiar with some of the matters he was dealing with and had to consult the India Office representatives who were standing on the steps of the throne and he was also 'not in good voice'.[8]

[4] *Hansard*, House of Lords, vol. i (16 February–26 May, 1909), Col. 417.
[5] Ibid. Col. 175.
[6] Ibid. Col. 135.
[7] Godley to Minto, 26 February 1909. *M.C.*
[8] Godley to Minto, 26 February, 5 March 1909. Ibid.

Curzon was the strongest opponent of the Bill. In Morley's words, 'he hates the Bill and the whole policy of which the Bill is the instrument . . . His arguments . . . all of them rest on the view that the whole attempt is a blunder, and that we ought to have persisted in his policy of shutting eyes and ears to all "political concessions" whatever.'[9] But despite Curzon's and the Conservative Peers' dislike of the Bill it was not thrown out for it had the support of the Government of India. There was also the House of Commons which would have passed the Bill in any case. Relations between the two Houses were already strained and no one wanted to shoulder the responsibility of adding further bitterness. Besides, as Lansdowne wrote to Minto, 'Morley and I settled the [sic] matters out of Court after a somewhat stiff deal'.[1] It seems that the opposition had promised that they would make all 'attempts to nag and whittle it away,' but would not throw it out.[2]

But in the Committee stage, it became apparent that the Conservatives would not compromise on Clause 3 of the Bill, which empowered the Government to create an Executive Council in any province under a Lieutenant-Governor. Morley had emphasized that it was purely permissive and did not necessarily mean the creation of compulsory Executive Councils in Lieutenant-Governor's provinces. MacDonnell did not agree with this view and thought it an 'unnecessary innovation'.[3] Curzon and Lansdowne supported his view. Morley, Wolverhampton and Crewe tried to save the clause but the motion was carried by fifty-nine to eighteen votes. This happened on 4 March 1909.[4] Morley tried to restore the clause on 9 March when he presented the Government of India's telegram in which Baker's demand for an Executive Council for Bengal had been put forward. But the opposition remained adamant and Morley had to give way. The House of Commons, on the other hand, passed the clause intact.

[9] Morley to Minto, 5 March 1909. *M.P.*
[1] Lansdowne to Minto, 11 May 1909. *M.C.*
[2] Morley to Minto, 5 March 1909. Ibid.
[3] *Hansard*, House of Lords, vol. i (16 February–26 May 1909), Cols. 295–8.
[4] Ibid. Cols. 314–15.

Moreover, the appointment of S. P. Sinha, which was published on 23 March 1909, made Clause 3 seem in the eyes of its opponents a minor incident. Even then an assurance was given by the Government that Parliament should have effective control as regards the creation of Executive Councils in provinces other than Bengal. This compromise practically ensured the passing of the Bill intact when it again reached the House of Lords.

Thus the creation of Executive Councils in Lieutenant-Governors' provinces was restricted to Bengal in deference to the House of Lords. It was only Baker, the Lieutenant-Governor of Bengal, who had fought for the creation of an Executive Council for Bengal, so he was given one. The Government of India was not very enthusiastic about these Executive Councils. Its half-heartedness encouraged the House of Lords to throw the clause out in the first instance.[5] C. Y. Chintamani considered this compromise a big surrender to the House of Lords by Morley and regretted the disallowance of such a Council in U.P.[6]

The Bill was read a second time by the House of Commons on 1 April 1909 and went to Committee on 19 April. T. R. Buchanan, the Under-Secretary of State, piloted it, but he fell ill and C. E. H. Hobhouse took his place. The second reading in the House of Commons was not very impressive. The House took little or no interest. At one time there were about fourteen M.P.s on the Government benches and eight on the other side. The debate was 'spiritless'. It gave Morley the impression of listening 'to a band of disembodied ghosts—so far off did they all seem from the hard realities and perplexities with which we have been grappling all these months'.[7]

[5] *Hansard*, House of Lords, vol. i (16 February–26 May 1909), Lansdowne's speech, 9 March 1909, Cols. 340–42.

[6] The *Hindustan Review*, vol. xix, Nos. 107–8, May–June 1909, pp. 552–69.

[7] Morley to Minto, 2 April 1909. *M.P.* The following members took a prominent part in the debate in the House of Commons:

| Conservatives | Liberals |
| --- | --- |
| A. J. Balfour | H. H. Asquith, P.M. |
| Sir F. Banbury | T. R. Buchanan. Under S. of S. |
| Captain Guy Baring | Sir Henry Cotton |
| E. H. Carlile | Sir Charles Dilke |

*continued overleaf*

On 25 May 1909 the Bill became an Act. Though it modified its predecessors of 1861 and 1892, its text does not seem very revolutionary. But it was a clear step forward.

During the formation of the Rules and Regulations for election to the newly constituted councils under the India Councils Act of 1909 the question arose whether deportees ought to be able to take their seat in the Assemblies. Morley was of the same opinion as Minto that some control was necessary over the actions of admittedly seditious persons, but was not willing to permit any permanent disqualification to a deported person after he had been freed. He, therefore, suggested that he was ready to approve a veto on all elections[8]; and Godley thought it 'a very considerable change—I was going to say, of opinion, but perhaps I should rather say—of mood on his [Morley's] part'.[9] Morley wanted Minto's opinion in this regard, as Buchanan was expected to make a statement in the House of Commons.[1] Minto did not like any discussion in the House of Commons of any part of the Regulations, which were under the Government of India's consideration, before they were finalized. He also asked Morley 'why it is impossible to defend attachment of a political disqualification to deportation after the deported man is released?' He thought public opinion in India would regard such a disqualification from standing for election as a natural consequence of deportation and that the Government of India could not disregard it

| Conservatives | Liberals |
|---|---|
| Sir Henry Craik | John Ellis |
| W. Joynson Hicks | George Gooch |
| W. J. MacCaw | T. Hart-Davies |
| E. C. Meysey-Thompson | C. E. Hobhouse |
| Earl Percy | Sir J. Jardine |
| Earl of Ronaldshay | A. Lupton |
| | F. C. Mackarness |
| Labour | C. J. O'Donnell |
| Keir Hardie | J. D. Rees |
| Nationalist | Dr. V. H. Rutherford |
| John Dillon | D. M. Smeaton |

[8] Morley to Minto, telegram, 24 March 1909. *M.C.*
[9] Godley to Minto, 26 March 1909. Ibid.
[1] Morley to Minto, telegrams, 24, 30 March, 7 April 1909. Ibid.

with safety. Moreover, if a deported person was admitted to the Council, soon after his release, 'it would be a serious blow to the position of Government and the Council'. He, therefore, suggested that a complete list of classes of persons disqualified should be issued along with 'power of "waiver" by the Viceroy, or possibly, for Provincial Councils, by the Lieutenant-Governor'. He requested Morley that pending finalization of the Regulations, no pledges should be given in the House of Commons.[2] Morley replied that as the question of disqualification was so important the Government could not evade it. Any attachment of a political disqualification to deportation after the deported man had been released would turn the Bill into a measure for widening the scope of the Regulations of 1818. The Executive Government would then have the power not only of detaining a person without charge or trial but also of excluding him, at its own discretion, from effective public life without limit of time. Such a wide power in the hands of the Executive Morley would not like. He, therefore, informed Minto that 'after consulting the Prime Minister, I have decided that the Government cannot evade the responsibility of informing the House of Commons plainly to-day that His Majesty's Government do not intend that the fact of a man having been deported shall, after his release, of itself be a ground for disqualifying him for election to a Legislative Council.'[3]

Minto admitted the difficulties besetting the matter in the House of Commons but insisted that his first duty was to consider India. He urged Morley to realize that while Parliament should make the Bill, it was for the Government of India to formulate the Rules and Regulations.[4]

As was expected Mackarness moved an amendment during the

[2] Minto to Morley, telegram, 17 April 1909. *M.C.* Mary, Countess of Minto, op. cit., p. 301. See also Minto to Godley, 29 April 1909. Minto informed Godley about his views as well.

[3] Morley to Minto, telegram, 19 April 1909. *M.C.* Mary, Countess of Minto, op. cit., p. 301.

[4] Minto to Morley, 21 April 1909. Ibid. Morley himself admitted this fact in his speech in the House of Lords. *Hansard,* House of Lords, vol. i, 23 February 1909, Cols. 123-4.

Committee stage of the Bill in the House of Commons. The amendment was to the effect that no one should be disqualified from membership of any Legislative Council 'by reason of his having been deported and imprisoned without having been charged with and convicted of any offence'.[5] In Mackarness's view it would be a gross injustice to disqualify those persons who had been deprived of the right of defending their innocence in a court of law. They had not been charged, convicted and told of their crime.[6] C. E. H. Hobhouse, who had assumed the responsibility of piloting the Bill during Buchanan's illness, explained the need of disqualification and the right of the head of the Government to waive disqualification in favour of an individual. But as regards the deportees, he made it 'quite clear' that the Government did not intend 'that the fact of a man having been deported shall, after his release, of itself be a ground for disqualifying him for election to a Legislative Council.'[7]

When Minto came to know of Hobhouse's statement, he sent a strong protest from the Government of India. He told Morley that this pronouncement had been made before the Government of India had had a full opportunity to consider the matter in consultation with Local Governments. He also informed Morley that the Local Governments were unanimous in holding that deportees should be disqualified from standing for election and that Sinha, the Law Member and a member of Minto's Reform Committee, had 'taken a very strong line, insisting that disqualification was absolutely necessary in the case of deportees'. The Government of India was of the opinion that a general power of veto vested in the Governor-General, or the head of a Province, would not safely meet the case of deportees. They were afraid that 'if deportees were put up for election there would be violent political excitement during the election. If, after the election, they were vetoed, their wire-pullers would be almost

---

[5] *Hansard*, House of Commons, vol. iii (29 March–23 April 1909), 19 April 1909, Col. 1267.

[6] Ibid. Mackarness's speech, Cols. 1268–71.

[7] Ibid., Hobhouse's speech, Cols. 1273–5.

certain to arouse the populace, whether voters or not, and the probable result would be dangerous disturbances such as occurred in Bombay when Tilak was arrested'. As regards Morley's objections that the attachment of disqualification would widen the scope of the Regulations of 1818, and that it would imply that deportation was a normal process, the Government of India forcefully contended that it could equally well be argued that the disqualification of a convict would add to the scope of the Penal Code, and that deportation, though not a normal, was an actual process, recognized by law and in actual operation and therefore a process that it was necessary to provide for. The Government of India's recommendations, thus, were for the disqualification of deportees from standing for election subject to a 'waiver' by the Governor-General, or the head of the Government which passed the order of deportation. They were even prepared to limit this disqualification to a period of five years from the date of release. They further urged that this application or non-application of the 'waiver' should not be subject to the sanction of any higher authority than the head of Government. It should be finally decided by the authorities in India.[8]

It was during the third reading of the India Councils Bill that Earl Percy asked searching questions about the Government's policy with regard to the deportees. 'Are persons who have been deported on a charge of suspicion of sedition to come under a separate category of disqualification?' he asked. He wanted Hobhouse to be more precise than he had been when he had told the House in the Committee stage 'that deported persons were not to be regarded *ipso facto* as disqualified'.[9] Explaining the exact attitude and intentions of the Government, Hobhouse told the House that the Government had no intention of sanctioning the disqualification of deported persons as a class and they could not allow any regulation by the Government of India having an effect of that sort. But if the Government of India desired a power to

[8] Minto to Morley, telegram, 3 May 1909. *M.C.*
[9] *Hansard*, House of Commons, vol. iv (26 April–14 May 1909). Earl Percy, 26 April 1909, Cols. 95–96.

exclude any undesirable person from standing for election, His Majesty's Government would not refuse such power.[1] A. J. Balfour agreed with the policy of the Government.[2]

Godley informed Minto that 'it is now settled that you may, by Regulation, give to yourself and to the Local Governments the power of preventing the nomination of *any* irreconcilable; and this is, surely far better than the exclusion of deportees *as such*.'[3]

Morley had thus turned down Minto's suggestion in deference to the House of Commons, as he himself admitted, 'we could not have defended the measure which you desired'. The solution to which he was prepared to agree was 'a general power by Regulation to disallow candidature of any person whose antecedents and character are such that his election would, in the opinion of the Government of India, be contrary to public interests, whether he has been deported or not'. Deportation was his sore point as he insisted that 'the Regulations should not mention or refer to deportation'.[4] Minto had earlier informed Morley that 'this is a wider power than we asked for, but our impression is that, although the proposal avoids mention of deportation, which is a settled fact, it offers a law of political restraint exactly parallel to the law of personal restraint contained in the Regulations of 1818, and we are convinced that it will be regarded in India with greater disfavour than our proposals relating to deportees'.[5] Minto felt very strongly about the interference of the House of Commons and 'disregard of the opinion of the Government of India, in deference to the wishes of a certain political section at home unacquainted with conditions here'. He considered this procedure, if taken as a precedent, 'as extremely dangerous to

[1] *Hansard*, House of Commons, vol. iv (26 April–14 May 1909). Hobhouse, Cols. 98–99.

[2] Ibid. Balfour, Cols. 99–100. C. Y. Chintamani, writing in the *Hindustan Review*, vol. xix, Nos. 107–8, May–June 1909, regretted Hobhouse's statement and stated that any disqualification in connexion with deportation was an 'unjust punishment'.

[3] Godley to Minto, 30 April 1909. *M.C.*

[4] Morley to Minto, telegram, 11 May 1909. Ibid.

[5] Minto to Morley, telegram, 3 May 1909. Ibid. Mary, Countess of Minto, op. cit., p. 304.

the future of this country'.[6] Morley argued that 'the Government of India is no absolute or independent branch of Imperial Government. It is in every respect answerable to the Cabinet as any other department is; and if the Cabinet, for reasons of its own, decides that no political disqualification shall attach to deportation, that ends the matter. You are mistaken in laying all the blame on Parliament. If the Cabinet had gone the other way, nothing would have induced *me* to assent.'[7]

The Regulations which were promulgated after all this discussion were that 'No person shall be eligible for election as a Member of the Council if such person . . . has been declared by the Governor-General in Council to be of such reputation and antecedents that his election would, in the opinion of the Governor-General in Council, be contrary to the public interest'. Thus the Government of India obtained a wider power than they had asked for. Now they could declare any person, whom they considered undesirable, as ineligible for election. Morley had secured his point at the cost of making the Government of India more powerful. He objected to the word 'deportation'. He could not digest and would not like to see it in any form in his Bill or Regulations. *The Cambridge History of India* gives an erroneous account of this episode. It conveys the impression that the Governor-General in Council was given the power he was asking for, 'to declare that in his opinion a person was of such reputation and antecedents that his election would be contrary to the public interest'.[8] This power was not what the Governor-General in Council had wanted. It was given to him by the Secretary of State, because the latter could not allow the words 'deportees' and 'deportation' in the list of disqualifications.

There were still a number of hurdles to be crossed. During the debate on the Address in reply to the King's speech in the House of Commons, Mackarness moved an amendment to the Address that the success of the reform proposals in India 'is

[6] Minto to Morley, 13 May 1909. *M.C.*
[7] Morley to Minto, 13 May 1909. Ibid.
[8] *The Cambridge History of India*, vol. vi, p. 571.

gravely endangered by the fact that British subjects in that country are subjected to imprisonment and deportation without having had any charge made against them, and without having been convicted of any crime.'[9] Buchanan defended the Government policy and the amendment was defeated by 195 votes to seventy-six—of whom thirty-three were Irish, twenty-five Labour, three or four Liberal Unionist and other Liberals. Morley was pleased with the result and wrote to Minto, 'so, you see, the Mother of Parliaments is not such a bad step-mother after all'.[1] But the question of deportees could not be postponed very long. The letters and telegrams that passed between Minto and Morley during the last months of 1909 and early January 1910 amply show Morley's anxiety as to the effect the continued detention of the prisoners would have on public opinion in England. He thought that this continuance of detention contradicted their policy of reform and as time passed by his insistence on the release of some, if not all, grew.

Besides his own dislike of deportation Morley was under pressure from the House of Commons.[2] Some 150 members wrote to Asquith in protest against deportation and Morley informed Minto that Asquith would 'give them a judicious reply but you will not be able to deport any more of your suspects— that is quite clear.'[3] A few days later Morley again wrote, 'A pretty heavy gale is blowing up in the House of Commons about deportation and shows every sign of blowing harder as time goes on.' He implored Minto that besides Tories and Radicals some of the moderate Liberals were becoming uneasy and though he intended 'to sit tight just where we are, uncomfortable as is the saddle', it would be wise to release these deportees.[4] Minto did

[9] *Hansard*, House of Commons, vol. i, 1909 (16 February–5 March 1909), 24 February 1909. Col. 807.

[1] Morley to Minto, 26 February 1909. *M.P.*

[2] J. O'Grady, F. C. Mackarness, Keir Hardie, A. Lupton and others asked questions about deportations, see *Hansard*, House of Commons, vol. iv (April 26–May 14), Cols. 879, 880, vol. v (May 17–June 4), Cols. 227–9, 996–9, 1001–3, 1017–20, 1030–1.

[3] Morley to Minto, 5 May 1909. *M.P.*

[4] Morley to Minto, 27 May 1909. Ibid.

not like this interference by the House of Commons. 'I daresay you think me oversensitive as to the House of Commons action in respect to India, but I feel that I cannot exaggerate the importance of saving India just now from ill-considered expressions of opinion in Parliament. Every little twopenny-half-penny question which can be taken to indicate sympathy with agitation and discredit to the Government of India is magnified a hundredfold here.' He told Morley that the 'anarchical undercurrent'[5] still existed and the Government could not afford to neglect it for a moment, but 'these pin-pricks at home *do* shake us'.[6] Minto was very clear in his mind with regard to his policy towards deportees. He had repeatedly informed Morley that his duty was 'to secure British administration in India and the welfare of the populations over whom we rule'. Indians must be given a share in the administration but the supreme guidance must remain in British hands. Considering the present ticklish situation he was not willing to permit any outside influence, even that of Parliament. The release of deportees under Parliamentary pressure would not improve the situation. His intention was to consider 'without a hint to the outside world, the possibility of release simultaneously with the opening of the New Imperial Legislative Council, after the elections'. The release of deportees before election would have created an embarrassing situation. Some of the deportees were prominent Indians and they were likely to stand for election for the enlarged Legislative Assemblies. Minto did not want them to stand for election or to influence the election of others. Moreover with the inauguration of new Legislative Councils, he wanted to begin with 'a clean sheet' and 'let bygones be bygones', but if the deportees were released before, 'our assent [to release the deportees], no matter what the reason for it might be, would be looked upon as a surrender to political pressure and nothing else . . .'[7]

[5] Minto presumably used these words loosely; what he meant was terrorist undercurrent. The terrorists did not want anarchy, neither were they anarchists.

[6] Minto to Morley, 10 June 1909. *M.P.*

[7] Minto to Morley, 17 June 1909. Ibid.

Though not completely convinced, Morley agreed to wait for some time. Morley had never shared Minto's views upon Parliamentary interference. He had repeatedly told Minto that Parliament was the real master and a positive check on the autocratic actions of the Government of India. Minto never disputed Parliament's supreme authority but always submitted that his first task was to discharge his duty of governing India judiciously and that as the man on the spot he knew better the policy to follow in India than the critics of the Government at Westminster. He did have supporters of his policies in Parliament. When the radicals in the House of Commons criticized some of his repressive policies, the Conservatives in the House of Lords wished he had more power to crush 'sedition'. The debates on the Seditious Meetings Act and the Press Acts in both Houses clearly bear out this point.[8] This counter-balancing of influences was essential, in a way, for Minto's administration because after all Morley and he differed in their political training and outlook as well. Morley was not a radical himself, but he was conscious of the views of his radical supporters. Whenever he, under the influence of the radicals, put pressure on Minto to revise his policy, Minto, knowing full well that the Conservatives would support him, insisted that his views be made public. Likewise when Minto was insisting on an Indian member for his Council, and Morley, because of Conservative opposition, was reluctant, the possible reaction of radical opinion on Morley's refusal made him ask Minto whether it was possible to keep it a secret that the suggestion was ever made and that Minto supported it.

Fear of Parliamentary pressure again forced Morley to write to Minto in August. He suggested the release of deportees at the time of the announcement of the Regulations. 'The release of our *détenues* at such a time would be a mark of our confidence in our policy and our position.'[9] Minto considered in the Council the revision of the cases of deportees. The Lieutenant-Governors of Bengal and Eastern Bengal and Assam had strongly opposed their

[8] See Chapter III.
[9] Morley to Minto, 20 August 1909. *M.P.*

release for security reasons and the Council too came to the same decision. It was, therefore, decided that they should not be released for some time. Minto's consideration in maintaining their detention was that besides Bengali sympathy, he had to consider Anglo-Indian opinion, the views of the Rulers of Native States and 'A huge population whose loyalty to us depends largely on their conviction of our strength, and that, to Anglo-Indian, Ruling Chief and loyal Native, the release of the deportees at present would mean nothing but weakness'.[1] Minto maintained that to release the deportees on the announcement of the Regulations would mean turning them 'loose on the country at the most inopportune moment that could be chosen'. It would provide the strongest temptation to political agitators to induce them to come forward as candidates for the newly-constituted Councils. He was afraid that the Government would come into disrepute because 'we might be forced to detract from the generosity of our new administration by refusing to accept certain candidatures as contrary to the public interest'. So in his opinion the best time to release them would be after the inauguration of the new Councils in January.[2] Morley could no longer remain patient. He enquired whether the decision was taken by a committee of the Council or the full Council and who were the members responsible for the decision[3]; in particular he enquired whether Sinha attended the proceedings.[4] He also asked Minto to send the reports of the Local Governments.[5] Minto sent the reports, and explained that the decision was taken by the full Council and that Sinha agreed with it.[6]

Minto had suggested that for the time being discussion should

[1] Minto to Morley, 1 September 1909. *M.P.*
[2] Minto to Morley, 9 September 1909. Ibid.
[3] Morley to Minto, telegram, 8 September 1909. Ibid.
[4] Morley to Minto, telegram, 10 September 1909. Ibid.
[5] Morley to Minto, telegram, 14 September 1909. Ibid.
[6] Minto to Morley, telegrams, 9, 13, 15 September 1909. 'Sinha declared his inability to criticize reasons of high policy affecting deportations, and concluded by saying, "if the Order of December 1908 is held to be right I agree that the release should be deferred till the new Councils are formed" '. Minto to Morley, telegram, 13 September 1909. Ibid.

not centre round the rights and wrongs of the policy of deportation, but this action must be considered in respect of the effect
their release may have on the safety of India. Morley agreed, but
suggested that although the release of all of them might lead to
mischief, at least some could be released against whom the case
was comparatively weak. He did not agree with the views that
their release might lead to further trouble, expressed by Baker
and Hare for the continuation of detention, and reminded Minto
that Ibbetson had had the same sort of view when Lajpat Rai's
release was being considered. In his opinion Baker and Hare
would say the same things if they were consulted 'six months, or
twelve months or twenty months hence'. With regard to some
'unpleasant candidates', Morley agreed that it would be awkward
to let any one of them come to the Legislative Councils, but
maintained that it would be just as awkward for them openly to
accept the obligation to co-operate with the Government. They
would lose all respect in the eyes of their followers 'by the fact
of their joining the hated Raj, even to a moderate extent'. He
further asked Minto whether he had 'thought of the possibility
of an anti-deportation discussion being brought forward in your
L.C.?' Thus, in his opinion, as a 'wise accompaniment of the
next stage of Reforms', at least two of the men should be released
and 'the speedier the better'.[7]

Morley returned to the subject later, and again asked Minto to
come to some decision about the release of deportees soon, as
'their continued detention makes a mockery of the language we
are going to use about Reforms. It makes a thoroughly self-
contradictory situation'. He thought it a 'matter of policy of the
highest moment'.[8]

Minto considered the release of the deportees in the Council but
the Council again decided to stick to its previous decision and
maintained that their release was not justified for security rea-

[7] Morley to Minto, 30 September 1909. *M.C.* From the very beginning
Morley was asking for the release of Aswini Kumar Dutt and K. K. Mittra,
as in his opinion the cases against them were weak.
[8] Morley to Minto, 20 October 1909. Ibid.

sons. He did not agree with Morley's argument that the continued detention of the deportees 'makes a thoroughly contradictory situation'. He explained that the main purpose of the Reform Scheme was to rally the moderates, but if these 'firebrands' were released it would jeopardize the chance that 'the reasonable and stable elements in Indian society' would come forward. To him their release would create a 'self contradictory situation'. He assured Morley that he realized 'the difficulties which surround you at home and the pressure you have faced so bravely', but it was wrong to assume that his main consideration in continuing the detention of the deportees was European and official feeling. He was much concerned about the effect their release would have on the opinions of loyal Indians. In his view they did not want them to be released.[9] He therefore remarked that 'it would be lamentable if we, at the last moment, ruin the results we expect by attempting to meet sentiment quite unsuited to the present position in India'. This Morley would not tolerate. Morley was aroused. He immediately asked if all the members of Minto's Council agreed with him in his policy. Furthermore he not only threatened that the Cabinet was against it but asked Minto if he was prepared to 'reject the unanimous suggestion of the Cabinet'. He tried to refute all of Minto's arguments. To his mind they were all based on flimsy grounds. All of Minto's fears, i.e. Hindu-Muslim disturbances, fears of the Ruling Chiefs, British opinion of the opponents of reform in England and the fear that the moderate cause would suffer if the deportees were released, were not valid arguments. He even told Minto that 'an important moderate leader [Gokhale] explicitly says that to continue detention would give a trump card to extremists'. In other words Morley suggested that as far as Indian opinion was concerned Minto's reading was wrong and that he knew much more than Minto. Thus if they wanted to win the support of the moderates, they must do as the moderates wanted. He therefore suggested that either on 15 November, the day when the

[9] Minto to Morley, telegram, 22 October, letter, 21 October 1909. M.C.

Reforms were to be introduced, or on 9 November, the King's birthday, an amnesty be granted to them.[1] This was the harshest threat Minto had received from Morley, but he remained adamant. He refused to agree with Morley and frankly said that 'there can be no question of an amnesty on a certain date'. His Council and the Lieutenant-Governors were unanimous that their release was not in the interests of 'the internal peace of India'. So he took a bold stand against Morley. He, however, tried to pacify him by saying that he had always served the Government loyally and recognized the importance of unity on all matters, but it was the duty of the Government of India to express their views with regard to the safety of the Empire. In his opinion the views of Gokhale, or for that matter any other person, were 'perfectly valueless and misleading', because they did not possess all the information. The Government of India, being in possession of all the material against deportees, was the best judge to decide about their release. He admitted that he understood 'British odium to detaining men without trial', but 'that feeling cannot be expressed from Indian populations—the vast majority of whom desire to live in peace', and outside Bengal people 'would simply marvel at release'. Hence the Government of India thought it was not safe to release them now. If, however, Morley insisted, the Government would obey him but 'they could not be held responsible for the results.'[2] Minto's own view was that he could not conceive 'at the present moment anything more dangerous than that disregard should be had to the matured opinions of the Government of India and Local Governments.'[3] He further submitted in a letter that, 'whilst I and my Council would endeavour to do our duty as best we could, we should be entitled to ask that our communications to the Secretary of State should be made public . . .'[4] But Morley's anger and pressure subsided even before the receipt of the letter. Minto had

[1] Morley to Minto, telegrams, 27, 31 October 1909. *M.C.*
[2] Minto to Morley, telegram, 31 October 1909. *M.P.*
[3] Minto to Morley, telegram, 2 November 1909. Ibid.
[4] Minto to Morley, letter, 2 November 1909. Ibid.

threatened to absolve himself of responsibility should things go wrong, Morley could not take the risk of being blamed for forcing the Government of India to do a thing which they did not want for security reasons. He admitted the force of Minto's argument and sought a compromise by asking him to fix a date for their release. In this connexion he pointed out that Minto had earlier expressed his willingness to release them on 1 January 1910.[5] Now Minto had won his day after a great fight and endless worry, he did not want to make any commitment so he refused to fix any definite date. His main objection was that if the date of release was made public in advance, the Government would be accused of refusing release simply on account of elections and also that it would seem to imply amnesty. In his view the release should appear not as an amnesty, but as a logical consequence of the causes of deportation having ceased to exist.[6]

On 13 November an attempt was made on the Viceroy's life while he was touring Ahmedabad. On 21 December A. M. T. Jackson, Collector of Nasik, was murdered. Some minor incidents of crime also took place in other places. Morley, who had not ceased to ask Minto to release the deportees, was informed that because of these incidents it would be impossible for the Government to modify their orders. Minto admitted that the deportees had no hand in these incidents, but their release would be misunderstood and loyal Indians particularly would consider it as a weakness on the part of the Government.[7]

After the elections to the new Councils, Morley again took a very strong line. In his opinion Minto had no more justification for not releasing the deportees because the Government of India intended to acquire more powers to suppress 'sedition' under the new Press Act of 1910. Moreover, Minto had promised to

[5] Morley to Minto, telegram, 3 November 1909. *M.P.* See Minto to Morley, 9 September 1909; in this letter Minto had stated that the deportees could be released in January after the inauguration of new Councils, provided nothing went wrong.

[6] Minto to Morley, telegram, 5 November 1909. Ibid.

[7] Minto to Morley, telegrams, 6, 26 December 1909; 2, 5 January 1910. *M.C.*

release them after the new Councils had met.[8] He also threatened that, 'it will be intensely disagreeable to me to have to send you an official instruction, but I fear there can be no alternative if you should continue your present objection'.[9] Now Minto gave way and advised his Council to revise its decision. He informed Morley that they would be released immediately after the passage of the Press Act.[1] Morley heaved a sigh of relief.[2] The Act was passed on 8 February 1910 and the deportees were released on 9 February. If, however, Morley had failed to persuade Minto to release them early, he had succeeded in convincing him that it would not be possible to deport any more. So Minto disallowed the deportation of fifty-three persons recommended by the Government of Bengal.[3]

Lady Minto is wrong when she states that Morley had no prior intimation of their release.[4] A general impression was also created amongst officials in India that Minto had been forced to take this decision. After all, Shams-ul-Alam, the Deputy Super-

[8] Morley to Minto, telegrams, 22, 23 January 1910. *M.C.* The new Imperial Legislative Council met on 25 January 1910.

[9] Morley to Minto, telegram, 28 January 1910. Ibid.

[1] Minto to Morley, telegrams, 5, 8, 9 February 1910. Ibid.

[2] Morley to Minto, telegram, 6 February 1910, letter, 10 February 1910. Ibid.

[3] Government of Bengal to the Government of India, 1 February–28 February 1910 and Government of India to the Government of Bengal, 7 March 1910. *Home Progs.* Political, January–July 1910, 8430.

[4] *My Indian Journal*, 1910, vol. i, p. 52. 'The announcement of the release came as a complete surprise to everyone with the exception of his Executive Council. Neither Sir Edward Baker nor Mr. Butler were aware of Rolly's decision, and one and all imagined that he had given way to undue pressure from home. Although Morley has never ceased agitating about the deportees for the past year, he himself did not know that this moment had been selected to release them. Rolly is quite certain that he had done the right thing from a political point of view.' 'Mr. Chirol told me that he had been with Morley twelve hours before reading in the papers of the release of the deportees, and that Morley had never hinted that they were to be released. I told him he could not have done so, as he knew nothing about it himself until it was a *fait accompli*,' p. 88.

See Minto's note about the release in the above *Journal* as well (pp. 69–72). The account from her *Journal*, which Lady Minto gives in her book on page 377, is not found in the *Journal* itself.

intendent of Police, had been murdered on 24 January 1910 and
the situation had not improved so much as to justify Minto's
action, neither had the terrorist movement died down. Minto
was conscious of it as well. He wrote a note in which he stated
his reasons for taking this action. In this note Minto stated that
he took the decision on his own and that he did not inform Morley
beforehand.

Minto is incorrect in saying that he did not inform Morley
beforehand. He did inform Morley and he was really pressed
very hard. Morley's telegram of 28 January 1910, threatening
him with 'official instruction', must have made him think hard.
The decision to release them on 9 February was decidedly his.
The reason for this decision, according to him, was not Morley's
pressure, but 'whether it was advisable to refuse release and
alienate a large body of influential Indian public opinion, whilst
at the same time having to face a hostile Council in the early days
of its existence, whose demands we should have eventually to
recognize—for we could not have kept the deportees imprisoned
indefinitely'. He was also informed that a deputation was being
organized to wait on him. So 'independently of any influences in
England', he 'acted in Indian interests alone' and decided to
release them. He risked even severe criticism of Anglo-Indian
society.[5] The way he had been resisting pressure from home
suggests that there is some truth in his statement that his main
consideration in releasing them was Indian public opinion. The

[5] Note by Minto, 1 March 1910, in Lady Minto's *My Indian Journal*,
1910, vol. i, pp. 69–72, vol. ii, pp. 338–41. This note was sent to Dunlop
Smith, who was Political A.D.C. to Morley at that time. Lady Minto gives two
reasons for Minto's decision—to begin 'with a clean sheet' and before 'the
Labour members' in the House of Commons 'raised a hue and cry', 'making
martyrs of the deportees'. Because, according to her, Minto thought that their
utterances in the House of Commons would be published and 'copied into
every vernacular paper' and would affect Indian public opinion. *My Indian
Journal*, 1910, vol. i, p. 52.

Minto mentioned in his note that he was conscious of the composition of
the present Government which depended on Labour votes. Questions might
have been asked in Parliament, compelling the Government to force the
Government of India and this he thought would have been most unfortunate.
Ibid, vol. i, pp. 69–72.

Indian Press received the news with relief and was generally pleased. Even the Anglo-Indian papers were not critical of Minto's action. The *Civil and Military Gazette* stated that 'the release of deportees would seem to show that the Government was willing to trust the influential classes of the people and to rely upon their co-operation and loyalty'.[6]

Minto, no doubt, had stuck to his earlier decision that the deportees should be released as soon as the reforms were in operation. He resolutely resisted the greatest pressure from Morley and felt very strongly about it.

It seems that amongst officials this impression that Morley was under great pressure from the Labour members was very common. Lady Minto refers to Labour members many times. After Jackson's murder she wrote in her *Journal*, 'owing to this [murder of Jackson] Rolly will not be able to discharge any of the deportees, and I expect this will greatly annoy the authorities in England, as unless the deportees are released the Government will lose many of the Labour votes'.[7] Presumably by Labour members she meant the Radical members as well. Minto seems to have felt the same.

Morley very much resented this when he came to know of it. He wrote to Minto, 'What I disliked was the pretty distinct implication that I was urging release, because His Majesty's Government, as you suppose, is 'largely dependent' on the votes of the Labour Party, and the Labour Party might have cried out against persistent and indefinite detention. That is to say, I should not have overruled you because I thought indefinite detention bad in Indian interests, as lowering Indian respect for British legality and strict regard for justice, but simply because I was afraid of being turned out of office by Labour men, *plus* Radical stalwards, *plus* Irish, *plus* a certain Tory contingent . . .' Then he recounted various instances—like the appointment of

[6] See also The *Statesman*, 9 February 1910; the *Leader*, Allahabad, 9 February 1910; The *Civil and Military Gazette*, Lahore, 9 February 1910; the *Tribune*, Lahore, 9 February 1910; the *Madras Mail*, Madras, 9 February 1910; the *Times of India*, Bombay, 9 February 1910.

[7] Lady Minto, op. cit., 1909, vol. ii, p. 377.

Sinha—where he fought for Minto's policies even 'against the Palace'. He also emphasized that constitutionally he was empowered to overrule the Government of India.[8]

Minto tried to pacify him by saying that he had misunderstood him. He informed Morley that he wrote the note of 1 March 1910 in reply to an accusation by one of his colleagues that 'the Government of India had lost credit in this country because it had surrendered to orders from home'. He stated that this was the general impression amongst Anglo-Indians. He avoided the reference to the Labour Party, but pointed out that there was no need to bring in constitutional issues, otherwise it would tempt one to wonder 'whether a Parliamentary Government, as it now exists, is suitable for the administration of a great Empire.'[9] Minto had always wondered about it.

This incident, however, shows how much Morley interfered in the internal policy of Indian administration. Instead of suggesting the broad lines of policy only he tended to interfere in the details. But this also suggests that without Minto's consent and agreement he was unable to alter his policy however distasteful it might be to him. His threats and his authoritative tone had not much effect on Minto. He could not go beyond that because the House of Lords would not have let him overrule the Government of India. For the success of all his policies co-operation and loyal support of the Government of India were essential. And Minto could not be persuaded to deviate under any pressure from any policy which he thought was justified in the interests of the British administration of India.

The Congress mood of jubilation changed into a more critical attitude, particularly in connexion with the regulations to be issued under the scheme. In 1909, the Congress, meeting at Lahore under Madan Mohan Malaviya, passed a resolution which regretted that 'the regulations framed under the Act have not been framed in the same liberal spirit in which Lord Morley's despatch of last year was conceived'. The Congress objected to

[8] Morley to Minto, 17 March 1910. *M.C.*
[9] Minto to Morley, 7 April 1910. Ibid.

'the wide, arbitrary, and unreasonable disqualifications and restrictions for candidates seeking election to the Councils; the general distrust of the educated classes that runs through the whole course of the regulations; and the unsatisfactory composition of the non-official majority in Provincial Councils rendering them ineffective and unreal for all practical purposes'. The Congress urged the Government to revise the Regulations, 'remove the objectionable features and bring them into harmony with the spirit of the Royal Message and the Secretary of State's despatch of last year'.[1]

Surendranath Banerjea and Madan Mohan Malaviya, who had welcomed with great enthusiasm the Reforms outlined in Morley's Despatch of 27 November 1908, condemned in strong terms the Regulations issued by the Government of India to give effect to the Reforms. In moving the resolution Banerjea put the blame for practically wrecking the reforms on the shoulders of the bureaucracy. In his opinion they had converted 'that promising experiment into a dismal failure'.[2] Madan Mohan Malaviya in his presidential address argued that when in Britain at least two persons, Michael Davitt, once convicted of sedition, and John Burns, once sentenced to six weeks' imprisonment, could become M.P.s and one of them even a Cabinet Minister, there existed no reason why Indian nationalist leaders whom the Government had once deported should be prevented from becoming members of the Indian Legislative Councils.[3] The *Bengalee* criticized the exclusion of deportees as in entire conflict with the spirit of English political practice.[4]

Despite this Congress criticism, the Morley-Minto Reforms were introduced and in Minto's words they marked 'the close of a system of administration which . . . has contributed much to the prosperity of India and to the glories of her history', but they also opened 'a new era with the inauguration of broader principles

[1] *Report of the I.N.C.*, 1909, Resolution IV, p. 47.
[2] Ibid. pp. 22–23, 48–52.
[3] Ibid. p. 29.
[4] The *Bengalee*, 28 February 1909.

of government'.[5] Under these reforms the strength of each Legislative Council was increased. Election was officially recognized. Under the principle of representation of interests, separate Muslim representation along with weightage was established. The official majority, prevalent in every province except Bombay, was done away with. More time was provided for budget discussion and supplementary questions were allowed. Two Indians in the Secretary of State's Council and one in the Viceroy's Executive Council were introduced.

These reforms have been praised and denounced with equal vehemence. Amongst their bitter critics is the *Montagu-Chelmsford Report*. The *Report* criticized them for the narrowness of franchise, and for giving no power and no responsibility to the Legislative Councils. The *Report* was also critical of the composition of the Councils, particularly the presence of too many lawyers and the introduction of separate representation of various communities. It considered the presence of an official block in the Imperial Legislative Council a hurdle, which irritated the Indian members and created a sort of racial discrimination as this block drove the Indians into another block.[6]

Some of this criticism is accurate. But the authors of the reforms had no intention of transplanting British institutions wholesale into India. Their aim was to admit Indians, on a very restricted basis, to consultation and a modest share in the administration. The reforms were neither calculated nor expected to end the activities of the extremists and terrorists, but they were definitely intended to strengthen the hands of the Government in dealing with them by winning more support from the moderate section of the Indian people. In this aim they were successful. They also showed that however slow and tardy the path of constitutional progress was, it was better than the dangers of revolutionary violence. These discredited the revolutionists and made it easier for moderate Indian leaders like Gokhale to resist

[5] Minto's Speech in Legislative Council, 25 January 1910.
[6] The *Montagu-Chelmsford Report*, 1918, Cd. 9109, pp. 70, 71, 73, 76, 186–8.

the extremists in the Congress. Though Morley and Minto tried their best to emphasize that these were not intended to establish a parliamentary system in India, the Indian leaders interpreted them as an advance towards parliamentary government. Though the Government of India continued for some time to be a 'bene- volent despotism', even after their introduction, these reforms were the highlight of the policy of association. In this, with all their drawbacks, they were a definite step forward.

## APPENDIX I

# MUSLIM REPRESENTATION IN THE CONGRESS, 1885–1910

| Congress Session | Place | Total Delegates | Muslims |
|---|---|---|---|
| 1885 | Bombay | 72 | 2 (Both Bombay attorneys) |
| 1886 | Calcutta | 440 | 33 (27 from Bengal) |
| 1887 | Madras | 607 | 79 (59 from Madras) |
| 1888 | Allahabad | 1,248 | 219 (152 from N.W.P. and Oudh) |
| 1889 | Bombay | 1,889 | 248 (80 from Bombay) |
| 1890 | Calcutta | 677 | 116 (82 from N.W.P. and 29 from Bengal) |
| 1891 | Nagpur | List not available | |
| 1892 | Allahabad | 625 | 91 (81 from N.W.P. and Oudh) |
| 1893 | Lahore | 867 | 65 (51 from the Punjab) |
| 1894 | Madras | 1,163 | 23 (17 from Madras) |
| 1895 | Poona | 1,584 | 25 (21 from Bombay) |
| 1896 | Calcutta | 784 | 54 (42 from Bengal) |
| 1897 | Amraoti | 692 | 57 (53 from Berar) |
| 1898 | Madras | 614 | 10 (10 from Madras) |
| 1899 | Lucknow | 789 | 313 (308 from N.W.P. and Oudh) |
| 1900 | Lahore | 567 | 56 (52 from Punjab) |
| 1901 | Calcutta | 896 | 74 (54 from Bengal) |
| 1902 | Ahmedabad | 417 | 20 (19 from Bombay) |
| 1903 | Madras | 538 | 9 (5 from Madras) |
| 1904 | Bombay | 1,010 | 35 (25 from Bombay, 1 from Bengal) |
| 1905 | Benares | 756 | 20 (9 from U.P.) |
| 1906 | Calcutta | 1,663 | 45 (24 from Bengal out of 686 delegates) |
| 1907 | Surat. Adjourned *sine die*. | | |
| 1908 | Madras | 626 | 10 (3 from Madras) |
| 1909 | Lahore | 243 | 5 (3 from Bengal, 2 from Punjab) |
| 1910 | Allahabad | 636 | 19 (8 from U.P.) |

# SIGNATORIES OF THE MUSLIM ADDRESS

1. H.H. Aga Sir Sultan Mohamed Shah Aga Khan, G.C.I.E. (Bombay).
2. Shahzadah Bakhtiar Shah, C.I.E., Head of the Mysore Family, Calcutta (Bengal).
3. Honourable Malik Omar Hayat Khan, C.I.E., Lieut., 18th Prince of Wales' Tiwana Lancers, Tiwana, Shahpur (Punjab).
4. Honourable Khan Bahadur Mian Mohamed Shah Din, Bar.-at-Law, Lahore (Punjab).
5. Honourable Maulvi Sharf-ud-din, Bar.-at-Law, Patna (Behar).
6. Khan Bahadur Syed Nawab Ali Chowdhry, Mymensingh (Eastern Bengal).
7. Nawab Bahadur Syed Amir Husan Khan, C.I.E., Calcutta (Bengal).
8. Naseer Husain Khan Khayal, Calcutta (Bengal).
9. Khan Bahadur Mirza Sujaat Ali Beg, Persian Consul-General, Murshidabad, Calcutta (Bengal).
10. Syed Ali Imam, Bar.-at-Law, Patna (Behar).
11. Nawab Sarfraz Husain Khan, Patna (Behar).
12. Khan Bahadur Ahmed Mohiuddin Khan, Stipendiary of the Carnatic Family (Madras).
13. Maulvi Rafiuddin Ahmed, Bar.-at-Law (Bombay).
14. Ebrahimbhoy Adamji Peerbhoy, General Merchant (Bombay).
15. Abdurrahim, Bar.-at-Law (Calcutta).
16. Syed Alahdad Shah, Special Magistrate and Vice-President, Zamindar's Association, Khairpore (Sindh).

17. Maulana H. M. Malak, Head of Medhi Bagh Bohras, Nagpur (C.P.).
18. Mushirad Dowla Mumtaz-ul-Mulk Khan Bahadur Khalifa Syed Mohamed Husain, Member of the State Council, Patiala (Punjab).
19. Khan Bahadur Col Abdul Majid Khan, Foreign Minister, Patiala (Punjab).
20. Khan Bahadur Khawaja Yusuf Shah, Honorary Magistrate, Amritsar (Punjab).
21. Mian Mohamed Shafi, Bar.-at-Law, Lahore (Punjab).
22. Shaikh Ghulam Sadik, Amritsar (Punjab).
23. Hakim Mohamed Ajmal Khan, Delhi (Punjab).
24. Munshi Ihtisham Ali, Zamindar and Rais, Kakori (Oudh).
25. Syed Nabi-ullah, Bar.-at-Law, Rais, Kara, Distt., Allahabad (U.P.).
26. Maulvi Syed Karamat Husain, Bar.-at-Law, Allahabad (U.P.).
27. Syed Abdur Reoof, Bar.-at-Law, Allahabad (U.P.).
28. Munshi Abdur Salam Khan, Retired Sub-Judge, Rampur (U.P.).
29. Khan Bahadur Mohamed Muzammil-ullah Khan, Zamindar, Secretary, Zamindar's Association (U.P.) and Joint Secretary, M.A.O. College Trustee, Aligarh (U.P.).
30. Haji Mohamed Ismail Khan, Zamindar, Aligarh (U.P.).
31. Sahabzada Aftab Ahmed Khan, Bar.-at-Law, Aligarh (U.P.).
32. Maulvi Mushtaq Husain, Rais, Amroha (U.P.).
33. Maulvi Habib-ur-Rahman Khan, Zamindar, Bhikanpur (U.P.).
34. Nawab Syed Sirdar Ali Khan, son of the late Nawab Sirdar Dilar-ul-Mulk Bahadur, C.I.E., Hyderabad (Deccan).
35. Maulvi Syed Mahdee Ally Khan (Mohsin-ul-Mulk), Honorary Secretary, M.A.O. College, Aligarh, Etawah (U.P.).

*M.P.*

# MEMBERS OF THE PROVISIONAL COMMITTEE OF THE ALL-INDIA MUSLIM LEAGUE APPOINTED AT ITS DACCA SESSION 1906

Joint Secretaries:

Nawab Viqar-ul-Mulk.
Nawab Mohsin-ul-Mulk.

Members:

Eastern Bengal:

The Honourable Nawab Salimullah of Dacca.
The Honourable Chaudhry Nawab Ali (Mymensingh).
Moulvie Himayatuddin (Barisal).

Assam:

Moulvie Abdul Majid, B.A., B.L. (Sylhet).

Western Bengal:

Mr. Abdul Rahim, Bar.-at-Law (Calcutta).
Nawab Nasiruddin Khayal (Calcutta).
Nawab Amir Hossein Khan (Calcutta).
Mr. Shamsul Huda, *Vakil* (Calcutta).
Mr. Serajul Islam, *Vakil* (Calcutta).
Mr. Abdul Hamid, Editor, *Moslem Chronicle* (Calcutta).

Behar:

Mr. Ali Imam, Bar.-at-Law (Patna).
Mr. Mazhar-ul-Haque, Bar.-at-Law (Chhapra).
Mr. Hasan Imam, Bar.-at-Law (Patna).

Oudh:

Mr. Nabi-ullah, Bar.-at-Law (Lucknow).
Mr. Hamid Ali Khan, Bar.-at-Law (Lucknow).
Nawab Imad-ul-Mulk (Bilgram).
Munshi Ihtisham Ali, Rais (Lucknow).
Mr. Zahoor Ahmed, B.A., LL.B. (Lucknow).
Mr. Mahomed Nusim, *Vakil* (Lucknow).
Mr. Ghulamus Saqlain, B.A., LL.B. (Lucknow).
Raja Nowshad Ali Khan (Lucknow).


Agra Province:

Nawab Mohsin-ul-Mulk (Aligarh).
Nawab Viqar-ul-Mulk (Amroha).
Sahebzada Aftab Ahmed Khan, Bar.-at-Law (Aligarh).
Mr. Mohamed Ishaque, B.A., LL.B. (Allahabad).
Moulvie Kiramet Hussein, Bar.-at-Law (Allahabad).
Mr. Abdur Raoof, Bar.-at-Law (Allahabad).
Mohammed Raoof, Bar.-at-Law (Allahabad).
Haji Mahomed Moosa Khan (Aligarh).
Khan Bahadur Muhomed Mozammil-ullah Khan (Aligarh).
Mr. Abdullah Jan, *Vakil* (Saharanpore).
Mr. Abdul Majid, Bar.-at-Law (Allahabad).
Haji Ismail Khan (Aligarh).
Sheikh Abdullah, B.A., LL.B. (Aligarh).
Mr. Mahomed Ali, B.A. (Oxon.).


Punjab:

Mr. Mahomed Shafi, Bar.-at-Law (Lahore).
Mr. Fazle Hussein, Bar.-at-Law (Lahore).
Mr. Abdul Aziz, Editor, *Observer* (Lahore).
Khaja Yousoff Shah (Ludhiana).
Hakim Ajmal Khan (Delhi).
Sheik Gholam Mohammed Sahib, Editor, *Vakil* (Amritsar).
Mr. Ghulam Sadiq (Amritsar).

Frontier Province:

Mufti Fida Mahomed Khan, Bar.-at-Law (Peshawar).

Sindh:

Mr. A. M. Dehlavi (Hyderabad).

Kathiawar:

Mr. Ghulam Mohammed Munshi, Bar.-at-Law (Rajkote).

Bombay Presidency:

Nawabzada Nasir-ullah Khan, Bar.-at-Law (Bombay).
Mr. Rafiuddin, Bar.-at-Law (Bombay)

Madras Presidency:

Khan Bahadur Abdul Hadi Badshah.
Khan Bahadur Ahmed Mahi-uddin (Madras).
Mr. Yakub Hussein, Proprietor of the *Moslem Patriot* (Madras).
Nawab Gholam Ahmed (Coromandel).
Mr. Abdul Hamid Hasan, B.A., LL.B., Editor, the *Moslem Patriot* (Madras).

Orissa:

Mr. Naur-ul-Huq, Secretary, Mahommedan Association (Cuttack).

Central Provinces:

Khan Saheb Mahomed Amir Khan, Pleader (Nagpur).
Mr. H. M. Mullick (Nagpur).

Burma:

Mr. A. S. Rafique (Rangoon).

> *Proceedings of the Home Department (Public),*
> *January-April* 1907, vol. 7587. February 1907.

# THE LONDON BRANCH OF THE ALL-INDIA MUSLIM LEAGUE, FOUNDED ON WEDNESDAY, 6 MAY 1908

President: S. Ameer Ali.

Hon. Vice-Presidents: 1. Sir Henry Seymour King, K.C.S.I., M.P.
2. Sir Raymond West, K.C.S.I.
3. Harold Cox, Esq., M.P.

Ordinary Vice-President: C. A. Latif, Esq.

Hon. Secretary: Ibni Ahmed, Esq.

Joint Secretary: S. Zahur Ahmad, Esq.

Asst. Sect. and Asst. Treasurer: M. Masudul Hasan, Esq.

Committee: Dr. Abdul Majid, B.A., LL.D., Bar.-at-Law.
Dr. Mohammed Ikbal, M.A., Ph.D.
Dr. M. A. Ansari, B.A., M.B.
S. A. A. Tabrizi, M.A., B.L.
Latafut Husain Khan.
Mohammed Shakir Ali, F.S.S.
M. K. Azad.
Mirza Mohammed Rafi.
Mohammed Yakub.
M. A. Hafiz.
Mohammed Sharif.
A. H. Khudadad Khan.
A. M. Khwaja.
Musharraful Hakk.

Major S. H. Bilgrami was elected *ex-officio* member of the Committee.

*I.O.L.* Tr. 1113(a).

# SOME IMPORTANT LETTERS

1

*From W. A. J. Archbold to*          Corstorphan's Hotel,
        *Dunlop Smith.*                  Simla.
                                 9 August 1906.

Dear Colonel Dunlop Smith,

I have written to the Nawab Mohsin-ul-Mulk, telling him to do nothing till he hears from me, and asking him to write to Syed Husain Bilgrami suggesting that he should wait too. There is one consideration which I am sure you will not overlook in thinking what had best be done. The Dacca Mohammedans are very much interested in the matter we were talking of, and will certainly join in any deputation of the kind suggested in the Nawab's letter; we have had a good deal of communication with them of late. It might be a good thing if in their present excited state, their energies could be directed in a natural and legitimate direction, and it would, I am sure, quiet things if some reassuring statement could be made to the deputation, all of which need not involve injustice to the Hindus or to anyone else.

If the Mohammedans were informed (privately) that a deputation would be received and a statement made, what would happen would be that representative Mohammedans from various parts of India would come to Simla and present a carefully drawn-up petition. The number would not be very large, as the people who ought to be on it are very well known. From my knowledge of those who would lead I am sure that nothing in the slightest degree disloyal or objectionable would be brought forward. There is no wish on the part of the Mohammedans to give trouble to the Government in any way, only, if I may judge, a certain widespread nervousness and uneasiness as to the future, a fear lest they should be left out in the cold.

Please forgive this long letter. When I read of the meeting and uneasiness in Dacca, and saw the names of those concerned, I was very anxious to suggest the deputation as a solvent of the difficulties there, as well as possibly elsewhere.

Yours sincerely,<br>
(Sd.) W. A. J. Archbold.

'I have told him His Excellency will agree to receive the deputation.'

(Sd.) J. R. D. S.<br>
10-8-6.

2

*From W. A. J. Archbold to*          Corstorphan's Hotel,
    *Dunlop Smith.*                  Simla.
                                     20 August 1906.

Dear Dunlop Smith,

I see and hear that things in Eastern Bengal and Assam are still in a very unhappy condition. If there is any danger of trouble from the side of the Mohammedans at any time, I need hardly say how glad I should be to go and talk with the leaders, and do my best to keep them within bounds.

What I am thinking of is this. His Excellency the Viceroy has consented to receive the Deputation, provided all is in order. I have drawn up the 'formal request' for the Mohammedans, and they are by this time, I hope, busy getting it signed. It would be quite easy to show the leading people how fatal to their own cause any violence would be, and how much better it would prove to stick to the constitutional course, even though they may feel it difficult in the present excited state of feeling to do so.

We are all very anxious that the Mohammedans should not put themselves in the wrong; it is just what their enemies would like. As you know, they are rather backward in the arts of political agitation, and the danger is that they may go wrong through ignorance. I am very glad that they have restrained themselves as well as they have done.

Yours sincerely,<br>
W. A. J. Archbold.

P.S. In the above suggestion I do not of course mean that I should have any sort of commission or authority. It would be absurd to think of such a course. The plan will, I sincerely hope, prove unnecessary.

*Dunlop Smith to Archbold*—21 August 1906. Politely turned down Archbold's offer to go to Dacca to pacify the Muslims.

3

*From W. A. J. Archbold to*          Simla.
*      Dunlop Smith.*              22 August 1906.

Dear Dunlop Smith,

Many thanks for your letter.

The enclosed from Mohsin-ul-Mulk I obtained permission to show. It might be worth while having a copy sent to Mr. Hare for his *private* information, so that he might have it before him, not that it contains anything that he will not know.

So much for the dark side of things.

I have just had a wire from S. Husain Bilgrami of Hyderabad, saying that he fully agrees with a long letter I sent to him, so that he is on the side of order and constitutional action. This is a great moral gain, as he will have much to say, and is in many ways a leader. I hope that he will now keep the rather excited Mohammedans of Bengal within bounds. Bilgrami is going to meet Mohsin-ul-Mulk at Bombay.

I have written a long letter to Syed Nawab Ali Chowdry of Dacca, telling him to keep all his friends quiet and talking about the coming deputation. I have had letters from him before.

Please don't trouble to write, as I know how busy you must be, but, when you have done with Mohsin-ul-Mulk's letter, you might send it back to me.

Yours sincerely,
(Sd.) W. A. J. Archbold.

P.S. Of course, if a copy of Mohsin-ul-Mulk's letter is sent to Mr. Hare, it will be marked strictly confidential.

4

*Mohsin-ul-Mulk to*      Bombay.
*Archbold.*               18 August 1906.

My dear Archbold,

Thanks for your letter of the 14th instant, together with a draft of the formal application. I am sending it to a few of my friends, but I am sure nobody will like the opening phrases which give an assurance of a deliberate aloofness from political agitation in the future. Probably also they will not like me to represent their cause to Government without the means of a political association. I shall, however, let you know what is decided.

I find that Mohammedan feeling is very much changed, and I am constantly getting letters using emphatic language, and saying that the Hindus have succeeded owing to their agitation, and the Mohammedans have suffered for their silence. The Mohammedans have generally begun to think of organizing a political association and forming themselves into political agitators. Although it is impossible for the Mohammedans, on account of their lack of ability and union and want of funds, to attain any success like the Hindus, and they are likely to lose rather than gain by such a course, it is yet impossible for anybody to stop them. The Mohammedans of Eastern Bengal have received a severe shock. I have got a letter from Syed Nawab Ali Chowdry of Dacca who gives utterance to the extremely sorrowful feeling prevailing there. He says: '... up till now the Mohammedans of

Bengal have been careless. They have now begun to feel the consequences of their carelessness. If only the Mohammedans of Bengal, instead of following the Government, had agitated like the Hindus and had enlisted the sympathies of the Mohammedans of the whole of India, and raised their voice up to the Parliament, they would never have seen these unfortunate consequences.

'The resignation of Sir Bampfylde Fuller has produced an unrest throughout the Mohammedans in the whole of Bengal, and their aspirations for higher education and increased rank and responsibility are being subsided. Looking at it from one point of view the Government has taught a good lesson to the Mohammedans by accepting Sir Bampfylde's resignation. It has served to awaken them after a sleep of carelessness. We shall now have to proceed on the same lines as the Hindus, not only in India, but in England.'

This is only a brief quotation of what I am getting from the whole of India. These people generally say that the policy of Sir Syed and that of mine has done no good to Mohammedans. They say that Government has proved by its actions that without agitation there is no hope for any community, and that if we can do nothing for them we must not hope to get any help for the college; in short, the Mohammedans generally will desert us, because the policy of the college is detrimental to their interests. My dear Archbold, nobody can say that the present state of Mohammedan feeling is without its justification. The Liberal Government is at the bottom of it, and is responsible for it. I consider it a wrong policy arising out of the ignorance of the real conditions in India. Mr. John Morley is a philosopher and might well have been contented to give lessons in philosophy; and one cannot but feel sorry that the destiny of India has been placed in his hands.

His policy has done a lot of injury to India and may do much more. Is it right for the Government to allow an important section of the Indian population, which has always supported and even depended on Government to safeguard its interests, to be disappointed and get up a spirit of agitation like the Hindus? I only hope that the Government of India will do something to subside the growing Mohammedan feeling and to remedy their hopelessness.

Yours sincerely,

(Sd.) Mohsin-ul-Mulk.

P.S. I have informed Sir James La Touche of the proposal to send a memorial and deputation to the Viceroy because I thought it was necessary.

5

*Dunlop Smith to*                    Simla.
  *Moulvi Syed Mehdi Ali Khan.*    13 September 1906.

Sir,

I have the honour to acknowledge the receipt of your letter, dated the 7th instant, forwarding a memorial requesting that His Excellency the Viceroy will permit a Deputation of leading Mohammedans to wait upon His Excellency to present an address. 2. In reply, I am directed to inform you that His Excellency will have much pleasure in receiving the Deputation, and trusts that the 1st October at 11 A.M. will be a convenient day and hour for the Deputation. I am to request that a copy of the proposed address may be furnished to me for His Excellency's information as early as possible.

I have etc. etc.,

(Sd.) J. R. Dunlop Smith.

Minto received the address sometime before 26 September —Minto to Morley—26 September 1906—draft of address received.

*Mohsin-ul-Mulk to*  Simla.
   *Dunlop Smith.*  7 October 1906.

My dear Sir,

The members of the Committee appointed to consider what improvements may be effected in the constitution of the Legislative Councils, with especial reference to the strength and position therein of the non-official Members, were so good as to give me an opportunity of discussing with them the question of Mohammedan representation on those bodies, and I beg to state my views on the subject for submission to His Excellency's Government.

Both on the Supreme and the Provincial Councils an adequate number of seats should be reserved exclusively for the Mohammedans. The present system of election applicable to the general body of the people need not be interfered with, and it should remain open, as hitherto, to all communities. For the seats on the Legislative Chambers reserved for the Mohammedan community separate electorates should be created, and the franchise in their case may be distributed on the following basis:

A—For the Provincial Councils—

   (1) Every Mohammedan British Indian subject paying income-tax on an income of Rs.1,000 a year,

   (2) Every Mohammedan landowner having a net rent roll of Rs.1,000 a year, to be ascertained on the basis of Revenue assessments as obtaining in different Presidencies and Provinces,

   (3) Every Mohammedan member of the Senate of a University,

   (4) Every Mohammedan graduate of five years' standing, shall each have a vote, but no single individual should have more than one vote, though he may happen to combine several qualifications. With reference to (1) and (2), the standard might be adapted to the circumstances of each Province.

Each Presidency or Province should, where local conditions require it, be divided into two or more electoral divisions or constituencies in accordance with its particular needs and circumstances. Every one of these constituencies or a combination of them will be entitled to return a Member at each election, or by turns, as may be determined in view of the number of seats reserved on the particular Provincial Council. For instance, West Bengal ought to be divided into Behar, and the rest of West Bengal, the United Provinces, into Oudh, and the rest of that Province, and so forth. This, I think, is necessary in order to safeguard against an unequal distribution of the privilege. In this connection, it may also well be considered whether important cities like Calcutta, Bombay, Madras, Lahore, Delhi, Lucknow, Allahabad, Aligarh, Patna, and Dacca should not be given separate franchise so far as their Mohammedan citizens are concerned. In every electoral division or constituency, each district should form a unit, but the number of votes which a particular district should be entitled to ought to be proportionate to the number of votes it may contain.

B—The Supreme Council:

The Mohammedan Members of different Provincial Councils, and the Mohammedan Fellows of the Indian Universities, and Mohammedans having an annual income, say, of Rs. 25,000 a year should be given the right to elect men out of their own body, or outside it, for the seats reserved on the Supreme Council. But in order to make sure that the interests of the Mohammedans of any particular Province may not be over-looked, it will in my opinion be necessary to lay down that the choice of the electors should be confined in terms to the Mohammedan inhabitants of a particular Province or Provinces.

With regard to the registration of voters and the method by which votes ought to be recorded, or poll taken, these are matters of detail which I need not enter into.

The above outline of my views is neither full nor final and it is possible that, on further reflection, I may be in a position to make suggestions in addition to, or in modification of them.

I am . . .

(Sd.) Mahdee Ally.

7

*Dunlop Smith to*                    12 October 1906.
  *Mohsin-ul-Mulk.*

Dear Nawab Sahib,

I submitted your letter of the 7th to the Viceroy, in which you sketch various improvements proposed to be effected in the constitution of the Legislative Council. I am to thank you for this frank expression of the views of your Committee, and to inform you that a copy of your letter has been sent to the Committee of the Executive Council now sitting for their careful consideration.

The Viceroy will be glad to receive any further communication which you may find it possible to make on this subject later on.

I am . . .
(Sd.) J. R. Dunlop Smith.

8

*G. K. Gokhale to*                    21 September 1906.
  *Wedderburn.*

Putting aside all other quarrels which are more or less personal, the main line of division in the Congress Camp at this moment is as regards our ideal and our plan of campaign. Mr. Bipin Chandra Pal and his party have openly unfurled a new banner and have taken up a position which makes any compromise with them impossible. They want the Congress to declare that it demands autonomy, absolute and immediate, without British control, and in their opinion nothing less is worth having. They openly urge that our present agitation for reforms is suicidal, because the success of this agitation means an improved and therefore a prolonged foreign rule. Our policy, they say, should be to make this rule as hateful as possible so that the necessary momentum to overthrow it before long may be forthcoming . . .

It is extremely unfortunate that this activity should show itself just at a time when the Government of India and the Secretary of State are contemplating a forward move in associating the people of the country with the work of administering their affairs and it is even probable that the proposals which are at present under consideration may assume a less liberal form on its account than they would otherwise have done. But as you know so well the growth of this school of irreconcilables is really Lord Curzon's legacy to the country. The utter contempt with which he used to brush aside all Indian public opinion and his insolent imperialism have created in the country an amount of anti-Government and anti-English feeling, which will not subside until Mr. Morley and Lord Minto steadily persevere for some time, in spite of every discouragement, in their proposed liberal policy . . .

9

*Tilak to*                  21 September 1906.
    *Wedderburn.*

In short the issue is—Does the Congress mean to confine itself solely to focussing public opinion and educating the British public; or whether it would extend its usefulness by developing the methods of self-reliance suggested by the last year's experience. I hold the latter view. But whatever be the view I hold, I can assure you this much, that I shall be the last person to see the cause of the Congress suffer in any way. Suppose that the Liberal Government grants us any concession, even then it will be necessary to resort to methods of self-reliance in order that the concessions now granted may not be withdrawn in future by the Conservative party.

                                          *M.C.*

# BIBLIOGRAPHY

## A. PRIVATE PAPERS

### 1. India Office Library

#### (a) MORLEY PAPERS

Copies of letters from Morley to Minto, 1905–10. 5 Vols.
Letters from Minto to Morley, 1905–10. 19 Vols.
Letters from Hardinge to Morley, 3 March–25 May 1911. 1 Vol.

*Telegrams*
Private Telegrams. Secretary of State to Viceroy and Viceroy to Secretary of State, December 1905–November 1910. 2 Vols.

*Files on specific subjects*
India. Council Reforms, October 1906–August 1907.
India. Council Reforms, October 1908–May 1909.
India. Council Reforms, July 1909–December 1909.
Question of Muhammedan Representation, October 1906–November 1909.

*Miscellaneous Correspondence and Notes*
Letters to Morley from Sydenham and to Sydenham from Morley.

#### (b) DIARIES OF F. A. HIRTZEL, 1906–9

4 Vols. Home Misc. 864.

#### (c) KILBRACKEN COLLECTION

Letters from Lord Morley to Sir Arthur Godley, 1906–9.
Letters from Lord Minto to Sir Arthur Godley, 1906–9.

#### (d) HAMILTON PAPERS

Letters from Curzon to Hamilton. Vols. xvi–xviii.

### 2. British Museum

#### (a) CAMPBELL-BANNERMAN PAPERS

41223. Vol. xviii (ff. 288).
Correspondence between Morley and Campbell-Bannerman. 1 Vol.

#### (b) DILKE PAPERS

43895. Vol. xxii (ff. 274).
Correspondence between Sir Charles Dilke and Morley. 1 Vol.

### 3. Indian Institute, Oxford

Lady Minto, *My Indian Journal.* 9 Vols.

### 4. National Library of Scotland, Edinburgh

*Minto Collection*

Summary of Administration, 1905–10. 27 Vols.
Letters to Persons in England and Abroad, 1905–10. 2 Vols.
Letters to H.M. the King, 1905–10. 1 Vol.
Correspondence regarding Council Reforms, n.d. 2 Vols.
Notes and Council Committee Reports, 1908. 1 Vol.
Correspondence regarding Council Reforms, 1909. 3 Vols.
Correspondence regarding Executive Council, n.d. 1 Vol.
Letters and Telegrams—India, 1905–10. 10 Vols.
       England and Abroad, 1905–10. 2 Vols.
       H.M. the King, 1905–10. 1 Vol.
Telegrams—Secretary of State, 1905–10. 5 Vols.
Letters—To and from the Secretary of State and Sir A. Godley, 1905–10. 6 Vols.
Engagement Book of His Excellency, 1906–10. 6 Vols.
Engagement Book of Her Excellency, 1906–7, 1907–10. 4 Vols.
Diary of Events, 1907. 1 Vol.
Proceedings of the Legislative Council, Calcutta, 1910. 1 Vol.
Proceedings of the Legislative Council, Simla, 1910. 1 Vol.
Papers connected with report of the Council's Committee, 1906. 2 Vols.
Ahmedabad Outrage, 1909. 1 Vol.
Speeches of the Earl of Minto, 1905–10. 1 Vol.
Correspondence between Minto and Chiefs for suppression of sedition. Foreign Department Serial No. 178. Calcutta, 1910. 1 Vol.

*Unbound Papers*

Official Diary of Events in India, 1907–10.
Punjab Colonization Bill; Viceroy's decision to withhold his consent, 1907.
Legislation in connexion with sedition, 1906–10. Comments of certain newspapers on the correspondence between H.E. Lord Minto and Ruling Chiefs regarding measures to be taken for the suppression of sedition.
Speech by the Hon. S. P. Sinha, First Member of the Viceroy's Council, delivered at Calcutta Town Hall, April 1909.
Memorandum of an interview between H.E. the Viceroy and Mr. Gokhale, January 1908.
Correspondence between Tilak, Gokhale and Sir W. Wedderburn, September 1906.

Notes on Indian Affairs, given to Lady Minto on her visit to England, 1906.
Notes on Indian Affairs, given to Sir James Dunlop Smith on his departure for England, 1908.
One packet containing various newspaper cuttings regarding Indian affairs.
Packets of letters containing:

1. Correspondence relative to the offer and acceptance of the Vice-royalty of India, 1905.
2. Letter and telegram from H.M. the King on appointment to Vice-royalty, 1905.
3. Congratulations from friends upon appointment to Viceroyalty, 1905. 3 packets.
4. Miscellaneous letters in connexion with appointment to Viceroyalty, 1905.
5. Correspondence with the Hon. St. John Broderick. 1905-6. 2 packets.
6. Correspondence with Lord Curzon, previous to arrival in India, 1905.
7. Correspondence with Sir Arthur Bigge, 1906-7.
8. Correspondence with Sir Arthur Bigge, 1910-13.
9. Correspondence with Viscount Morley, 1907-13. 2 packets.
10. Letter to Sir Arthur Bigge, 3 January 1908.
11. Secret notes sent to Lord Morley *re* Sinha. 12 August 1909.
12. Letter from H.R.H. the Prince of Wales, 4 August 1910.
13. Letter from Mr. Harcourt Butler, 15 November 1910.
14. Extract from Speech by Lord Minto to the East India Association, 24 April 1912.
15. Correspondence with Sir Arthur Godley, 1906.
16. Correspondence with Native Ruling Princes, 1910-13, 1910-14.
17. Correspondence with Sir Harcourt Butler, 1911-13.
18. Correspondence with Col. Sir James Dunlop Smith, 1908-12.
19. Correspondence with Lord Kitchener, 1906-11.
20. Miscellaneous letters of farewell from India and England, 1910.
21. Correspondence, 1916-17, between Lady Minto and the following regarding Lord Morley's Book *Recollections:*
   Lord Morley,
   Sir James Dunlop Smith,
   Sir Harcourt Butler.

## B. OFFICIAL RECORDS

### *India Office Library*

India Public Proceedings, July 1905–December 1910. 16 Vols.
Political and Secret Records (Home Correspondence), 1906–10. 7 Vols.
Public Letters from India, 1906–10. 5 Vols.

Public Despatches from England, 1906–10. 5 Vols.
India Confidential Proceedings–Political, July 1907–December 1910. 5 Vols.
Indian Legislative Council Proceedings, 1905–10.
Provincial Native Newspaper Reports, 1905–10.
Parliamentary Debates on Indian Affairs, 1905–10.
Report on Indian Constitutional Reform, 1918 (London).
Sedition Committee Report, 1918 (Calcutta, 1918).

## C. PARLIAMENTARY PAPERS

House of Commons, 1905. Vol. 58, C2658. Eastern Bengal and Assam Papers relating to the Reconstitution of the Provinces of Bengal and Assam.
House of Commons, 1906. Vol. 81, C2746. Reconstitution of Provinces of East Bengal and Assam: Further Papers.
House of Commons, 1906. Vol. 81, C3242. Resignation of Sir J. B. Fuller.
Parliamentary Papers Collection 345; 1907, 1908, 1909. Cd. 3710, Cd. 4426, and Cd. 4652. Papers relating to the Advisory Council and Provincial Advisory Councils, the enlargement of Legislative Councils and the discussion of the Budget.
Parliamentary Papers Collection 345A., 1909. Cd. 4652. Representation of Muhammadans on the Legislative Councils and Cd. 4987: Regulations &c. for giving effect to the Indian Councils Act, 1909.

## D. REPORTS, PERIODICALS AND TRACTS

*Reports of the All-India National Congress,* 1905–10.
*Report of the Inaugural Meeting of the All-India Muslim League, London Branch,* 1908. London. Tr. 1113(a).
*Presidential Address–All-India Muslim League,* 1907. Karachi. Tr. 1042.
*Speech at the All-India Muslim League Session at Amritsar by Syed Ali Imam,* 1908. Bankipur, 1908. Tr. 1113(a).
All-India Muslim League, *The Indian Mohamedans and the Government,* 1909. Tr. 1113(b).
*Proceedings of the All-India Muslim League,* Nagpur, Allahabad, 1911, by M. M. Aziz Mirza.
All-India Muslim League, Lahore, *The Indian Constitution Communal Electorates,* Lahore, 1929.
*India's Demands–A collection of the speeches delivered on the platforms of the Indian National Congress and the All-India Muslim League,* 1916.
*The Partition of Bengal–An open letter to Lord Curzon,* 1905. By 'One of the People', Dacca. Tr. 955.
*The Unrest in India Considered and Discussed,* 1907, by S. A. Khan. Bombay. Tr. 1001.

*All About Partition,* Calcutta, 1905. Tr. 1037.

*The Case Against the Break-up of Bengal,* Calcutta, 1905.

*The Congress Split,* 1908: *The Surat Congress,* 1908, Madras. Tr. 1042.

*Canadian Historical Review,* April 1907.

*Contemporary Review,* London, 1907–9 and also November 1923. Gooch, G. P., 'Lord Morley'.

The *Economist,* London, 6 October 1906, 27 February 1909.

*Edinburgh Review,* Edinburgh, 1907, 1910.

*Empire Review,* London, 1906, 1907, 1909.

*English Historical Review,* London, April 1961. Dr. Mary Cumpston, 'Some Early Nationalists and Their Allies in the British Parliament, 1851–1906'.

*Fortnightly Review,* London, 1909, 1911.

The *Hindustan Review,* 1907, 1909, 1911.

*Imperial and Asiatic Quarterly Review,* London, 1907, 1909.

*Indian Review,* Madras, 1905–10.

*Indian World,* Calcutta, 1906–10.

*Modern Review,* Calcutta, 1910.

The *National Review,* London, 1906, 1911.

*New Statesman,* London, 29 September 1923, 'John Morley'.

*Nineteenth Century,* London, 1906, 1907, 1909, 1910, September 1912.

*Pacific Historical Review,* vol. xvii, 1948, Giles. T. Brown, 'The Hindu Conspiracy, 1914–1917'.

*The Quarterly Review,* London, 1906, 1909, 1911 and also January and April 1924, J. H. Morgan, 'The Personality of Lord Morley'.

The *Spectator,* London, 1906, 1909, 1910.


### E. NEWSPAPERS

*The Times,* 1905–10.

The *Manchester Guardian,* 1905–10.

The *Bengalee,* Calcutta, 1905–10.

The *Pioneer,* Allahabad, 1905–10.

The *Civil and Military Gazette,* Lahore, 1905–10.

The *Englishman,* Calcutta, 1905–10.


### F. UNPUBLISHED THESES

AHMED, SUFIA. 'Some Aspects of the History of the Muslim Community in Bengal, 1884–1912.' Ph.D. 1961, University of London.

AZIZ, K. K. 'Britain and Muslim India—A Study of British Public Opinion vis-a-vis the Development of Muslim Nationalism in India, 1905–1947.' Ph.D. 1960, University of Manchester.

## BIBLIOGRAPHY

243

CHAKRAVARTY, SASADHAR. 'The Evolution of Representative Government in India, 1884–1909, with reference to Central and Provincial Legislative Councils.' Ph.D. 1954, University of London.

HASSAAN, R. B. M. R. 'The Educational Movement of Sir Syed Ahmed Khan, 1858–1898.' Ph.D. 1960, University of London.

GHOSH, S. 'The Influence of Western, particularly English, political ideas on Indian political thought, with special reference to the political ideas of the Indian National Congress, 1885–1919.' Ph.D. 1950, University of London.

JONES, I. M. 'The Origins and Development to 1892 of the Indian National Congress.' M.A. 1947, University of London.

McLANE, J. R. 'The Development of Nationalist ideas and tactics and the policies of the Government of India, 1897–1905.' Ph.D. 1961, University of London.

SANDERS, I. L. 'Indian Nationalism: with special reference to Nehru's Career and influence.' M.Sc. (Econ.) 1959, University of London.

ZAKARIA, R. A. 'Muslims in India: a Political Analysis, 1885–1906.' Ph.D. 1948, University of London.

## G. AUTOBIOGRAPHIES AND BIOGRAPHIES

AZAD, ABUL KALAM. *India Wins Freedom: An Autobiographical Narrative* (Calcutta, 1959).

BANERJEA, S. N. *A Nation in Making* (London, 1925).

BUCHAN, JOHN. *Lord Minto: A Memoir* (London, 1924).

CHAMBERLAIN, SIR AUSTEN. *Politics from Inside: An Epistolary Chronicle, 1906–1914* (London, 1936).

CHAUDHURI, N. C. *Autobiography of an Unknown Indian* (London, 1951).

CLARKE, (SIR G. LORD SYDENHAM). *My Working Life* (London, 1927).

DURAND, MORTIMER. *Life of the Rt. Hon. Sir Alfred Comyn Lyall* (London, 1913).

GODLEY, SIR ARTHUR, BARON KILBRACKEN. *Reminiscences of Lord Kilbracken* (London, 1931).

GORE, JOHN. *King George V: A Personal Memoir* (London, 1941).

GRAHAM, G. F. I. *The Life and Work of Sir Syed Ahmed Khan* (London, 1909).

HAMILTON, E. R. *The Life of Henry Fowler, First Viscount of Wolverhampton* (London, 1912).

HAMILTON, LORD GEORGE. *Parliamentary Reminiscences and Reflections* (London, 1917).

HARDINGE, LORD, of PENSHURST. *My Indian Years, 1910–1916* (London, 1948).

HUGHES, EMRYS. *Keir Hardie* (London, 1950).

KHAN, THE AGA. *Memoirs* (London, 1954).

KHAN, SYED SIRDAR ALI. *The Life of Lord Morley* (London, 1923).

LYTTON, THE EARL OF. *William Scawen Blunt; A Memoir by his grandson* (London, 1961).

MAGNUS, PHILIP. *Kitchener, Portrait of an Imperialist* (London, 1958).

MARY, COUNTESS of MINTO. *India, Minto and Morley (1905–1910)* (London, 1934).

MASANI, R. P. *Dadabhai Naoroji* (London, 1939).

MODY, H. P. *Sir Pherozshah Mehta*, 2 vols. (Bombay, 1921).

MORGAN, J. H. *John, Viscount Morley* (London, 1924).

MORLEY, VISCOUNT. *Recollections*, vol. ii (London, 1917).

NATESON, G. A. *Sir Henry Cotton* (Madras, 1912).

NEVINSON, H. W. *More Changes, More Chances* (London, 1925).

NICOLSON, HAROLD. *Curzon: the Last Phase* (London, 1937).

——*King George V: His Life and Reign* (London, 1952).

O'DWYER, MICHAEL. *India as I Knew It, 1885–1925* (London, 1925).

PARVATE, T. V. *Gopal Krishna Gokhale* (Ahmedabad, 1959).

POPE-HENNESSY, JAMES. *Lord Crewe, 1885–1945: The Likeness of a Liberal* (London, 1955).

RATCLIFF, S. K. *Sir William Wedderburn and the Indian Reform Movement* (London, 1908).

RONALDSHAY, LORD. *Life of Lord Curzon*, vols. i and ii (London, 1928).

THAMANKAR, D. V. *Lokamanya Tilak* (London, 1956).

WEDDERBURN, W. *Allan Octavian Hume* (London, 1913).

YAJNIK, I. *Shyamaji Krishnavarma* (Bombay, 1950).

ZUBAIRI, M. A. *Tazkira-i-Mohsin* (Urdu, Delhi, 1935).

## H. OTHER PRINTED WORKS

ALBIRUNI, A. H. *Makers of Pakistan and Modern Muslim India* (Lahore, 1950).

ALI, ABDULLA YUSUF. *A Cultural History of India During the British Period* (Bombay, 1940).

ALI, MOHAMMED. *Thoughts on the Present Discontent* (Bombay, 1907).

ANDREWS, C. F. and MUKERJI. *Rise and Growth of the Congress in India* (London, 1938).

AYYAR, SIR S. SURAMANIA. *Constitutional Reforms* (Madras, 1917).

BAGAL, J. C. *History of the Indian Association, 1876–1951* (Calcutta, 1953).

BAHADUR, LAL. *The Muslim League; its History, Activities and Achievements* (Agra, 1954).

BANERJEE, A. C. *The Indian Constitutional Documents*, 2 vols. (Calcutta, 1948).

BARTARYA, S. C. *The Indian Nationalist Movement* (Allahabad, 1958).

BILGRAMI, S. H. *Addresses, Poems and Other Writings* (Hyderabad, Deccan, 1925).

BLUNT, W. S. *My Diaries* (London, 1919).

BOSE, N. S. *The Indian Awakening and Bengal* (Calcutta, 1960).

BUTLER, SIR HARCOURT. *India Insistent* (London, 1923).

CHAILLEY, JOSEPH. *Administrative Problems of British India* (London, 1910).

CHATTERJEE, RAMANANDA. *Towards Home Rule*, Part I (Calcutta, 1917).

CHAUDHRI, B. M. *Muslim Politics in India* (Calcutta, 1946).

CHAUDHURY, R. C. *The Congress Split* (Calcutta, 1908).

CHINTAMANI, C. Y. *Indian Politics Since the Mutiny* (London, 1940).

CHIROL, VALENTINE. *Indian Unrest* (London, 1910).

CHIROL, SIR V. *India, Old and New* (London, 1921).

CLARKE, (SIR G. LORD SYDENHAM). *Studies of an Imperialist* (London, 1928).

COTTON, Henry. *New India or India in Transition* (London, 1885; rev. 1907).

COUPLAND, SIR REGINALD. *Report on the Constitutional Problem of India* (London, 1942).

CROSS, C. M. P. *Development of Self-Government in India, 1858–1914* (Chicago, 1922).

CUMMING, SIR JOHN (ed.). *Political India, 1832–1932* (London, 1932).

CURZON, LORD. *The Place of India in the Empire* (London, 1909).

—— *Speeches* (Calcutta, 1901).

DESAI, A. R. *Social Background of the Indian Nationalism* (Bombay, 1956).

DODWELL, H. H. *Cambridge History of India,* vols. v. and vi (Cambridge, 1932).

—— *India,* 2 vols. (London, 1936).

—— *A Sketch of the History of India* (London, 1925).

DUFFERIN, MARQUIS OF DUFFERIN AND AVA. *Speeches Delivered in India, 1884–1888* (London, 1890).

ELLIOT, MURRAY KYNYNMOND (GILBERT JOHN) 4TH EARL MINTO. *Speeches by Minto* (1905–1910) (Calcutta, 1911).

FARQUHAR, J. N. *Modern Religious Movements in India* (New York, 1918).

FRASER, LOVAT. *India Under Curzon and After* (London, 1911).

FULLER, J. B. *Some Personal Experiences* (London, 1930).

GARRATT, G. T. *An Indian Commentary* (London, 1928).

GHOSE, H. P. *The Newspaper in India* (Calcutta, 1952).

GHOSE, R. B. *Speeches with Biographical Note* (Madras, n.d.).

GHOSH, P. C. *Indian National Congress* (Calcutta, 1960).

GOKHALE, G. K. *Speeches* (Madras, n.d.).

GOPAL, RAM. *Indian Muslims, 1858–1947* (London, 1959).

GOPAL, S. *The Viceroyalty of Lord Ripon* (London, 1953).

GRIFFITHS, P. *The British Impact on India* (London, 1952).

HARDIE, J. K. *India: Impressions and Suggestions* (London, 1909).

HIRST, F. W. *Early Life and Letters of John Morley,* 2 vols. (London, 1927).

HUNTER, W. W. *The Indian Musalmans* (London, 1884).

ILBERT, C. *The Government of India* (Oxford, 1922).

AN INDIAN MAHOMMEDAN. *British India from Queen Elizabeth to Lord Reading* (London, 1906).

*The Indian National Congress—its Origin, History, Constitution and Objects* (Madras, 1888).

*The Indian National Congress, Speeches and Addresses, 1885–1908* (Madras, n.d.).

Indian National Party. *British Rule in India Condemned by the British Themselves* (London, 1915).

KABIR, HUMAYUM. *Muslim Politics, 1906–1942* (Calcutta, 1943).

KARIM, REZAUL. *Muslims and the Congress* (Calcutta, 1941).

KEITH, A. B. *A Constitutional History of India* (London, 1936).

—— *Speeches and Documents on Indian Policy* (London, 1922).

KHAN, THE AGA. *India in Transition* (London, 1918).

KHAN, SIRDAR ALI. *India of Today* (Bombay, 1908).

KHAN, SIR SYED AHMED. *The Causes of the Indian Revolt* (1873).

—— *The Present State of Politics, Speeches* (Allahabad, 1888).

—— *Review of Dr. Hunter's Indian Musalmans* (London, 1872).

KHAN, SYED SIRDAR ALI. *Lord Curzon's Administration of India: What he promised? What he reformed?* (Bombay, 1905).

—— *The Unrest in India* (Bombay, 1907).

KRISHNA, K. B. *The Problem of Minorities* (London, 1939).

LAJPAT RAI. *The Story of My Deportation* (Lahore, 1908).

—— *Young India* (New York, 1917).

LOVETT, SIR V. *History of the Indian Nationalist Movement* (London, 1921).

MACCULLY, B. T. *English Education and the Origins of Indian Nationalism* (New York, 1940).

MACDONALD, J. RAMSEY. *The Government of India* (London, 1919).

—— *The Awakening of India* (London, 1910).

MAJOR, E. *Viscount Morley and Indian Reform* (London, 1910).

MAZUMDAR, A. C. *Indian National Evolution* (Madras, 1917).

MEHTA, A., and PATWARDHAN ACHYUT. *The Communal Triangle in India* (Allahabad, 1942).

MIRZA, M. M. AZIZ. *A Talk on Muslim Politics* (Lucknow, 1910).

MORLEY, VISCOUNT JOHN. *Indian Speeches* (London, 1909).

MUKHERJI, P. *Indian Constitutional Documents* (1918).

NATESAN, G. A. *Eminent Musalmans* (Madras, n.d.).

—— *The Swadeshi Movement* (Madras, n.d.).

NAWAZISH ALI, SYED. *Hayat-i-Sir Syed. A Life of Sir Syed* (Urdu, Lahore, 1904).

NEHRU, J. L. *Discovery of India* (London, 1956).

NEVINSON, H. W. *The New Spirit in India* (London, 1908).

NOMAN, M. *Muslim India* (Allahabad, 1942).

O'DONNELL, C. J. *Causes of Present Discontent in India* (London, 1908).

PANNIKAR, K. M. (and an Indian Student). *Indian Nationalism: Its Origin, History and Ideals* (London, 1920).

PHILIPS, C. H. *Historians of India, Pakistan and Ceylon* (London, 1961).

—— *India* (London, n.d.).

RAJPUT, A. B. *Muslim League, Yesterday and Today* (Lahore, 1948).

RAMANA RAO, M. V. *A Short History of the Indian National Congress* (Delhi, 1959).

RAY, P. C. *The Case Against the Break-up of Bengal* (Calcutta, 1905).

RONALDSHAY, LORD. *The Heart of Aryavarta* (London, 1925).

—— *India: A Bird's Eye View* (London, 1924).

—— *Psychology of Indian Unrest* (London, 1925).

SHARMA, J. S. *Indian National Congress* (Delhi, 1959).

SINGH, G. N. *Landmarks in Indian Constitutional and National Development,* vol. i. 1600–1919 (Benares, 1933, and Delhi, 1950).

SITARAMAYYA, B. P. *History of the Indian National Congress* (Madras, 1935).

SMITH, W. C. *Islam in Modern India* (London, 1946).

SMITH, W. R. *Nationalism and Reform in India* (New Haven, 1938).

SPEAR, T. G. P. *India, Pakistan and West* (London, 1958).

STAEBLER, WARREN I. *The Liberal Mind of John Morley* (Princeton, 1943).

SYMONDS, RICHARD. *The Making of Pakistan* (London, 1950).

THOMPSON, E., and GARRATT, G. T. *Rise and Fulfilment of British Rule in India* (London, 1934).

TILAK, B. G. *Bal Gangadhar Tilak: His Writings and Speeches* (Madras, 1918).

TUFAIL, AHMED MANGLORI. *Mussalmanon ka Roshan Mustaqbil* (Urdu, 'Bright Future of the Muslims', Badaun, U.P., 1938).

WELLCOCK, WILFRED. *India's Awakening: Its National Significance* (London, 1922).

WILSON, F. W. *The India Chaos* (London, 1932).

WILSON, S. G. *Modern Movements Among Muslims* (London, 1916).

WINT, GUY. *The British in Asia* (London, 1954).

WOODRUFF, P. *Men Who Ruled India,* vol. ii (London, 1954).

ZACHARIAS, H. C. E. *Renascent India, from Ram Mohan Roy to Mohandas Ghandhi* (London, 1933).

# INDEX